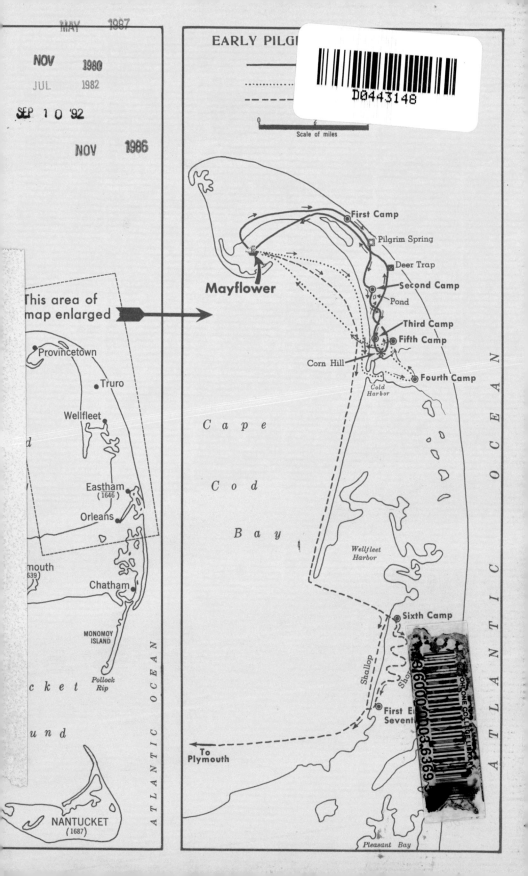

EARLY PILGRIM

Scale of miles

First Camp

Pilgrim Spring

Deer Trap

Mayflower

Second Camp

Pond

Third Camp

Fifth Camp

Corn Hill

Cold Harbor

Fourth Camp

C a p e

C o d

B a y

Wellfleet Harbor

A T L A N T I C   O C E A N

Sixth Camp

Shallop

**First E
Seventh**

← To
Plymouth

Pleasant Bay

This area of
map enlarged ➤

Provincetown

Truro

Wellfleet

Eastham
(1646)

Orleans

mouth
639

Chatham

MONOMOY
ISLAND

Pollock
Rip

ket

und

A T L A N T I C   O C E A N

NANTUCKET
(1687)

The Mayflower

Mayflower II in full sail. (PLIMOTH PLANTATION)

KATE CAFFREY

THE MAYFLOWER

STEIN AND DAY/*Publishers*/New York

First published in the United States of America in 1974
Copyright © 1974 by Kate Caffrey Toller
Library of Congress Catalog Card No. 73–91855
All rights reserved
Designed by David Miller
Printed in the United States of America
Stein and Day/*Publishers*/Scarborough House, Briarcliff Manor, N.Y. 10510
ISBN 0–8128–1679–X

The which I should endeavour to manifest in a plain style, with singular regard unto the simple truth in all things; at least as near as my slender judgment can attain the same.

—William Bradford

What makes a nation in the beginning is a good piece of geography.

—Robert Frost

The Pilgrim saddle is always on the Bay horse.

—Old New England saying

All sources are suspect.

—A. J. P. Taylor

To Bryen, Sadie and Lorna Gentry

Contents

LIST OF ILLUSTRATIONS

PART ONE

A Great

Design

The English spring is clearly in sight of summer when the hawthorn trees come into flower. As soon as those clusters of blossom cast their delicate scent across field or garden or municipal park it is safe, as the ancient English proverb has said for centuries, to put away one's winter clothes and let one's thoughts rove happily ahead to cricket and tennis on shaven lawns, chairs in the garden, strawberries and cream. As with the chestnut trees, the white hawthorn usually appears earlier than the pink and it is of the white that one instantly thinks. Nothing is more English than the flowering may, and it is interesting that in the seventeenth century many English ships, among all the rest with names like *Lion* or *Fortune, Hopewell* or *Discovery,* were called *Mayflower.*

One ship bearing this name was sailing from Leigh in 1606 and London in 1607 to the wine ports of Bordeaux and La Rochelle, bringing home barrels of France's best-loved export. It was a sizable ship for its time, about ninety feet long (only twelve feet longer than a tennis court), just over twenty-six feet at its widest (shorter than the world record long jump), and 180 tons in weight. Four hundred and fifty such vessels would add up to the tonnage of the *Queen Mary;* eleven such, in a line, would not equal the *Queen Mary*'s length.

No one knows what ports this *Mayflower* belonged to in the earlier years, but between 1609 and 1611 she was designated "of Harwich" in the port books. Harwich, situated beyond Roman Colchester at the outermost tip of Essex, is still one of the smallest of English ports, and certainly one of the most attractively set, its harbor facing north to Suffolk across the beautiful estuary of the River Stour, and its little old town around the corner toward the flat pale expanse of the North Sea still has something of a Dutch flavor about it. But before 1620 the ship was again based at the Port of London.

In 1620 Oliver Cromwell came of age. Charles Stewart, whose death warrant Cromwell would sign a generation later, was twenty. Descartes was twenty-four, Izaak Walton twenty-seven, Robert Herrick twenty-nine. Among the children, La Rochefoucauld was seven, Samuel Hudibras Butler eight, Turenne nine, Milton twelve. Corneille was fourteen. Richelieu was thirty-five, John Donne approaching fifty, Francis Bacon nearly sixty. Galileo was fifty-six. Shakespeare had been dead four years, Raleigh two. In the following year La Fontaine and Andrew Marvell would be born; within eight years Molière, Wren, George Fox, John Bunyan. King James I, that somewhat distressing monarch who dribbled and spat over his food, wrote a book about witchcraft and a blast against tobacco, was fifty-four in the year that saw the births of such ill-assorted characters as John Evelyn, Ninon de l'Enclos, and Cyrano de Bergerac. It was also, of course, the year the *Mayflower* sailed on her most celebrated voyage.

· 2 ·

The sixteenth century had been an age of expansion. Impelling curiosity and the wish for conquest and riches caused European governments to finance expeditions to the New World. Columbus's thirty-three-day voyage ended among beautiful varied scenery, lush growth, simple kindly generosity from the natives, and an apparently unlimited potential. Since then the leading colonial power had unquestionably been Spain, with her big navy and merchant marine, large tough army, and dauntless priests. By 1550 Charles V could lay claim to many Caribbean islands, to Mexico by right of conquest, to a vast undefined area north of the Rio Grande, and to all South America except Brazil, which belonged to Portugal. The first atrocious cruelties to the Indians were curbed by church and king and the settlers showed no hesitation in intermarrying; they also peppered the territories with mission stations, even as far north as the coast of California, where they named these after such people as St. Francis, St. Barbara, and Our Lady Queen of the Angels. Treasure fleets sailed regularly home, carrying gold and silver worth tens of millions of pesos a year, the Spanish peso being rated then at a particularly high value. Spain had, in fact, raced ahead so that by the time England was getting seriously interested in colonies there were over two hundred settlements in South America and Mexico, many of them flourishing towns with schools (the University of Mexico was started in 1551), printing presses and bookshops, and cathedrals, all backed up by the mines, ranches, and sugar plantations.

This early and spectacular expansion of Spain stirred France to emulation, expressed sarcastically by King François I, who said he would like to see a copy of the will of the original owner, Adam, bequeathing Spain the lands she claimed as hers. In 1524 François sent John Verrazano to look for the Northwest Passage. He did not find it, but reported on return that there was a lot of land free for the taking. Several years later, Jacques Cartier discovered the St. Lawrence and grandiosely named an Indian village Mont Réal.

When Drake's raids on the Spanish forts and treasure ships brought twelve million pounds into Elizabeth Tudor's exchequer, England belatedly began to take notice. It was true that Henry VII had financed the Cabots in 1497 and 1498 when they made expeditions to the New Found Land and to Chesapeake Bay, where they planted the English flag and Henry promptly claimed what he called "a domain of unknown size and character," later correctly described as the biggest land development and investment opportunity in Western history. It was true that when his son Henry VIII broke with the Pope, rivalry sharpened between England and the Catholic countries. But domestic dissensions held back overseas expansion until the last quarter of the century. By then, England, facing increased demands for wool to supply the cloth weavers, increased unemployment through the shift from agriculture to manufacture and trade with common lands turning into fenced sheep pastures, higher prices—the country was full of pestilence, penury, and "sturdy beggars"—needed outlets for her energies and sources for the luxury goods her multiplying merchants were requiring. In 1583 Humphrey Gilbert briefly settled a group in Newfoundland but soon withdrew them, which will surprise no one who has ever seen that inhospitable-looking land. In 1587 Walter Raleigh settled a colony on Roanoke Island. One hundred and fifty stubborn, brave people, twenty-five of them women and children, went out, the English ships sailed away and left them, a girl was born called appropriately Virginia Dare, but in 1591 the ships came back to find an empty fort with the word CROATAN scratched on the wall. The mystery of the lost colony has haunted American song and story ever since; Raleigh said he would live to see Virginia an English nation yet, but the Old Dominion was hardly that by the time he knelt at the block in 1618.

All the same, there was a colony in Virginia. Realizing that such enterprises needed proper planning, the English started forming joint stock companies, one of which was the London Company of 1606, the year *Macbeth* was first produced. It was chartered by James I to colonize America between the 38th and 41st parallels —approximately the territory of Virginia, Maryland, and New Jersey—and about 150 men and boys sailed out in three small ships, the *Susan Constant,* the *Godspeed,* and the *Discovery,* reached Chesapeake Bay, where they thought the Pacific must be very near, and set up the colony of Jamestown in 1607. They found the flat watery landscape of the Tidewater rich in grass and tall trees, large strawberries and abundant game, but the swamps brought malaria and fevers with all the alarming concomitants of swelling and fluxes, the Indians were hostile and killed many settlers, they quarreled among themselves, and food ran short. Captain John Smith saved them so that by 1619 each freeman of Virginia was granted 100 acres of land. A Dutch ship brought "twenty negres" as slaves. Ninety well-chosen and well-chaperoned women came out to marry the bachelors, who paid their passages in tobacco. The first legislative assembly on the American mainland met, roughly modeled on Parliament, with a Council of six members and a House of Burgesses numbering twenty, who met under the chairmanship of the governor. They established a common-law code, the basis of the future Virginia constitution.

Most of the English settlers in Virginia were what might be called establishment supporters. They were generally members of the Church of England, royalist by inclination, and had fled from no persecution. They were there to make money and set up a new colony, not to express any particular ideology. The open landscape, with its slow-moving rivers, mild winters, and hot summers, lent itself to the plantation system. The way to the West was not, as far as they could see, barred by awesome mountain ranges.

It was a very different matter farther north. There, the climate had warm summers, but bracing cold winters; the land was hilly, with dense forests and a rocky coastline full of bays and inlets; the rivers were swift and strong, and at the back lay the Appalachian Mountains, obviously hard to cross. So any settlements there would be small clustered communities, clinging together for protection, and growing thick and firm before their more daring members started to press westward. The fast rivers prompted the eventual development of electricity and water power. Big houses set in broad plantation fields were not possible. The very geography of North America shaped the contrasting patterns of life that clashed two and a half centuries later in the Civil War.

One factor, however, was common to both. It is possibly the basic element in American history: the push westward, the magnet of the frontier. The wish to find what lies over the hill is so ingrained in the American ethic that it was inevitable that the United States should go into space. Space, after all, presents the frontier on the grand scale.

· 3 ·

By 1620 enough expeditions had reported back to make it clear that settlement in the northern part of America was possible. Europeans could survive the climate: indeed, it was healthy. There was plenty of game and fish. The principal European crops, wheat, barley, rye, oats, would grow. Two new valuable foods grew on the spot already: potatoes and Indian corn. This last, also called maize, gave an unequaled yield; planted in May it was ready to eat by July, and it could be the staple cattle food too. Even the voyage, which seemed to some people a powerful deterrent, was not such an obstacle as all that, according to the glowing accounts sent back from Virginia: it was neither too long nor too tedious, lasting at most six weeks, and most of it in the open sea, a place clear of rocks and of governmental tyranny.

One Englishman who interested himself in the subject of developing plantations in the New World was Sir Ferdinando Gorges. He came from Somerset, though the Gorges family originated in Devon. The head of the family at this time was Ferdinando's cousin Tristram, living at the principal Gorges house of St. Budeaux: today a part of Plymouth, but then a separate manor and village. (It was in the parish church of St. Budeaux that Francis Drake was married.) Another Gorges cousin was an aspiring but unsuccessful poet named Arthur, who kept up the family practice of choosing flamboyant names by calling his sons Carew, Egremont, and Timoleon. This Arthur was a friend of Raleigh. Their long and unwaveringly cordial acquaintance began in the Marshalsea prison, where both high-mettled young men worked out short sentences for crimes as colorful as their characters. Arthur Gorges was jailed for "giving the lie to the Lord Windsor in the Presence Chamber"; Walter Raleigh's offense was agreeably described as "a fray beside the tennis court." The Gorges were vaguely connected by marriage with the Raleighs and the Gilberts: the most celebrated of the latter was the navigator Sir Humphrey Gilbert, born in Devon in 1539 and granted a patent by Elizabeth Tudor in 1578 to discover and colonize in North America any land left unsettled, a spacious grant indeed. He voyaged twice to Newfoundland, and on the second expedition took possession of the harbor of St. John's. Soon after this he was lost in a storm at sea while attempting to explore the coast and, according to Hakluyt, encouraged his crew in the face of disaster by pointing out that they were as near to heaven by sea as by land.

Adrian Gilbert and Tristram Gorges joined in working on the charter for the Northwest Passage in 1583; Edward Gorges went to Roanoke in 1585, and one of Edward's sons sailed with Raleigh to Guiana.

Ferdinando Gorges started off as a professional soldier, for as a younger son he had to make his own way in the world. He served in Flanders, was taken prisoner at Ypres, was exchanged for an Armada prisoner of equal rank, fought in Normandy under Robert Devereux, Earl of Essex, with the troops of Henry of Navarre, who recommended him for promotion, and Elizabeth Tudor appointed him captain of the fort at Plymouth. He made the mistake of helping Essex in the mad rebellion led by that rash charmer, but wriggled out of trouble afterward, and James I gave him back his Plymouth command. Stationed there in the citadel, he watched the ships coming and going, fishing vessels heading for the Grand Banks and, now and then, explorers setting out to investigate the coasts of America. One such was Captain Martin Pring, who made a most exact survey of Massachusetts Bay. Pring's party took two mastiffs with them, named Gallant and Fool, who greatly frightened the Indians, though their fears were calmed by one young crew member who played a kind of guitar to which they danced. The Indians liked the music so much that they showered the performer with gifts: tobacco, pipes, and snakeskin belts six feet long. The crew admired the Indian crops of maize and cucumber, tobacco and pompions (pumpkins today), and brought home with them an Indian canoe. They loaded their ship, the *Discoverer,* with samples of all the unusual supplies they could find, and Pring's reports attracted Gorges more than ever before to the prospect of American colonization.

His interest increased when Captain George Weymouth returned from a voyage to Maine, bringing back five Indians, three of whom he presented to Gorges. James Rosier, who wrote a commentary on this expedition, stated plainly:

> The first and chiefest thing required for a plantation is a bold coast and a fair land to fall with. The next, a safe harbour for ships to ride in.

Weymouth's investigations showed that this was abundantly true of those parts of the Atlantic seaboard he examined, which seemed to him to afford conditions excelling those of Europe. Gorges was delighted with his Indians, too, and during the three years they stayed with him he dragged out of them every scrap of information they could provide. They told him of great rivers, safe harbors, and beautiful islands; of Indian government and Indian chiefs; of allies and enemies. They even helped him to rough out maps of parts of the mainland. Naturally Gorges was eager to see the rapid formation of charter companies to promote plantations, in which ambition he was closely associated with another Somerset man, the Lord Chief Justice Sir John Popham, formerly recorder of the city of Bristol. The only problem, and it was considerable, was that Gorges and Popham wanted to establish a strong West Country influence in the companies, whereas the West Country ports were interested in fishing rather than in planting settlements. They made a bold beginning, however, by sending out two ships. One of the ships, ordered to head for Cape Breton, went wrong and arrived in the West Indies, where the Spaniards captured the crew. The other, with Pring as master, reached Maine successfully and brought back a glowing account that converted a number of West Country gentlemen to the plantation idea.

Gorges had organized the very first expedition to New England as far back as 1603, the year Elizabeth Tudor died. Authorized by Raleigh, with the details arranged by Gorges, a party of twenty-four gentlemen and eight sailors chartered the *Concord* and sailed from Falmouth on March 26. Twelve of them proposed to settle, the rest returning with samples of produce. The captain of this expedition was Bartholomew Gosnold, and among the passengers who had received grants of land from Gorges were Bartholomew Gilbert, Gabriel Archer, and John Brereton, a professional soldier with the rank of major-general, from Cheshire. Their destination was Massachusetts Bay, and Gosnold struck it precisely, having made the crossing so directly that he estimated saving almost three thousand miles. On May 15, after a fifty-day voyage, the *Concord* rounded a headland which Gosnold named Cape Cod. They had enjoyed the crossing, with "not a man sick two days together." Gosnold and Brereton with two others stepped ashore on the white sands, but did not stay there, taking the ship on past what are now Nantucket, Martha's Vineyard, and Dover Cliff, into Buzzard's Bay, which they called Gosnold's Hope, and anchored off a likely-looking island which they named Elizabeth's Isle. Within less than three weeks they had built a fort and storehouse in the middle of a lake three miles wide and had traded with the local Indians in furs and sassafras. The Indians were able to speak "divers Christian words," presumably learned from other exploratory expeditions, and made the travelers welcome. One group, led by their chief, came to greet them; Archer walked forward and embraced the chief, whereupon the Indians all sat down "in manner like grey-hounds upon their heels," and Gosnold's men instantly "fell a-bartering." They gave the chief a pair of knives, so sharp and glittering that the chief was much impressed, and a straw hat, which he delightedly wore right away. It seemed that the Indians liked everything about their new friends, except for their English mustard, which made them pull sour faces.

Leaving most of the party in the fort, *Concord* went off to load up a cargo of cedarwood. The party planted wheat, barley, and peas, finding to their amazement that within two weeks the seeds had sprung up nine inches. They eked out their food with "alexander and sorrel pottage" and nuts, and smoked tobacco, but by the end of a month they faced the fact that their numbers were too small and their stocks too low to guarantee survival. The ship's return was hailed with deep relief. There was quite a lot of quarreling between the crew and the would-be planters before they decided to go home. After an uncommonly quick crossing—five weeks—they landed at Exmouth on July 23.

The supplies they brought back realized a handsome profit, the sassafras alone selling for £336 a ton. Sassafras rapidly became the wonder plant: sassafras tea, hot or cold, sweetened with honey or sugar and brewed from the roots or bark, apparently cured gout, fevers, and headaches, and acted as a general tonic. General Brereton wrote an account of the expedition under the title *A Briefe Relation of the Description of Elizabeths Ile, and some others towards the North Part of Virginie.* It had a powerful effect upon the twenty-three-year-old Captain John Smith, and made him determined to cross the Atlantic himself. Smith's two and a half years in Virginia, which he left forever at the age of twenty-nine, had an influence out of all proportion to its length; and when he was fifty-one he wrote his *Advertisements for the unexperienced Planters of New England or anywhere.* He it was who gave New England its name, to balance Drake's New Albion in Guiana.

With the best will in the world, such early accounts as these were misleading. The voyages had been made in summer; it was not possible to imagine what New England would be like when winter began to spread its iron crust over the land. England could not draw upon the superior knowledge of the Spanish, still regarded as the enemy. Indeed, one doubt voiced at the start was that the Spaniards might come up the coast to wipe the English out. This fear was crisply dealt with by one William Wood, who said that the Spanish would hardly bother to travel thousands of miles with a fleet simply to attack small settlements not yet worth pillaging. He boldly suggested that when they were sufficiently prosperous to tempt assault, their defenses would be equally formidable: "When the Bees have honie in their Hives, they will have stings in their tailes."

In tracts like *Nova Britannia,* written in 1609, the beauty and richness of the wide-open spaces across the Atlantic appeared in the rosiest light. The rivers, deep and broad, swarmed with fish; the climate was healthy; the Indians were loving and gentle and the colonists could not only befriend them but raise their standard of living; the woods were endless and the land bursting with luscious fruits. Among natural resources the writer listed mulberry trees and silkworms, thick furs, pitch, tar, resin and turpentine, sturgeon and caviar, an abundance of game, fruit, and plants.

Mineral resources were also hinted at, and the dream of the poor London apprentice was to find wealth and adventure overseas. Raleigh's and Drake's voyages created a trail of legends: mountains of gold, river sands where diamonds and pearls could be picked up in handfuls, magic herbs to cure all diseases, fountains of eternal youth. Sassafras, as we have seen, was one wonder plant: tobacco was another. James I might write in 1604 his famous *Counterblast,* describing the death of a smoker whose body when opened contained a bushel of soot; the legends spoke louder. In 1588 Thomas Harriot wrote *A Briefe and True Report of the New Found Land of Virginia,* and in it pointed out that tobacco would purge superfluous phlegm, open pores and body passages, cure ague and gout, reduce fatigue and hunger, cool the system, and stop hangovers. Other writers said it would relieve headaches and toothache, rheumatism and pains in the joints, swellings, wounds, snakebite, and halitosis. It could be smoked, chewed, rolled into pills, steeped in water like a tisane, powdered for cuts, made into poultices. There was nothing, apparently, that it would not do.

The lure of gold was well illustrated in a play called *Eastward Ho!* produced in 1605. In it a character named Captain Seagull gave a spirited commercial for the western voyages:

> I tell thee gold is more plentiful there than copper is with us, and
> for as much red copper as I can bring, I'll have thrice the weight
> in gold. Why, man, all their dripping pans and their chamber pots
> are pure gold, and all the chains with which they chain up their
> streets are massy gold; all the prisoners they take are fettered in

gold. And for rubies and diamonds, they go forth on holidays and gather 'em by the seashore to hang on their children's coats.

It was Captain John Smith who dealt the deathblow to the gold delusion when, after sailing up to Maine in 1614, he wrote in words published two years later that New England's wealth would come from fish, and that there was the country for men of "great spirits but small means."

But the astonishing fertility of America continued to dazzle aspiring explorers. Six weeks' sail away, they said, were wild boar and venison as plentiful as mutton and bacon in London. Even when the first settlements were established the prodigality of the country charmed beholders: the Reverend Francis Higginson, who landed at Salem in April 1629 and was to die of tuberculosis within a year, wrote in *New Englands Plantation,* published in 1630, that God had arranged the four elements in America to be specially favorable to human life. One sip of New England's air was better than a whole draft of Old England's ale. There was plenty of good wood for fuel; one could eat roast game all winter; pigeons, geese, and duck were very plentiful, partridge as big as English hens, turkeys bigger than English ones and "exceeding fat, sweet and fleshy" abounded. Strawberries, big and juicy, grew richly, like other fruits.

These accounts, and others like them, described the Earthly Paradise indeed: it all sounded as attractive as a modern travel brochure or the write-up on a new car. Like both of these, however, it left out the undeniable disadvantages.

Word of some possible or actual drawbacks did filter through to Europe. People had been known to starve in the midst of plenty. New territories contained disease, perhaps new diseases. Women and children, who must go along if any colony were to survive, might not live through the voyage, let alone the first months of settling. The Indians were not always loving and gentle—horrifying stories of torture and massacre were reported. The whole undertaking was enormous anyway. There was room and to spare for doubt.

• 4 •

Apart from what might be described as purely material considerations, there was the spiritual question, which had arisen naturally out of the religious controversies of the sixteenth century and bulked larger as time went on.

The Protestant ethic, the idea that each man should make up his own mind according to his conscience, dealing direct with God rather than through the medium of the accumulated wisdom and experience of the church, was set free in England by the Reformation, though for years there was little or no verbal or outward difference. Church services went on word for word unchanged, except that the monarch's name was substituted in prayers for that of the Pope. The Latin mass was said as it had ever been. But the concept was spreading that a single human soul, or a group of them, could stand apart and think for itself. This linked with the growth of nationalism—the awareness that instead of a supranational church dealing impartially with its flock no matter what country they came from and doing so in the supranational common language of Latin, each separate colony could establish its own church and therefore its own spiritual attitude. In England the coping stone of this growing belief was the translation of the Bible, crowned, between 1604 and 1611, with the Authorized Version, which gave the English Bible to the English people as the supreme literary achievement of the age.

The fact that the Bible could be read and discussed, its precepts interpreted afresh in the light of each man's experience and personal creed, created, or helped to create, the individual groups known as Separatists. Study of the Scriptures opened their eyes abruptly to their own ignorance and folly, and naturally aroused in them a deep sense of sin. The next logical step was self-reform. After that came the reform of others by evangelistic preaching. Now there can be no doubt that the spectacle of an ostentatiously godly neighbor, forever pointing an accusing finger at the impiety and frivolity of others, is an unbearable nuisance. The Separatists were objected to and persecuted as the assembly of Jerusalem set upon Stephen, and for much the same reasons, except that church writs in this case took the place of stones.

Faced with this opposition, the Separatists' will hardened to the point where they stated bluntly that it was wrong to submit to a parcel of dictatorial bishops and other unenlightened church dignitaries. One particularly tenacious cluster of Separatists lived in a comparatively small area of north Nottingham and the Lincolnshire border, a countryside of wide shallow hills and open fields of trim agriculture, rising eastward to the Lincoln wolds and leveling out southeastward into the flat plain of Holland, as that part of England is appropriately called. This group formed a nonconformist meeting under the leadership, first, of an elderly pastor, Richard Clifton, and then of one John Robinson, born about 1576 at Sturton-le-Steeple on the old Roman route from Lincoln to Doncaster. Of yeoman stock, Robinson was educated at Cambridge, where he stayed for twelve years from 1597 as a Fellow of Corpus Christi College. During those twelve years the great controversies of religion engaged his full attention, but when James I became king in 1603 and a more repressive regime appeared to have come in, Robinson resigned his fellowship and went home. At the same time he gave up the living of St. Andrew's, Norwich, which he had held for a year, because he refused to subscribe to the revised Thirty-nine Articles.*

Half a mile from Sturton-le-Steeple, at Fenton, lived Bridget White, whom Robinson married. They went to live at Gainsborough (George Eliot's St. Ogg's), an old market town huddled down on the banks of the River Trent, across which it looked into the county of Nottingham. In due time three children were born to them, John, Bridget, and Isaac. The religious group led by Robin-

---

* The Thirty-nine Articles are a statement of the particular points of doctrine maintained by the Church of England, and all candidates for ordination as clergymen of the Anglican church must subscribe to them. First drawn up in 1562–63, they were subsequently revised in 1604.

The article that condemns Separatist sects was the principal one Robinson shied at.

Manor Farm, Scrooby, where Separatist Meetings were held.
(PHOTO NICHOLAS SERVIAN FIIP, WOODMANSTERNE LIMITED)

son met twelve miles west of Gainsborough in the village of Scrooby, to which they walked to meetings, a distance soon too great for Clifton to manage.

Scrooby, where Cardinal Wolsey had halted on his last journey north and planted a mulberry tree, was one of the manors belonging to the Archbishopric of York. John Leland uncompromisingly called it "a mean townlet," though he did admit that St. Wilfred's church was well built. It stood on the Great North Road, a misnomer at that time because the way was nothing but a meandering unfenced track on which no one traveled farther than a few miles without a guide, and although Elizabeth Tudor had ordered the clearing of undergrowth and brushwood for a depth of two hundred feet on both sides of all main roads, highway robbery and murder were still everyday occurrences. Nearby Bawtry was a rendezvous for bandits and ruffians of all kinds. The manor of Scrooby provided a posthouse for travelers, where they could change horses and, if they wished, stay the night. Records exist of a charge of seven shillings for bed and breakfast, supper, and a bedtime hot drink of wine with spices, sugar, egg, and bread; eight shillings for a horse for eight miles; two shillings for beer, bread, burned sack and sugar (a kind of mulled wine). The manor contained several small houses, a bakehouse and a brewhouse, a forge, a granary, stables, kennels, and dovecotes, all within the moated area of the manor house, which had forty rooms and a private chapel. It stood near a hummocky field between the mill on the Ryton stream and the River Idle, into which it flowed.

The steward and bailiff was John Brewster, who had come there after a Cambridge education. His son William, born in 1566, was also educated at Cambridge, a contemporary of two dazzling undergraduates: Christopher Marlowe and Robert Devereux, Earl of Essex, both two years his senior. In those days Cambridge, according to Dr. John Caius, was a perfect nest of idlers, "the abodes of sloth and luxury, monasteries whose inmates yawn and snore, leading their lives in vanity and folly," devoted to gambling and cards, drink, fashionable clothes, and the company of disreputable women.

Cambridge was more than this, though: it was the center of heated religious controversy and debate. One celebrated son of the university was Robert Troublechurch Browne, most notable of Separatists, so influential that Separatists were known as Brownists for years. He had left Cambridge for Holland, where he lived at Middelburg, in 1582 publishing two tracts that were widely read in England and gained many adherents for the ideas they expressed. One was entitled *A Treatise of Reformation without Tarrying for Any,* and the other *A Book which Showeth the Life and Manner of all True Christians.* The core of Browne's belief came in the precept that the Kingdom of God would not be established, or begin to be established, by whole parishes or communities at large, "but rather by the worthiest, were they ever so few." These should separate from the rest and follow their own inner light.

Ideas such as these appealed to William Brewster, but as a young man he seemed likely to follow a career in the diplomatic service. Sir William Davison, chosen to go to the Netherlands on a special mission, picked Brewster as a confidential servant and spe-

cial messenger. Davison's mission was to take possession of the
so-called cautionary towns of Flushing and Brielle, ceded to England as a guarantee of the cost of the Earl of Leicester's expedition
in 1585 and not handed back for thirty years. The embassy was
successful: in token Davison was given the keys of Flushing, which
he handed to Brewster for safekeeping; Brewster slept with them
under his pillow. Esteemed by Davison more as a son than as a
servant, employed in every matter requiring the greatest trust and
secrecy, Brewster was well thought of too by the Dutch, who
presented him with a gold chain. It seemed as though a glittering
career lay ahead for William, but Elizabeth Tudor involved Davison in her search for a scapegoat after the execution of Mary
Queen of Scots, and by the end of 1587 Davison was held prisoner
in the Tower and Brewster, his prospects in pieces, was back at

William Brewster's cottage, Scrooby. (PHOTO NICHOLAS SERVIAN FIIP,
WOODMANSTERNE LIMITED)

Scrooby helping his father, who had been there then for twelve years.

Within three years William Brewster had taken over the full duties of postmaster, which he held for eighteen years, and had become a Separatist, which he remained for life. He built up a following of fellow thinkers who at first worshiped in Scrooby church with its century-old chancel screen carved in patterns of vines and grapes, but who later met on Sundays in Brewster's house. He also established a solid family with his wife Mary, two years younger than he, and various children, including a son Jonathan, born in 1593, and two daughters, Patience, born in 1600, and Fear, born in 1606. Dismissed from his job in 1607 because of his religious activities, he was still able to afford some shares in the Virginia Company two years later, despite a fine levied on him for what was called disobedience in matters of religion and the loss of his salary at Scrooby, nominally recorded at thirty pounds eight shillings and fourpence a year (almost ten times that of his father thirty years earlier).

Robinson found a kindred spirit in Brewster and joined in the group activities, rapidly rising to a leading position. Meetings for worship were austere: there was no organ music—organs were considered "the Devil's bagpipes"—and the only singing was in unison, for part singing was said to be "frivolous and unbecoming the House of God." Prayers were said with the congregation standing, for kneeling was a Popish practice according to Separatist belief: perhaps this was as well since bouts of prayer might go on for as long as two hours.

Among the recruits to the group at Scrooby appeared a young man called William Bradford, born on March 19, 1589, in the village of Austerfield three miles to the north on the Yorkshire border. After his father's death and his mother's remarriage he had been brought up by his grandfather and two uncles. The solitary life he had led from childhood caused him to think for himself more than most children do, and when barely into his teens he began to question spiritual matters. He became convinced that the Refor-

William Bradford's birthplace, Austerfield. (PHOTO NICHOLAS SERVIAN FIIP, WOODMANSTERNE LIMITED)

Austerfield Church where Bradford was baptized. (PHOTO NICHOLAS SERVIAN FIIP, WOODMANSTERNE LIMITED)

mation had not worked fast enough and determined to withdraw from his local parish assemblies. This bold resolve was not easily reached. He read tracts and pamphlets on all aspects of the subject, discussed them with anybody who would listen, attended meetings and heard sermons, lectured his uncles, who did not take it at all kindly, prayed earnestly for guidance, and withstood the angry or worried protests of his friends to the point where he set out to find a group that went by what he called the written Word of God. At Scrooby he found the answer.

It is to Bradford that we owe most of our information about the Pilgrim Fathers of 1620, for he kept the journal later published under the deceptively laconic title *Of Plymouth Plantation*. He also wrote part of the Pilgrim chronicle given the entirely misleading name of *Mourt's Relation*. It is impossible not to develop a warm liking and admiration for Bradford on reading his writings, however exasperated one becomes at some of the opinions he expresses. It is a classic document—the annual summing up, obviously written without a calculating eye to posterity as he leaves out a good deal of priceless information, yet a clear picture emerges of a sincere, brave, simple man of sense and compassion without sentimentality, who wrote his reflections in strong and dignified language and attributed the smallest gleam of good fortune to the watchful providence of God.

Not for some years did Bradford reveal himself fully as the great Pilgrim leader. At first he was merely a young member of the group, ardent, intelligent, and thoughtful. As the Scrooby Separatists established themselves and began more and more to behave in a manner the conformists found objectionable, so opposition to them stiffened and positive action against them began. This in turn of course made the Separatists more certain than ever that they were God's elect, destined to suffer for their faith like the martyrs so vividly described in Foxe's book. They were watched, criticized, informed upon, dismissed from official posts, sometimes imprisoned, until they decided that the area was too hot to hold them and they must move elsewhere.

Where indeed they could go to find safety was not in doubt for long. One place they knew existed where freedom of religion for all men was possible: the Netherlands.

· 5 ·

The seven United Provinces (Holland, Zeeland, Utrecht, Guelders, Friesland, Overijssel, and Groningen) had wrested their independence from their Spanish overlords only a few years before. They had declared themselves a republic governed by Their High Mightinesses the States-General sitting as a parliament under the chairmanship of the Grand Pensionary, with the ruling prince of the House of Orange-Nassau as titular head, or Stadtholder. After they had flung defiance in the face of Catholic Spain with startling success it was not surprising that they should uphold the principles of religious toleration. The Separatists interpreted this as pro-Protestant, for one of the basic tenets of their creed was that Satan was a Catholic. Bradford opens his journal with an explicit statement that England, first to break free from the darkness of popery, had naturally provoked the envy of Satan, who began to persecute the elect in the harshest manner.

It is essential to realize how literal and positive was Satan at this period. It was, after all, the age of the witch craze in Europe, when demoniacal possession was as firmly believed as the precepts of psychiatry today. Then, as now, sin wears different coats to different eyes, and to the English Protestants it came clad in the full panoply of Rome. Too close to Rome for comfort seemed the vestments of the English bishops, who stopped such activities as Brewster's efforts to appoint Puritan clergymen to local livings. Liberty of conscience might be found in the freer air of the Low Countries, where Satan's power was weaker.

Friends were quick to emphasize the difficulties of such an emigration. It would be hard to leave their work, their friends and relations, their native land. They proposed to go to a country they only knew by hearsay. They would have to learn a new language and find fresh jobs, which might not be easy. The cost of living was high in Holland. At any moment war with Spain might break out. They were ignorant of trade, the staple of Dutch life. No one could leave England without governmental permission, which would probably be refused to Separatists.

This last argument was the only moderately effective one. The exodus from England was a cloak-and-dagger operation, a matter of bribery and secrecy to smuggle themselves out of the country, dodging the vigilance of port officials.

In 1607 it seemed as if they were going to be able to do it. A ship was found and passage arranged from Boston in Lincolnshire, and a group including the eighteen-year-old Bradford set out, carrying their personal belongings, to travel the sixty miles from Scrooby. The way was mostly by boat, along the Idle and Trent Rivers to Gainsborough, by the Roman canal called the Foss Dyke to Lincoln, then by way of the River Witham to Boston.

Boston, St. Botolph's town, birthplace of John *(Book of Martyrs)* Foxe and parent of the principal city of Massachusetts, was a prosperous trading port with Flanders. Built on utterly flat land by the river, its superb church tower nearly three hundred feet high was a landmark for miles to sailors and landsmen alike, mounting a beacon in its lantern to guide the shipping. The Stump, as it is called, still dominates the attractive old market town near the Wash, and its Guildhall still displays the cells in which some of the Pilgrims were confined.

For it all went wrong. The ship's captain informed on them, their scheme was revealed, and they were arrested and searched. Bradford, being young, was released; but the rest of the party languished in the lockup for a month, the last set free being Brewster, Robinson, and the venerable pastor Richard Clifton. They were sent back and told not to try such dangerous dealings again.

They did, though. The following spring, 1608, they managed

Boston Guild Hall. The cells where the Pilgrim Fathers were imprisoned.
(PHOTO NICHOLAS SERVIAN FIIP, WOODMANSTERNE LIMITED)

it, though for quite a while it appeared unlikely that they ever would. Bradford and a few others got aboard a ship for Zeeland, and reached it after a jumpy land journey and a choppy crossing. The rest heard of a Dutchman at Hull who owned his own ship, and made an arrangement with him. He told them not to worry, he would get them out all right, but not from a port. He picked a deserted bit of coast midway between Hull and Grimsby, and suggested that the women and children should come to the rendezvous by boat with all the luggage and the men should come by land.

The boat duly set off, but arrived early in a very rough sea. The women were so seasick that the sailors took refuge in a creek, where it was calmer: so calm, in fact, that the boat grounded at low water and could not be pulled off until noon the next day. Meanwhile the ship had punctually arrived, and so had the men, who were walking about on the beach. The Dutch captain sent a boat to fetch them off, and had got the first half of the party safely on board when he noticed a sizable body of mounted men and a whole lot more on foot, all carrying weapons, bearing down on the women and children in the creek. Hurriedly he scrambled the rest of the men on board, and swearing cheerfully *"Sacramente!"* (an interesting reflection of the years of Spanish occupation), he weighed anchor, hoisted his sails, and ran for it before a fair wind.

The men of the Pilgrim party were, of course, greatly distressed at their double predicament. There they were, with nothing but the clothes they stood up in, with hardly any money, and their wives and children and belongings in the hands of the Philistines. With tears in their eyes they begged the Dutchman to turn back, but he refused.

It was a terrible crossing. It took over a fortnight, with a great storm that blew the ship across almost to Norway. For over a week the clouds were so low and heavy that not a glimpse of sun, moon, or stars could be seen. At one point the waves lashed so furiously that the crew went hysterical and prepared to abandon ship, expecting her to founder at any minute. The storm blew itself out, however, and the Dutchman steered to the south, where at last they staggered to anchor in Holland. A large crowd stood on the quay to watch them come in, amazed at their survival through so severe a storm.

Though it did not look like it at the time, their departure leaving the women and children behind proved helpful. The Boston and Hull and Grimsby authorities, and any others appealed to as to what could be done with these people, passed the buck briskly from one to another. Confronted with a crowd of destitute women, frightened and in tears, with their terrified children clinging to them, all cold and unhappy, they finally decided that it was unreasonable to punish them for merely doing their Christian duty— obeying their husbands. They could not be sent home, for they had no homes to go to; the only solution was to pack them off to Amsterdam. This was done, the task organized by Robinson and Brewster, who volunteered to stay to the last to help the weakest over, and who crossed to Holland in the final group to depart.

Holland struck the women as most peculiar. They were neither the first nor the last to notice how foreign Abroad could be, but their reactions were pleasantly naïve: they found a richly fertile, flat land, miles of it painfully reclaimed from the sea, with well-planted fields, fat cattle, orchards standing in beautifully ordered rows; imposing walled towns, prosperous and strongly fortified, guarded by armed soldiers in quaint uniforms; long straight roads, better paved than those in England; strangely uncouth voices—so very different from the comparatively scattered, sloppy, piecemeal England of hills and tangled woods and hazy distances that they had known all their lives.

In his *Travels*, the young Sir William Brereton, future Civil War commander on the Parliament side, described Amsterdam as

a most flourishing city yet the air so corrupt and unwholesome especially in winter time, when most part of the country round about overflowed. Here no fresh water, no water to brew but what is fetched from six English miles distant. Hence they have much beer but no water to wash withal but rain water, little fire except turf, the most of the wood burnt here brought out of Denmark and Norway. The coals come from Newcastle.

And Sir Thomas Overbury found Amsterdam solidly prosperous.

So it was. Water was the natural Dutch element, as the Spaniards had found, for the fight against Spain had begun in 1572 when a group of Calvinist sea captains calling themselves the Sea Beggars captured Brielle and thereby triggered off a sequence of revolutionary risings throughout Holland and Zeeland during which the valiant Dutch did not hesitate to use water as a weapon. Despite the enormous comparative power of Spain, her wealth, and the merciless energy she brought to the struggle, the Dutch were never again subdued by the Spaniards north of the Scheldt. The Seven Provinces united in 1579 and declared independence in 1581. To mark this notable achievement they passed a notable law, that every citizen should "remain free in his religion, and no man be molested or questioned on the subject of divine worship." Spain still held the port of Antwerp, so it was to Amsterdam that the Dutch trade flowed, brought in by Jewish and Flemish refugees who set up the trade in diamonds and cloth, the great financial enterprises, and the whole apparatus of chartered companies, banks, and the Stock Exchange, all growing almost visibly richer with maritime expansion. Timber and pitch from the Baltic, furs from Scandinavia and Russia, spices, jewels, and silks from the East, even rare bulbs and plants fetching incredible prices to feed the Dutch passion for horticulture, proliferated in the prosperous port.

In Amsterdam the reunited party from Boston found other Separatists who had taken refuge there. So far from hailing these compatriots with relief and joy, they almost at once began to squabble. It was the eternal religious argument about "everybody is out of step but our Joe." Pastor John Smyth, already well established in the city, alienated the sympathies of the recent arrivals by some of his doctrines, including his belief in adult baptism.

Richard Clifton, who had crossed from Boston, had tried hard to hold the English together in Amsterdam, but Robinson and Brewster faced the fact that a fresh separation was inevitable. The city of Leyden had made no fuss about letting them settle, provided they behaved themselves and kept the law. Clifton stayed in Amsterdam, "a grave and fatherly old man having a great white beard" who understandably was "loath to remove any more." He died there in 1616.

Within a year Robinson's followers had moved to the city of Leyden, of which a professor at the university had remarked that, as the Low Countries formed the best part of Europe, and Holland the finest of the United Provinces, so unquestionably the most beautiful city of Holland was Leyden.

He had a point. Situated a dozen miles north of The Hague and half a dozen from the sea, it is to this day a dignified and charming old place, full of handsome brick houses with the characteristic stepped and curved gables of classic Dutch design reflected in mirror-smooth canals spanned by elegant bridges. The Pilgrims worshiped at St. Peter's Church, a vast brick bulk with a small square on one side and, on the other, the Kloksteeg, or Clock Alley, where Robinson lived. His partially restored house, Groene Port (Green Door), still stands just across from the church. It has a stone archway with a door painted dark green leading to the neat square garden patterned with narrow paths. Pigeons coo on the roof of the building, occupying three sides of a square, which Robinson extended to accommodate twenty-one families. Next door but one stands the Groenehuis (Green House). Here lived Thomas Brewer of Kent, described by Sir Dudley Carleton, the English Ambassador to The Hague, as "a gentleman of a good house, both of land and living, which none of his profession in these parts are." Sixteen years younger than Brewster, a Calvinist rather than a Separatist by belief, he provided the capital to set up a printing press for the Leyden congregation. He arrived there in 1615, and found the English families all living close to one another in a little network of streets overshadowed by the great bulk of the Pieterskerk. One of the leading Separatists, a wool carder from Canterbury called Robert Cushman, had bought a fairly large house in the Nonnensteeg (Nuns Alley) and settled in this his second wife Mary Singleton; William Brewster lived in the Stinksteeg, which name needs no translation.

At the west end of Clock Alley a bridge spans the canal; here is the Rapenburg Quay, the architectural high spot of Leyden. Beautiful, dignified houses of brick, trimmed with pale stonework and crowned with elaborate gables, line the quay on both sides of the gentle water. It was from that quayside by the bridge that the Pilgrims eventually embarked for the canal journey to Delftshaven, the first stage of their voyage to the New World.

Leyden at that time was so eminent a cloth center that even the English sent their cloth there to be finished. Looms clacked and hummed in every street. The English settlers were what would be described today as bourgeois or petty bourgeois, and the financial limitations of their circumstances forced them to take up somewhat humble trades. Peace of mind and freedom of conscience mattered more to them than material prosperity, which was as well since they had a struggle at first to make ends meet. Later their condition became fairly comfortable. They took up a variety of trades, working as weavers and silk workers, tailors, hatters, glovers, shoemakers, fellmongers, wool carders, and blacksmiths, and numbered fifty-seven different occupations among them. The total Pilgrim colony amounted to 473 men, women, and children. The adults worked long hours for very modest wages. One or two managed better.

Brewster's educational background permitted him to take up tutoring. Plenty of students in Leyden wanted to learn English, and Brewster interpreted it to them through Latin, which, of course, he had in common with them. He drew up an English grammar on the lines of the Latin primer. This was a great attraction: not only Dutch students but German and Danish, some of them noblemen's sons, found sufficient space in their college timetables to fit in lessons with Brewster. He wrote tracts, too, some of which were printed on the press he operated with Brewer.

The printing shop was set up in the Pieterskerk Koorsteeg, Choir Alley. One could leave the printing house by the back door and slip in to the back door of the Green House without going out into the street, which proved useful at times. The house imprint was, naturally, in Latin, and read as follows:

LUGDUNI BATAVORUM

APUD GUILJEMUM BREWSTERUM

IN VICO CHORALI

—meaning: "At Leyden in Holland, at the House of William Brewster in Choir Alley."

Their first publication was issued in 1617, and was *A Plain and Familiar Exposition of the Ten Commandments, with a Methodical*

Short Catechism. Actually it was in Dutch, as all the earliest works published in Choir Alley were.

Later, when Brewster, as editor in chief, and Brewer, as managing director, branched out into English pamphlets and tracts, some of these were smuggled into England, where they caused trouble, in particular a piece called *The Perth Assembly.* Written by one David Calderwood, it was a savage attack on James I for trying to impose bishops on the General Assembly of the Church of Scotland in 1618. James protested angrily through Sir Dudley Carleton, who alerted the Leyden authorities. Unwilling to offend the English government, yet holding to their principles, the Leyden magistrates did enough to make the Pilgrim press a nervous, hunted business, but Brewster contrived to lie sufficiently low to evade arrest. James, still smarting, sent a cross letter to the ambassador ordering him to "move the States General to take some strict order through all their Provinces for the preventing of the like abuses and licentiousness in publishing, printing, and vending such scandalous and libellous pamphlets." Brewer was arrested and kept for a time in the university lockup; later he went to London to face questioning, and the cost of his journey was paid, surprisingly, by James. After the questioning, which proved nothing, he was set free, but James had only paid his fare to London, not back again, so he quietly disappeared for a long time, while Sir Dudley kept on sending evasive reports to London in an attempt to conceal his failure to track down Brewster. Certainly the hunt for the editor in chief was a fumbling business that seems in retrospect singularly halfhearted.

Brewster had been appointed an elder of the Pieterskerk congregation, and he shared with Robinson, though unequally, the pastoral duties. They selected a widow of sixty as deaconess, and a good energetic worker she turned out to be, visiting the sick, collecting for the poor, finding domestic help where it was wanted, reporting to the deacons about any backsliding she found, and terrifying the children in church. She sat prominently near them, with a small birch rod at the ready. This holy terror was described mildly by Bradford as an ornament to the congregation.

Sunday exercises, or services, were held twice during the day, from about eight in the morning to noon, and from two to five or six in the afternoon, so there was plenty of time for the children to grow restless. Preaching was the core of every service. Beginning with prayer, the members would then read a chapter or two of the Bible and discuss the meaning at length. A speaker gave out a text and preached on it for an hour, and after him other speakers would enlarge at equal length on the same subject. It is interesting in the light of this form of worship to note that in 1603 the Puritan Millenary Petition addressed to James I had requested shortening the length of services.

In spite of difficulties the Leyden community prospered and lived contentedly. Religious dissensions never split them once they had moved from Amsterdam.

New adherents trickled to Leyden out of England, and some came from the French-speaking part of what is now Belgium. This was occupied Spanish territory, and Protestant believers found sanctuary over the border. Sometimes their views agreed with those of the Separatists so that they felt at home in the Leyden group. One couple to do this was Jean Pesijn and his wife Marie de la Noye, who in time left money for rebuilding and extending part of the Groene Port; it is called on modern street maps the Pesijnhofje. A young connection of theirs came too, Philip de la Noye, who crossed to America in 1621 at the age of sixteen and whose name eventually contracted to Delano.

The scrupulous honesty of the Pilgrims was appreciated by the Leyden tradesmen:

> Though many of them were poor, yet there was none so poor but if they were known to be of that congregation, the Dutch (either bakers or others) would trust them in any reasonable matter when they had no money. Because they had found by experience how careful they were to keep their word, and saw them so

hardworking and diligent in their callings, yet they would strive
to get their custom and employ them above others in their work.

Members of the Pieterskerk congregation married and had
children. Digerie Priest, who worked as a hatter to support his
motherless daughters Mary and Sarah, married on November 4,
1611, a widow, Sarah Allerton Vincent, whose brother Isaac on the
same day married Mrs. Mary Norris. Over the next seven years the
Allertons had three children, a son Bartholomew and two daughters
Remember and Mary. Moses Fletcher, who had come from Sandwich in 1608 with his six-year-old son (named after him), married
Mrs. Sarah Dingby in 1613. The Brewsters, despite their comparatively advanced ages, had two sons, Love and Wrestling (Wrestling was born approximately at the time of the exodus from England, which accounts for the quaint choice of name). Francis and
Esther Cooke had a son, John, in 1610; so did John Crackston of
Colchester, who already had a daughter. Edward and Ann Fuller
had a son in 1615, called Samuel after his doctor uncle. Dr. Samuel
Fuller married his third wife, Bridget Lee, on May 12, 1617.
Thomas Rogers' son Joseph was among the first born in the community. William and Susanna Fuller White had a son, Resolved, in
1615. Mr. and Mrs. Thomas Tinker had one son, and John Turner
had two. One member, John Tilley, then in his forties, married a
Leyden girl, Bridget van der Velde, his second wife. An astonishingly high proportion of the Pilgrims married, in due course, three
times: it is rare to find a survivor who did not marry twice, nearly
always to someone who had been married before, and third marriages were commonplace. Weddings were civil rather than religious ceremonies, like the Dutch weddings themselves among citizens of the Protestant persuasion.

Leyden at that time was a center of culture and a hotbed of
debate. Its university, founded in 1575, was already famous for its
brilliant scholarship. Given the choice between paying no taxes and
having a university, the citizens had with exemplary intelligence

chosen the latter. It was still small: William Brereton wrote of it, in a somewhat critical spirit:

> Here be only two colleges, in one about thirty students of Divinity, who have their diets and twenty guilders apiece, a square uniform little court or quadrangle; in the other, twenty students of Divinity who have therein their diets and fifty guilders apiece; these only go in the habit of scholars, so here is no face or presence of a university.

There might be little outward show, but it was renowned in European academic circles for all that. Naturally the main subject was religious studies. The professor of theology, Jacob Arminius, turned from the depressing Calvinism of predestination to a milder theory, declaring that any believer could win salvation and that God's elect included the repentant faithful. His adherents, known as Arminians, gained a new champion in his successor, Simon Episcopius, and vigorous opponents in two other professors, Gomarus and Polyander. Debates were frequent, crowded, and lively. Robinson, who had matriculated there in 1615 and thereby gained scholar's privileges, which included an allowance of beer and wine, formed the habit of turning up to listen to the discussions, although he was preaching to his own congregation three times a week and doing a good deal of learned writing besides. Encouraged by Robinson's interest to rise to the height of his powers, Episcopius announced various controversial propositions on which he was prepared to lecture against all comers in public. Robinson equally provoked the opposing standard bearer, Polyander, who challenged Robinson to argue against him. Robinson was shy at first, as a foreigner and a stranger, but Polyander insisted, and two or three public discussions took place, in which Robinson had the best of it: "he put him to an apparent nonplus," wrote Bradford, pleased. This created an enormous impression: Robinson would have been invited to join the faculty if the professors had not feared to offend the English government by thus favoring a Separatist. One offer they did make was that Robinson, when it was known that the Pilgrims planned to settle in the New World, should choose the colony of the New Netherland, then still in the planning stage. None of Robinson's followers felt surprise at this offer, but Robinson evaded a firm answer. As things turned out, he never left the Netherlands.

· 6 ·

The twelve-year truce between Spain and the United Provinces, signed on March 30, 1609, was due to run out in 1621. As the teens of the century went by, it was clear that the English community in Leyden had passed its peak in numbers and prospects. Holland, then as now, was overpopulated; the standard of living was low. If a better place to live could be found, recruits would come again, just as they had come in the beginning.

The Pilgrims saw that their members were aging prematurely. Worse, however, was the changing attitude of their young people. The parents' privations had made them harsher in their treatment of their children than they would have wished; some of these sons and daughters were old before their time, physically weakened in the years when they should have been in full vigor. Worst of all, many young people showed lamentable signs of breaking loose. They lived in a city (always more sinful than the country to Puritan thinkers), where they saw other young people pursuing pleasure; the Dutch did not keep the Puritan Sunday, but, once having been to church, made it a day of entertainment and good living, particularly for children. The Pilgrims' youngsters were in danger of becoming permissive. Some of them actually left to join the army, or went traveling abroad. Those who stayed seemed likely to lose their native language and their sense of nationality. Premature death and youthful corruption threatened everything the Pilgrims stood for.

Not only that. They were not really gaining adherents; there were no local innocents to convert. The Dutch were not interested in changing churches, and the Leyden English, to do them justice, saw no reason why they should. But God's work could not go on as it should unless the Pilgrims could propagate the gospel, however humbly, among the heathen. All these considerations moved them to think of transferring abroad, and to the most masterful spirits among them the empty spaces of America seemed the most suitable for their purpose.

This suggestion of crossing the Atlantic—almost certainly made first by Robinson—threw the Leyden community into a turmoil of argument and doubt. Although it was, as Bradford wrote, "a great design," all the protests from the more timid, more prudent, or simply more imaginative, envisaging the length of journey, the perils of the sea, the utter solitude of the group when landed, surrounded by unknown country full of savages and wild beasts, were voiced. The change of air and diet would spread weakness and disease. They would have to drink water, and everyone knew how dangerous that was. In any event, how could they afford such a huge project, poor and few as they were? It had been difficult enough to move from England to Holland in the first place, and Holland was not far off, uncivilized, and inhabited by cannibalistic Indians.

In reply, those in favor said simply that great designs produced great difficulties, also great courage with which to meet them. The hazards were immense, but not overwhelming, because men advancing into the unknown invariably feared many risks which never arose, and God was on the side of the elect. The Indians could hardly be worse than the Spaniards, who, as soon as the truce ended, would attack the Netherlands and visit their utmost cruelty and displeasure upon those who had been calling Satan a Catholic for years. And what a triumph for God and the right if they should succeed in the wilderness, or at the very least provide a stepping-stone for others to come after them!

This idealistic argument won the day with a Separatist group whose whole way of life was based upon the ideal of a persecuted but persistent elect. The financial problem, a particularly knotty question, could be solved by applying to one of the chartered companies.

It would be easier to get permission to emigrate to a new and remote plantation than to return to England: one of the strongest reasons for encouraging colonial settlement was (and remained for a very long time) that it solved the problem of difficult or undesirable characters. All sorts of dropouts could go: and the philosophy that transported convicts to Australia and ne'er-do-well younger sons to Rhodesia in the nineteenth century operated more than two hundred years earlier to send Quakers, Scottish and Irish rebels, and, as in this instance, Separatists, out of the way for good. Francis Bacon objected that this was like planting a field with thistles. A new argument was promptly advanced, that whatever sort of people populated them, the new colonies ought to become genuinely profitable. Once the settlers were self-supporting, they must produce goods for export to England; and not too hastily either, as some plantations had already been ruined by overquick attempts at profit. Bacon, who explained this principle in his essay *Of Plantations,* pointed out that logically the colonists ought to be gentlemen rather than traders, as the latter thought of nothing but money.

These ideas led to the framing of a colonial policy. Settlers were to be English citizens living abroad rather than agents of London merchants or financiers. Under English law, all colonial territory belonged to the Crown. The easiest way for the monarch to administer it was to grant it by charter to companies or proprietors, who would then be responsible for future development. This was where the gentlemen came in. At first they contented themselves with making the arrangements for the various plantations, possibly with several of their number acting as lords proprietors either in person or by deputy, much in the manner later worked out for governing India through a viceroy. The proprietors, licensed in ones and twos, could govern directly, though they were bound to permit every colonist a voice in lawmaking. The companies would be based in London, sending perhaps a few members out, either with the first settlers or fairly soon after them, to see how they were getting on.

From the moment they thought of moving somewhere else, the

Leyden Pilgrims had considered going to America. The question was, to which part? Their Dutch friends offered, through their own New Netherlands Company, free transport to their plantation at New Amsterdam on the Hudson River, with an escort of two warships for the voyage, homes when they got there, and cattle for every family. The Pilgrims themselves were attracted to Guiana, between the Amazon and the Orinoco, with its warm climate of perpetual spring, its fertile ground, and its legends of the City of Gold. Both of these ideas were abandoned. The Dutch were present and established as masters in the one place, the Spaniards near enough to be threatening in the other. Also, Guiana was believed unhealthy compared with cooler climates farther north.

The next place considered was Virginia, where the English were already securely settled. But these were orthodox English, members of the Church of England and establishment supporters, so the Pilgrims might be persecuted there, under worse conditions than in England, far from help or protection.

In the end the decision was cast for a hitherto undeveloped part of northern Virginia, where the Leyden community could set up its own colony, under the general government of Virginia yet separated by distance and freedom of religion from the other English. After much anxious debate, they determined to ask the Virginia Company to sponsor them. They drew up a statement. In it they played down the political and religious differences, promising to honor the King's authority and even that of the bishops. Even in this important matter they did not completely abandon their cherished beliefs: the Seven Articles of the statement included the affirmation that the King should be obeyed actively, if what he ordered did not go against God's Word, and obeyed passively if it did (it is not easy to see quite how one could be both passive and obedient in this context), always provided that according to the individual conscience there might be a hopeful prospect of pardon for any transgressions by the forces of law and by God. Also, although they promised to honor the bishops, they did not promise to obey them.

Two distinguished members, an English merchant in his fifties named John Carver and Robert Cushman, whose qualities of leadership had already raised them to positions of responsibility among the Leyden English, were chosen to go from Leyden in 1617 to open negotiations with the Virginia Company. Carver, whose precise place of origin is not clear, had attached himself to the very center of the group by his marriage to Catherine White, widow of George Leggatt and sister of Bridget Robinson. Their reception was more than favorable: anxious for eager colonists, the company welcomed them, willingly promised a charter with all possible rights and privileges, and said the King was sure to grant them religious freedom. James I, who does not seem to have read the Seven Articles very carefully, expressed the keenest interest in the proposed voyage, and approved the idea of the Pilgrims' enjoying, as they had tactfully put it, liberty of conscience under his gracious protection. When Sir Robert Naunton, principal Secretary of State, read out their promise to extend "by all due means" the land they held and the knowledge of the gospel, James approved it as a good and honest plan; and then asked what profits could be expected. With the answer, "Fishing," he was delighted: "It was the Apostles' own calling!"

Cushman and Carver, finding God going along with them, promptly struck a setback when James told them to consult the Archbishop of Canterbury and the Bishop of London. The King could not imagine taking any action involving religious questions, however remotely, without consulting dignitaries of the Church of England; but the two men from Leyden, privately resolved not to entangle themselves with bishops on any account, returned instead to the Virginia Company and told them that the King's reaction seemed favorable. The Virginia Company met in February 1619 to decide that the Pilgrims could have their patent, though exactly how long it might take to discuss and draw up they did not at that moment say.

Carver and Cushman at once threw open the expedition to any friendly merchants who might be interested. Either to invest money in the enterprise, somewhat on the lines of a modern shareholding for which members put up capital and gain profitable dividends (or at least hope to do so), or to come in person with the party across the Atlantic—this was the customary way in which these projected settlements were financed. Acting under instructions from Leyden, they promised not to commit anybody to anything without Leyden approval. One offer of help, from Captain John Smith himself, was refused. Smith's philosophical conclusion was that time and experience would teach them more sense.

· 7 ·

By the beginning of 1620 three companies were involved in making land grants to American colonists. They were the Virginia Company, the London Company, and the Plymouth Company, this last so called because many of its members were solid merchants from the southwest and from Plymouth in particular. Company officials called themselves collectively Merchant Adventurers.

The Merchant Adventurers agreed that their job was to finance the proposed transport of the Leyden "congregation of independents" to "the Northern parts of Virginia" under such protection and patronage from the government and the companies as they could get. The companies' territory stretched approximately from Chesapeake Bay up to the tip of Nova Scotia, leaving out those places already occupied. It was the Merchant Adventurers' job to sign all charter party documents of importance. There were about seventy men concerned, a mixture of gentlemen, merchants, and craftsmen, some investing a lot of money and some a little, each according to his means and the degree of his interest. They were not an ordinary corporation, but a voluntary combine of individuals united to do good, plant religion in faraway places, and make profits.

Some of the Adventurers were frankly self-seeking, like Edward Pickering, William Greene, James Sherley, who was one of the treasurers, and two who had a lot to do with the expedition, John Pierce and Thomas Weston. Pierce was the recognized representative in dealing with the London and Virginia Companies for New England affairs, especially concerning patents and charters. Weston was one of the principal negotiators between the Adventurers and the Pilgrims. The other was forty-year-old Christopher Martin of Billericay in Essex, also a treasurer, who was sailing with the party.

Some other Adventurers crossed the Atlantic—William Mullins of Surrey (who went on the *Mayflower);* brewer William Collier; Robert Keayne, who founded the Boston Artillery Company and bequeathed his books to start the first public library in America in 1656 in the same city; Samuel Sharpe, who came to Salem in 1629; John Revell, who crossed a year or so later in the *Jewel,* stayed a few weeks, disliked what he saw, and came home; Nathaniel Tilden of Kent, who settled at Scituate. Nathaniel's brother Joseph, citizen and girdler of London, did not go, but William Thomas did, settling at Marshfield, later the dwelling place of Daniel Webster.

Other active Adventurers included Robert Alden, who at first disapproved of the Pilgrims but later became one of their strongest supporters; Edward Bass, who lent them money; and the Andrews brothers, Richard and Thomas. Richard, a wealthy haberdasher of Cheapside, was an alderman; Thomas was lord mayor. There were two shipowners—Emanuel Altham, owner of the pinnace *Little James,* and Thomas Goffe, owner of the *Mayflower.*

Although the Pilgrims had got their patent, or charter, they were kept waiting by all sorts of irritating delays for its details to be properly worked out. On May 8, 1619, Cushman reported to Leyden in a letter reflecting his understandable exasperation. A squabble had broken out among the Virginia Company officials. Sir Thomas Smith, pleading pressure of business and overworry, had resigned as treasurer. The company accepted his resignation and elected a successor. In the ballot Alderman Johnson, with 24 votes, and Sir John Worstenholme, with 16, lost to Sir Edwin Sandys, who received 60 votes. Sir Thomas at once protested that Sir Edwin was unfit to hold the office, as he thought anybody but he would have

been, and the wrangle that resulted occupied the company's attention to the exclusion of other business, while Cushman kicked his
heels disconsolately on a three-week visit to Kent, hoping that Sir
Edwin would prevail and they could get on with the important
business.*

Cushman had plenty to think about. He had news from Captain
Samuel Argall, newly arrived from Virginia. Argall, an early settler
who had been deputy governor of Virginia for two years, reported
details of a recent and most disastrous transatlantic voyage. The
party had been led by one Francis Blackwell, who had split away
from the Leyden Separatists and settled in Amsterdam. There he
set up his own group, and eventually determined to remove to
America. All this time he had been observed sorrowfully from
Leyden as a man declining from the truth, bringing dishonor to God
and financial ruin to his flock; Robinson's comment had been that no
good would come of it. Mr. Blackwell traveled to London, where he
held an illegal private meeting with members of his godly group
who were informed on and arrested in a kind of police raid. Questioned by the bishops, Mr. Blackwell denied his previously affirmed
beliefs and placed the responsibility on the shoulders of others. For
this public-spirited action he was released and given the blessing of
no less a person than the Archbishop of Canterbury himself.

Deciding that the best place to find sanctuary was probably
Virginia, Mr. Blackwell engaged a ship at Gravesend, began to
provision it, and loaded it with 180 people, packed like sardines.
Exactly who these people were is not clear, but many of them were
doubtless his spiritual supporters, and the rest the usual collection
of more or less disreputable persons with reasons of varying ur-
gency for wanting to leave one country to try their luck in another.
The provisioning arrangements developed complicated difficulties.
The local merchants protested volubly and the Gravesend streets
rang with angry shouts of "It's all your fault!" When Captain

---

* It is not surprising that Cushman supported Sandys, who was son of the lord of the
manor of Scrooby. Contact with the Virginia Company was made by Brewster through
Sandys.

Maggner set sail he ran at once into trouble. There was not enough fresh water, the passengers had dysentery and infections so that 130 of them died, the ship was blown too far south and took much longer than expected to make the crossing. The master and six of the crew died, and those who were left struggled and beat about for days, trying to find the bay where they were supposed to land.

Mr. Blackwell was among the dead, which was of course only to be expected from one who had so provoked the judgment of God. At first Cushman wondered whether his party would be discouraged by this melancholy voyage, but found that they sturdily planned to learn from the folly and error of others. Bradford's eventual comment was typical of him: "If such events follow the bishops' blessing, happy are they that miss the same."

· 8 ·

The compact drawn up between the Merchant Adventurers and the planters was the seven-year agreement usual at that time. By it the Adventurers would provide the means and the Pilgrims would provide the colonists. All preparations were to be settled by Weston and Martin acting for the Adventurers and any colonists going from England, and by Carver and Cushman acting for the Leyden community.

The usual charter terms of the time embodied a grant of up to 80,000 acres with fishing rights, permission to trade with the local Indians, and considerable latitude in self-government and lawmaking. The Virginia Company granted forty-four such charters before 1624. The tracts of land were called hundreds, or particular plantations, and the precise location of each was never specified in its charter. Party leaders were supposed to report in person at Jamestown and there select their particular plantation from land available at that moment.

In the early stages of the negotiations, Sir Edwin Sandys wrote kindly to Robinson and Brewster, expressing his admiration for their delegates and his sympathy with the Pilgrims' aims. The reply he received out of Leyden summed up the key points as Robinson and Brewster saw them.* God was on their side; thanks to God they were welded into a close-knit group, hardworking and frugal; they were risking everything and staking their future on the great design. They wrote touchingly: "We are well weaned from the delicate milk of our mother country, and inured to the difficulties of a strange and hard land, which yet in a great part we have by patience overcome." And they added a noble sentence: "Lastly, it is not with us as with other men, whom small things can discourage, or small discontentments cause to wish themselves at home again."

This last point emphasizes the special quality that the early settlers everywhere possessed. The vast majority of men and women in Europe stayed put and endured their personal struggle for existence. War, persecution, poverty, and hardship could not move them to so drastic a step as emigration. Those who did set out into the unknown had something else—some special ingredient of daring the most people did not possess, and they realized it themselves: "It is not with us as with other men."

It follows that the earliest planters could not be drawn from the lowest levels of poverty. Nor could they be found among the powerful, wealthy, and secure. They were of two kinds: bourgeois families able to pay their passage, and indentured servants with enough skill and hardihood to make them valuable as pioneers. Two motives of overriding strength impelled them: space to build, live, and work honorably and decently; and freedom of worship. They were, in fact, moving away from church and state as these existed in the Old World, to establish both in their own image in the untroubled spaces of the New.

Both church and state that the settlers wished to leave made it possible for them to do so. In seventeenth-century society one could hardly move without the other; church approval was essential to a degree that amazes the present-day reader, and state funds sup-

* Appendix 3.

ported the church. Without clerical blessing the companies could not operate; without company backing the emigrants could not sail. The companies raised the money, paid for much of the freight, found ships, hired crews, prepared plans, and encouraged volunteers to go and make profitable use of all these assets on the other side of the world. The fact that such volunteers were anxious to leave the spheres of influence ruled by the very people they wanted to get away from, yet without whom they could not go, is agreeably ironic.

· 9 ·

On June 9, 1619, the promised patent was issued to the Pilgrims. Curiously enough, it was made out in the name of John Wincop, who was not one of the Separatists. On the contrary, he was one of three clergymen brothers, and lived in the household of Thomas Fiennes-Clinton, third Earl of Lincoln, where he was chaplain to the family—a person absolutely rooted in the establishment. The earl had died on January 15, but his daughters, Lady Susan Humphrey and Lady Arabella Johnson, were interested in New England. So was their steward, Thomas Dudley. In time all three became settlers under the Massachusetts Bay Company, Dudley rising to the dignity of governor of the Bay Colony. Wincop had expressed interest in the proposed Pilgrim voyage, and originally planned to go with them. It seems likely that his name was set to the patent as a prudent front for others who might well not appear quite so respectable.

A copy of the patent was sent to Leyden for the congregation to read and discuss. In preparation for so momentous a decision, they held what Bradford called a day of humiliation, with a full meeting for worship, during which Robinson preached on an apt text from First Samuel.

And David's men said unto him, see we be afraid here in Judah:
how much more if we come to Keilah against the host of the
Philistines? Then David asked counsel of the Lord again.

A great discussion then followed to determine how many should
go, and who they were to be. Far more wished to go than any two
ships could carry, but not all of them could be ready soon enough.
Those who knew they were staying begged Robinson not to leave
them. He agreed, whereupon those who knew they were going
asked Brewster to go too. He said that he would. Everybody
consented to both groups' being regarded as complete churches in
themselves, each able to make its own arrangements independently,
as it might be that they would be parted forever. If, however, any
members crossed later on, these should be accepted without question. If the New England party survived, the rest would join them
as soon as possible.

The Brewster and Carver families having decided to go, the
Allerton and Bradford members joined them, also Eatons, Fullers,
Tilleys, Tinkers, and Whites. Francis Cooke and John Crackston
would go with their sons but without their wives; John Turner
would take his two sons. Edward and Elizabeth Barker Winslow
expected their kinsman Gilbert to join them at the English port on
the way.

Thomas Weston now arrived from London. A citizen and
ironmonger of the capital, he was emphatically out for profit. He
had been in trouble over this before, when he and his friends had
organized unlicensed trading with Dutch merchants. This cut
across the legitimate dealing authorized by the London merchants
acting in council, so a complaint by them forced the Privy Council
to summon Weston and tell him to stop his bootlegging. Now he
had a fresh chance to make a quick turnover. Wanting all the trade
for himself, he began by warning the Pilgrims against the Dutch
and the Virginia Company, and told them they could depend on him
and his friends. Go ahead, make your plans, we will see that money
and shipping are provided, and, by the way, it would be a good idea

to draw up an agreement that my friends will be happy to invest in—that was the burden of his song. Relying on the good sense of Robinson and Brewster in Leyden, and of Carver and Cushman in London, the community drew up the articles, and Weston went back with it to England.

Various people in both countries were now employed in making inquiries and arrangements for the dozens of details that had to be arranged: money, shipping, provisions, exact figures for those proposing to travel. Difficulties multiplied. Some Pilgrims changed their minds. They preferred Guiana to Virginia. They were, after all, not quite sure about risking their money. Others said it must be Virginia or nothing—what were these rumors about a possible new destination?

The rumors were true. News came from Weston and from other acquaintances that a new grant of land had just been issued by the King for a huge region north of Virginia, called New England after Captain John Smith's name for it in 1614, to be separated from the existing Virginia government. Weston and his associates, scenting vast fishing profits, urged the Pilgrims to go there; the Pilgrims, hearing the magic word "separated," inclined to it at once.

The Council for New England now discovered that they were unable to obtain (and therefore grant) the fishing monopoly. Weston, seeing his magnificent profits threatened, at once suggested to the Pilgrims that they should close with the proposed terms, even if it meant modifying some of their original specifications. The terms of the charter, which strongly resembled those under which Jamestown had been settled, numbered ten, and were quite precise. This is what they laid down.

One share equaled ten pounds. Every member aged sixteen and over was rated at that sum. Young people between ten and sixteen equaled a half share each. Children under ten would each have fifty acres of unmanured land. Each emigrant taking ten pounds in cash or goods had a double share. The colony would operate on principles of pure communism: that is, their food, clothing, and all provisions would be drawn from the common stock. All profits from work and trade belonged to the common stock also for seven years, the settlers having on arrival divided the tasks among themselves, land or water, building, farming, fishing, and so on. Anyone joining them or investing in them during the seven years was to have a share in proportion. The share of anyone dying during that time was to be divided in proportion among his heirs. At the end of the seven-year period everything would be divided equally between the Adventurers and the Planters, and the original contract concluded.

The point that Leyden argued over was that such houses and gardens as they had by then built up in America ought to be theirs absolutely, not half theirs and half the Adventurers'. They also insisted on two days a week set aside for "their own private employment, for the more comfort of themselves and their families." They said this in a letter to Carver and Cushman on June 10, 1620.* Did Cushman, they asked, want to know what they objected to in the conditions? He must not assume they thought he had no brains: on the contrary, let him use them to remember Robinson's original postulations, and keep in mind that he was not supposed to make any firm commitment without their approval. To be sure, these doubts had not sprung from any specific word by Cushman; they had been voiced by Thomas Nash, just back in Leyden from a short visit to London, and backed up in the same week by Robinson himself, who wrote privately to Carver: * "We employed Robert Cushman who is known (though a good man and of special abilities in his kind) yet most unfit to deal for other men by reason of his singularity and too great indifferency for any conditions; and for (to speak truly) that we have had nothing from him but terms and presumptions." The letter of June 10 sent best wishes to Weston, in whom the writers hoped they were not deceived, and was signed by "your perplexed, yet hopeful brethren," Samuel Fuller, Edward Winslow, William Bradford, and Isaac Allerton.

Cushman at once replied. He was sorry that they were worried about what he was doing; but it was not his fault: he would explain

* Appendix 3.

everything. Weston was the only Adventurer who had read the conditions, and he had disliked the Leyden stipulation about the house property. One Virginia Company merchant, John Ferrar, had withdrawn his £500 investment in the project when he heard of it, and Weston said the rest would withdraw as well unless Leyden gave way on that point. Others, older and wiser than Cushman, had urged him to agree; the whole voyage might be jeopardized if he did not. There was poor Cushman, struggling with these problems, and to add to it all came complaints from Leyden that he was lording it over his friends and doing just as he liked, agreeing right and left to terms fitter for thieves and slaves than for honest men.

He went on to deal point by point with the Leyden objections. A man risking both his person and his money hazarded more than one who ventured only one of them. The settlers were not a charitable institution: they were furnishing a storehouse. It would be wrong to build elaborate houses at first; any dwellings should be so simple that, if need be, they might "with little grief set afire and run away by the light." If God made them rich they would first provide more men, ships, and weapons; communities declined rather than prospered when fine houses and fashionable clothes came before essentials. Any man who grudged equal conditions to his neighbor was not of good quality. If the houses proved to be worth little, all the more reason not to squabble over the money. Those who put profit first were ignoble. It was true that the Adventurers risked less than the Pilgrims, but after all no Adventurer had urged them to emigrate.

So, wrote Cushman firmly, nobody need grumble that he had given way; the only questionable clause was the property clause. As far as the two days a week were concerned, they could do as they liked; the Adventurers said the Pilgrims were reasonable people and could make what working arrangements seemed best.

At the end of his letter Cushman referred to the Amsterdam congregation, some of whom had proposed to join the Leyden Pilgrims. "I had thought they would as soon have gone to Rome as with us, for our liberty is to them as rat's bane, and their rigour as bad to us as the Spanish Inquisition." He thought it best that they stayed separate. He was personally willing to withdraw from the whole business, if the congregation thought him the Jonah in the ship: "only let us have quietness and no more of these clamours."

This honest outburst was wasted effort. John Carver read the letter and kept it, believing it would simply increase the members' offended feelings. Cushman, however, wrote another letter on June 11, and this one was sent. It opened disarmingly enough, saying that John Turner had delivered a letter from Leyden, and Weston a letter from Amsterdam, "savouring of the place whence it came." Cushman, who was still ready to drop out, said he had pulled himself together to make one final attempt at sorting matters with Weston. Weston himself had been irritated and kept on saying that only his original promise prevented him from abandoning the project, but he had agreed to try once more. The upshot was decisive. They had taken an option on a ship "till Monday."

· 10 ·

Monday was June 12, and the ship was not the *Mayflower*. What ship it was, nobody knows: the name was never mentioned. The important fact was that Cushman had taken positive action. It is clear from the exasperated tone of his letters that he felt harassed almost out of his wits by the conflicting orders he was receiving—the Adventurers anxious to clinch matters and get started, the Leyden congregation begging for reassurance, Weston hoping to come out of the business with a good solid profit for himself, no matter where he got it from—all bombarding their unfortunate emissary until he hardly knew whether he was coming or going. He went on in his letter that if the ship proved too small for all who intended to go, those who were put off by the least thing could stay behind, as they were the sort who would create all kinds of trouble before the seven years ran out. "If you had beaten this business so thoroughly a month ago," he wrote, "and writ to us as now you do, we could thus have done much more conveniently. But it is as it is."

He said the ship was a fine one, and could be completely provisioned in England, apart from salt and nets, which should be bought in Holland. Provisioning should take two weeks. Any details not made clear would be explained by John Turner, who was leaving for Leyden on Tuesday night. Cushman wanted to come with him, to answer questions in person, but was far too busy to travel just then. If they thought he didn't know what he was doing, it was their fault for employing anyone so stupid; they had only to say so and he would go back to his wool combing and leave them to find a more capable organizer. They should, however, be careful not to shout before they were hurt.

One piece of vital information came in this letter. Cushman and Weston had engaged their pilot: John Clarke of Rotherhithe. He had crossed the Atlantic before, sailing to Virginia in 1610. In 1611, when a Spanish caravel visited Chesapeake Bay, Clarke had piloted her. The Virginian settlers arrested some of the Spaniards, whereupon the Spanish captain arrested Clarke, and took him to Spain via Havana in the caravel. He was detained there for four years, at first declaring that he was thirty-five years old and "of the religion of his king," but he later stated that he was forty and a Roman Catholic, no doubt in an attempt to speed up his release. Freed in an exchange of prisoners, he returned to England in 1616, and was employed by the Virginia Company on their Irish cattle boats. He took cattle to Virginia in the 750-ton *Falcon* under Captain Christopher Jones. A quiet, reliable man, Clarke was by all accounts an excellent choice.

Cushman had spent a busy weekend. He dashed off a letter to Carver, saying that there was no need for Carver to accuse him of negligence, which Carver had apparently done, possibly under the impression that the badgered Cushman was getting into a fearful muddle. Everything would be all right. Weston had been bothered somewhat by Cushman's ordering provisions in Kent which would have to be sent on to Southampton, a distance of about 130 miles from Canterbury: this meant time and money. The supply details were many and complicated. Cattle, bought live, were slaughtered, and their meat salted down; wheat, bought in the ear, was ground into flour and made into ship's biscuit; casks for beer, water, and wine were ordered and made ready. Cushman, naturally, took his goods where he found them: some in London, some in Canterbury or Sandwich, over sixty miles from the capital, some in Southampton, nearly eighty miles from London; so Weston, seeing arrangements taking place in three widely separated localities, and tempers fraying among the London agents and the Leyden congregation, warned Cushman that the summer would be over before they were ready.

Cushman calculated that for about 150 people intending to make the crossing there was approximately £1200 in available cash and a small quantity of goods, chiefly cloth, stockings, and shoes, the total falling £300 or £400 below the required amount. The man responsible for ordering provisions in Kent, he said, was Christopher Martin; though, since Martin came from Billericay in Essex, and Cushman was a man of Kent, Carver was understandably skeptical about this. Carver, who had stayed in London throughout, had suddenly put in a demand for £500; if, said Cushman, Carver wanted this sum immediately, he could have it, but they (presumably the Adventurers) could whistle for the rest; and (Cushman scribbled on, dashing impatiently from one subject to another) it was to be hoped that none of the Amsterdam people *would* come, as Cushman would do nothing but quarrel with them. One Mr. Crabbe, a minister, had promised to join the party, but Cushman would believe this when he saw it. The general tone of this enchanting letter* is perfectly summed up in a Cornish saying: "As Sally Bennett said when her old man got cotched in the threshin'-machine, 'you'm in, my dear, an' you may so well go through.' "

Martin's arrival on the scene signaled that of a number of others, some from Essex, some from London, who were joining the party, although they were strangers to the Leyden congregation

* Appendix 3.

and to their friends. These were emigrants accepted in order to suit the Adventurers and to increase the number of colonists. They included a London family called Billington, a Kentish family called Chilton, and Stephen Hopkins with his pregnant wife Elizabeth and their son and two daughters. There were the Mullins family, from Dorking, and several unattached young men. Exactly why they wanted to cross the Atlantic is uncertain. Possibly they simply wished to try their luck elsewhere, and the Pilgrims happened to be going at the moment that suited them.

Robinson, perturbed at Cushman's volatile tone and hair-trigger temper, wrote on June 14 to Carver, soberly emphasizing the natural anxieties of the Leyden group. Weston was apparently dealing with the Adventurers' end of the business in London, but his method of doing so caused anxiety—he seemed far too ready to delegate jobs to others, and far too slow in producing precise results. His unsatisfactory dawdling about had been reported to Robinson by George Morton. It seemed as though Weston was far too quick to delegate jobs to others, and far too slow in getting organized. He frequently referred to George Morton, a York merchant who was interested in the Pilgrims. Morton was, in a way, connected with them: his wife Juliana Carpenter was the sister of Alice Carpenter Southworth of Leyden. Robinson wondered what was the real reason for Weston's vacillating attitude. Perhaps some investors had backed out; perhaps he was afraid the Pilgrims would be ready too soon and would run up storage charges; perhaps he simply intended to force decisions by holding back himself. Certainly it was desirable to complete the arrangements as quickly as possible. The most important point to remember was that fishing and trading would be almost full-time occupations in the colony. Building private houses and tending private gardens were really spare-time jobs. All the more reason, therefore, that when these houses and gardens were finished, simple as they must be and consequently low in value, they should belong absolutely to the men who had made them.

This vexed question was not explicitly settled when the party set out. One must guess here, but it seems that neither Adventurers nor Planters had pressed it to a firm conclusion. Perhaps they thought it would settle itself in time; perhaps they hoped, or believed, that the opposition had given way; perhaps they kept silent on the sleeping-dog principle. The likeliest answer is a combination of all these.

• 11 •

There were to be two ships. One, to bring the Leyden party to England; the other, to take them across the Atlantic. But from the first it was clear that *both* ships should go to New England. The one coming from Holland, which would be the smaller of the pair, would be endlessly useful, as Bradford wrote, "to stay in the country and attend upon fishing and such other affairs as might be for the good and benefit of the Colony."

In a period when no ships were built or set aside purely for passenger transport, any available vessel had to serve the needs of any charter, the cheaper the better. It was, of course, possible to buy a ship outright, and the sixty-ton *Speedwell* was purchased for an unspecified price. It is not clear whether the name *Speedwell* was one of the typical punning titles of the period like *Hopewell* or *Godspeed,* or whether it refers to the English wildflower with the tiny starlike blue petals.

At this point it might be helpful to mention briefly the development of ships. Before 1450 two separate types existed: the Atlantic and the Mediterranean. The Atlantic, or Northern, style had a straight keel, or bottom, allowing a ship to be run up on a shore for cleaning, and a straight stempost, or front. Originally clinker-built—that is, with overlapping planks—it gradually evolved added pieces at either end—the fore and after castles, often edged with battlements. By 1400 the raised deckhouse aft and the high triangular platform at the front were being built above the principal deck, which ran unbroken the full length of the ship. The Mediterranean style, on the other hand, had a curved keel, so that if a ship ran aground it could be refloated by shifting the weight of the cargo carried in the hold and thereby altering the balance.

Originally both types were fitted with the Roman square rig —one large square sail furled on the single yard, or crossbar, of the single mast, roped separately for raising and lowering, and for tacking. In the Mediterranean, however, ships quickly adopted the Arab lateen sail, the crescent-shaped rig as characteristic of Arab vessels as the crescent of Islam itself. Although lateen rig required a larger number of men to man it than square rig, its adaptable efficiency paid off. In time, of course, the two styles fused into one, and the Mediterranean shipbuilders, always more experienced and progressive than the rest, developed more yards and sails, learned to cut the square sails to make separate windbags on either side of the mast, and added two more masts: the foremast in front, the mizzenmast at the back, each with its sails, the mizzen invariably with a lateen sail as the ships sailed better with that rig. A period of about twenty years in the middle of the fifteenth century saw the real marriage of the two types, which produced the basic barque of the next three hundred years, varying only in size. It was not clinker-built but carvel-built, that is, with edge-to-edge planks, its seams were proofed with pitch, it was high at the back dipping to a waist in the middle, and three-masted.

These perfectly ordinary vessels, never specially built and often not outstanding specimens of their time, went on the great voyages of discovery. Immensely long passages over uncharted seas were made, and then repeated, by ships built for, and regularly employed in, the ordinary trade of Europe. This fact helps to explain why, quite often, the actual names of ships go unrecorded in contemporary accounts. Neither *Speedwell* nor *Mayflower* is mentioned by name in Bradford's journal. It also has a bearing on the comfort or discomfort of the crossing. If a ship had carried furs or food, it would smell worse than if it had carried wine.

Speedwell was berthed at Delftshaven, midway between Rotterdam and Schiedam. Before leaving, the Leyden congregation naturally held a very special day of prayer. Robinson preached, at great length, on a text from Ezra:

> And there at the river, by Ahava, I proclaimed a fast, that we might humble ourselves before our God, and seek of him a right way for us, and for our children, and for all our substance.

It was an emotional day. Prayers and tears poured out freely for hours. On Friday, July 21, the sixty-six who were going, and a large number of friends and well-wishers from Leyden and from Amsterdam, went along the Kloksteeg, crossed the bridge to the Rapenburg Quay, and embarked on boats for Delftshaven. Their route went by Vliet, Delft with its massive church towers and stepped gables, Schie, and Overschie. "So they left," wrote Bradford, "that goodly and pleasant city which had been their resting place twelve years; but they knew they were pilgrims. . . ."

It was this use of the word "pilgrims" that created the phrase "Pilgrim Fathers."

At Delftshaven, there lay the *Speedwell* alongside the quay, ready to set out the following day. Few people present got any sleep that night: they stayed talking, eating, and drinking, or, as Bradford put it, "with friendly entertainment and Christian discourse and other real expressions of true Christian love." It rained on Saturday morning, but the wind was fair as everyone crowded on board for the final farewells. The congregation had pledged its intention that as soon as the colony was established the rest of the Leyden English would come over to join them, but this parting, as they knew, might prove final for all that. So moving was the sight of these companions bidding one another goodbye that the Dutch spectators on the quay were moved to tears. Bradford, always able to find something hopeful to say, reflected how comforting it was to witness the genuine affection of the members.

When the tide was right, the master, one Reynolds, said it was time to go. Robinson knelt on the quay, and the rest who were staying knelt with him, calling down blessings and uttering prayers for heaven's protection, while tears ran unchecked down their cheeks. The departing brethren were similarly affected. An unexpectedly military touch came from a volley of small shot and the firing off of three pieces of ordnance as a parting salute. Wreaths of smoke curled up and blurred the view of the white flag with its red cross of St. George that hung at the stern. From the mainmast top streamed out the (comparatively) newfangled Union Jack, decreed by James I only fourteen years earlier. The big sails slammed up into place, the fresh breeze caught them, and the *Speedwell* moved out into the open water.

With a pleasant, moderate wind, the crossing took three days. By Tuesday evening the ship had entered the Solent, and she spent that night in the tranquil breadth of Southampton Water. On the sunlit morning of Wednesday, July 26, the *Speedwell* came to her anchorage off Southampton's West Quay. Close by lay another ship, with people busy about her, loading cargo. This was the *Mayflower*.

· 12 ·

The question is: which *Mayflower*?

The *Mayflower* of Armada year, 200 tons, commanded by one Edward Banks, actually took part in chasing the Armada up the Channel. She was commissioned and financed on that occasion by the City of London. One of her owners, John Vassall, of Stepney, moved in 1591 to Leigh-on-Sea, near Southend at the mouth of the Thames. A *Mayflower* of Leigh appears in the London port books of 1606, taking on a cargo of cloth for Middelburg in Holland; her master was Robert Bonner of Leigh. A year later, Robert Bonner was listed as master of the *Mayflower* of London, unloading a cargo of wine from Bordeaux. In 1608 Bonner was listed as master of the *Josian,* whose master in 1606 and 1607 was Christopher Jones. In

1609 Jones appeared as master and quarter owner of the *Mayflower* of London.

From then on, this *Mayflower* sailed fairly regularly to the French ports of La Rochelle and Bordeaux, carrying cloth, hose, and rabbit skins, and bringing back wine and brandy. In 1609 she brought furs from Norway, and twice in 1614 she fetched home silks from Hamburg. On Tuesday, May 23, 1620, she docked in the Port of London from La Rochelle, the second voyage to France that year. Something more than two weeks later, Weston chartered her for the crossing to New England.

The ship on which Weston and Cushman had taken an option over the weekend of June 10–12 was considerably smaller. *Mayflower,* sailing in all seasons and all weathers around the treacherous coasts of Brittany, was clearly tough enough to make a summer voyage across the Atlantic. Again, one must guess here, but the logical assumption is that Weston and Cushman did not hesitate to choose the better alternative as soon as it appeared.

Much meticulous scholarship has gone into building up an accurate picture of the Atlantic *Mayflower,* and into the model of the ship which is displayed in the Pilgrim Hall at Plymouth, Massachusetts. The first research in depth, by Dr. J. W. Horrocks in 1922, led Dr. R. C. Anderson of the Society for Nautical Research in 1926 to design the model. On the basis of this, Mr. William A. Baker, the naval architect who designed *Mayflower II,* began his work. Mr. Baker, curator of the Francis Russell Hart Nautical Museum at the Massachusetts Institute of Technology, referred also to the notebooks of the late-sixteenth-century master shipwright, Matthew Baker.

The original starting point of all this study was Bradford's comment that the ship's tonnage was "nine score." The trouble is that precise tonnage figures are so difficult to determine. The most convenient measurement for years was the Spanish tonelada, equaling two pipes of wine in cask. That is between forty and forty-five cubic feet of liquid, approximately 2000 English pounds. The English ton, derived from the wine tonneau of Bordeaux, was one tenth larger. One English ton equaled four large barrels, or hogsheads. On January 28, 1620, the *Mayflower* of London unloaded a cargo listed as 153 tons of French wines plus 4 tons of red wine and 16 hogsheads of unspecified wine. This totals 161 tons. According to Matthew Baker's reckoning, the length of keel and the breadth and depth of any vessel, multiplied together and divided by 100, gives the ship's burden. The *Ascension* of London, burden 160 tons, was about 54 feet long in the keel, 24 feet broad, and 12 feet deep. The *Adventure* of Ipswich, by Matthew Baker's measurements of 1627, was 63½ feet long, just over 26 feet broad, and 11 feet deep; and her tonnage was 182. Dr. Anderson, calculating from this, worked out his *Mayflower* model on a scale of 64 by 26 by 11, giving a figure of 90 feet exactly as the length from stempost to sternpost. The beautiful replica, *Mayflower II*, designed for Warwick Charlton by William Baker and built in 1957 by Stuart Upham of Brixham in Devon, is as close to the original as it is possible for scholarly research to make it.

It is a mistake to picture the ships of the period as too fat. Their proportions, listed by William Borough, comptroller of the Navy in the fifteen-nineties, are: length of keel twice to three times the breadth, depth half, eleven twenty-fourths, or two fifths of breadth. The *Crane*, built in 1590 and identical with an example in Matthew Baker's notebooks, gives a ratio of 2.31 to 1 for length-breadth, and prompted Mr. Charlton to suggest for *Mayflower II* a keel 58 feet long, breadth of 25 feet, and depth of 12½, giving, by the 1582 tonnage rules, 181 tons.

Ship designs of the period, drawn with a compass and a straight edge and nothing else, emphasized Baker's principle that a ship should have "a cod's head and a mackerel's tail"—a full bow and a fined-down stern. The widest point came just above the waterline so that the ship would not heel over too far under full sail, and just forward of midships to comply with Baker's principle of balance. In drawing a design, profiles and cross sections were shown. First came the keel, stem and stern, showing the degree of rake for both stempost and sternpost: the drawing looked as though the vessel had been cut in half lengthways. The front and back rakes added together gave the breadth, with the forward rake always the greater of the two. Next the maximum cross section was drawn. Matthew Baker wrote:

> First ther most be made with the bredth and depth of the ship a paralillogram whose half shall souffyes for this works.

It was necessary to decide the width of the ship's floor, that is, according to an early-seventeenth-century definition, what width the ship rested on when grounded on a beach. Normally this would be one third of the full breadth. The difference in width between bow and stern, known as the trim of the ship, worked out by Matthew Baker's "ruell of proportion" at about two feet in the structure of *Mayflower*.

Shipbuilding tools included axes and adzes for cutting, augurs and "gimblets" for boring, wood ramps, timber-girth measures and gauges, hammerlike mauls for driving in the long wooden bolts, or treenails, nearly two feet long and properly seasoned to prevent shrinking, that fastened the planking to the frame. The masts were approximately 58 (fore), 80 (main), and 42 (mizzen) feet tall, and the long bowsprit measured some 57 feet. These spars were all, of course, tapered, ranging in diameter from almost two feet thick at the base of the mainmast to less than eight inches at its top. The crow's nest, a wide shallow bowl, was about nine feet across. All the ropes (over 400 of them altogether) weighed eight tons, the biggest being the mainstay (the principal rope of the mainmast), over three inches thick, and the main towrope, more than 100 fathoms long. The sails were made of heavy flax canvas in three different weights, so finely woven that they were reputed to be as strong as chain armor. They were hand-sewn with flax twine, and the holes through which their ropes were slotted were bound with leather to prevent fraying. The ship carried the typical sails of the time: on the mainmast the great mainsail and main topsail, on the foremast the foresail and foretop, and on the mizzenmast the spritsail and lateen mizzen.

Up to twelve guns were mounted by the gunports, or openings in the sides, seeming, to the modern eye, dangerously near the water: four medium-sized guns and eight smaller ones. The ship carried three boats: the master's skiff, which held five or six people, and the longboat, holding twenty; these were tied in place on deck, and, according to custom, used on the voyage to keep rabbits and poultry in. The third boat was the shallop.

Shallops, in comparison with the vessel herself, were fairly big—thirty feet long, one third the length of *Mayflower*—and usually had a single mast with one or two sails as well as sets of oars. The Pilgrim shallop was large enough to hold thirty-two people, as it did on one occasion, or, on another, eighteen men with food, weapons, and supplies for several days. To be stored, as it was, below decks for the crossing, it was cut down and partially dismantled, leaving enough room for people to sleep in it and keep some of their belongings, but both the cutting down and the daily wear and tear made its eventual restoration a two-week job for the carpenter once they reached the other side.

Most of the sleeping and living space for the passengers was in the low-ceilinged great cabin, 25 feet by 15 at its largest, and on the main deck, 75 by 20 at most. Below decks anybody five feet tall could never stand fully upright. What this measurement really means is that the maximum possible space for each person would have been slightly less than the size of a standard single bed. In an area that size, depressingly similar to a grave space, each person had to sleep, eat, store his personal belongings, change such clothes as he could or did, keep as clean as possible, brush hair, trim beards and nails, mind the children, prepare the food, and survive for eight months—the time it took to get ready, make the crossing, and establish the settlement on the shores of the New World.

· 13 ·

It is difficult to grasp exactly how *basic* were the supplies loaded on board the *Mayflower*. Every contingency had to be provided for: it was no good depending on anything's being sent quickly after the Pilgrims, nor upon finding anything at all when they landed. They knew, of course, that there would be trees, and therefore timber, but it takes time to make furniture, especially when there are no houses to put it in, so they took enough to furnish, after a fashion, nineteen cottages: chairs, table chairs, stools, and benches; a few small tables and a lot of trestle tables which packed easier into a smaller space, along with their tablecloths; beds, cradles, cupboards, chests, chests of drawers and buffets (a kind of sideboard); boxes and trunks; the vital spinning wheels and hand looms; bedding, including the kind that could be used on board ship, lengths of coarse canvas of 26 or 16 feet according to whether they went by the English ell or the Flemish, made into bags stuffed with straw on which two people might sleep; blankets and rugs including one green rug later presented to the Indian chief Massasoit; cushions and pillows; fire irons; and fireplace shovels which they charmingly called slices.

Then there were all the household utensils: pots of iron, brass, and copper; baking kettles and frying pans; spits; mortars and pestles; lanterns, lamps, candlesticks, sconces, and snuffers; tubs, buckets, pails, baskets; leather bottles, earthenware crockery, wooden plates known as trenchers, pewter plates and mugs; salt cellars, knives, spoons; hourglasses and sundials; and steelyards, by which they meant measures.

Next came the tools and implements with which they were going to carve out the Earthly Paradise in the wilderness: hoes, spades, scythes and sickles, mattocks and billhooks, garden rakes, hayforks, axes, saws, hammers and chisels, gouges, iron and steel bars, vises (which they called simply holdfasts), smiths' and coopers' tools, ropes and nails, staples and locks, hatchets and shovels, lime for mortaring, seed grain and garden seeds, nets and seines, twine and fishhooks, and something Bradford called an iron jack screw, which proved a lifesaver on the voyage.

Then they took weapons. There were personal ones: muskets, both matchlock and flintlock, and fowling pieces, with powder and shot; armor including helmets, corslets and cuirasses, and bandoliers; swords and cutlasses, which they called curtlaxes, and daggers; flints, shot belts, knapsacks; and, rather endearingly, a drum and a trumpet. Then there were the big guns: two sakers, two minions, two bases. The sakers were ten feet long with a four-inch bore, fired a four-pound ball, and weighed 1500 to 1800 pounds each; the minions, or falcons, as they were also known, fired a three-pound ball through a three-and-a-half-inch bore and weighed 1200 pounds each; the bases fired a one-pound ball through a one-and-a-quarter-inch bore and weighed 300 pounds. There were also four small cannon, which were later mounted in front of the governor's house in Plymouth, facing along each direction of the two intersecting streets that by 1627 made up the town.

The Pilgrims, like many explorers before and after them, took along, hopefully, various trading goods: bracelets of beads and metal, rings and knives, scissors, copper chains and strings of beads, red and blue cloth, "red cotton horsemans coats laced," small looking glasses, and cheap glass earrings. Partly for trade and partly for themselves, they packed pipes and tobacco, an early example of importing previous exports.

Inevitably they took books, principally, of course, the Bible, English, Dutch, and possibly French, and Latin and Greek Testaments. Psalm books, which included Luther's great hymn, *Ein fester Burg;* doctrinal tracts by Robinson, Ainsworth, Clifton, and Ames, volumes from Brewster's persecuted press; hornbooks and Bible stories for the children, for even then education bulked large in their plans for the future; calendars and almanacs; agricultural handbooks. Bradford carried with him Robinson's *Justification of Separation,* published in 1610, with his own name signed on the flyleaf. Dr. Fuller took a few medical books and a lot of religious ones, perhaps anticipating that the power of prayer would be more required than medical knowledge in the New World. Francis Cooke brought "one great Bible and four olde bookes," and Isaac Allerton had enough and to spare, for he gave a book to Giles Heale in Plymouth later. Captain Standish carried with him Caesar's *Commentaries,* Bariffe's *Artillery,* a history of the world, and, surprisingly, a history of Turkey.

As more and more citizens of the United States became ancestor-conscious and interested in tracking down relics of the Pilgrim Fathers, so legends grew up that such objects as Brewster's chair, Standish's sword, Winslow's pewter, and Peregrine White's cradle still existed. As with all holy relics, however, such opportunities exist for chicanery that one must treat these with the deepest skepticism.

William Mullins took 126 pairs of shoes and 13 pairs of boots. Clothes of all sorts had to go: oiled leather and canvas suits, stuff gowns and leather and stuff breeches, shirts, jerkins, doublets, neckcloths, hats and caps, hose, stockings, belts, piece goods, and what was nicely called "haberdasherie." The predominating colors were russet or deep green, but many of the women had saffron or dark-blue dresses, fairly low-necked with wide white collars and split or deeply cuffed sleeves, and Brewster had a violet coat, a red cap, a quilted cap, a lace cap, and a pair of green drawers among his belongings. Captain Standish wore a rust-brown doublet with shoulder caps, braid stripes down the sleeves, and buttoned tie fastenings, with white cuffs—Cromwell's russet-coated captain—and all the men wore knee-breeches with knitted stockings and buckled shoes. The crew, in a period before naval uniforms, wore leather jerkins and loose breeches above stockings or bare feet, and wool caps of the shape known as Monmouth. The older women had caps tied under their chins, but the girls pinned their caps to their hair. The children, with almost three centuries to go before clothes would be specially designed for them, dressed like tiny copies of their elders.

Apart from some salt, nets, cheese, and "strong waters"

brought from Holland, the ship was entirely victualed in South-ampton. Boxes of smoked herring, dried ox tongues known as neats' tongues, sacks of turnips, parsnips, onions and beans, also cabbage, which would be boiled with meat, barrels of spiced and salt beef, salt pork, peas and pease pudding, hogsheads of oatmeal and rye meal, wheat flour and Spanish rusk, tubs of pickled eggs and firkins of butter each holding 56 pounds, were loaded. There was a good deal of dried salt cod known as "haberdyne," smoked beef and pork. Lime juice was still unknown to combat scurvy, but lemon juice was recommended as a powerful specific. Spices were, of course, all-important, and the passengers provided themselves with ginger, pepper, cinnamon, mace, nutmeg, wormwood and green ginger, conserves of roses and clove-gilliflowers, sugar, raisins and what they wrote as currence, prunes to stew, and burned-wine (spiced wine used in small quantities as seasoning). The vital salt was carried in plenty. Tea and coffee were not yet known, but there were pipes of Holland gin and French brandy, and casks of beer and wine.

The ship carried no cattle, no beasts of draft or burden, but there were pigs, goats, and poultry, kept on the spar deck forward, a few sheep and some rabbits and more poultry, some of these for use during the journey, kept in the boats, and family pets, princi-pally cats and cage birds. Peter Browne took his large bitch mastiff and John Goodman took his little spaniel. Would all the pets survive the crossing?

Meals on board were cooked by the firebox, an iron tray with sand in it on which a fire was built. This was kept in the waist of the ship, and provided a considerable risk. The food was cooked for a group at a time, passengers making their own meals from the rations issued daily.

All these bulky stores were housed in the hold, with its base of ballast. The best-kept ships had stone ballast; the majority had sand or gravel, which held sewage and became sloppier as the voyage progressed. Sanitation was rudimentary: mostly its provisions con-sisted of open boxes slung over the rails, which passengers were understandably reluctant to use. On long voyages, with bad weather, sewage and waste of all kinds seeped into the ballast, creating filthy smells all too easy to imagine. Even today, on a short journey, only sheer necessity will drive a moderately squeamish passenger to the washrooms: anyone who wants to know what early voyages were like has only to select a choppy day on that most notoriously unreliable of waters, the English Channel, and make the crossing in the school-party season. Seventeenth-century ships carried pumps, two as a rule, square-built of wood and designed to draw off the bilge. They only partially succeeded in completing this task. When conditions below decks reached the point where even hardened sailors were complaining, the ship had to be cleaned out. This process, called rummaging, meant beaching the vessel, shoveling the ballast overboard to be washed by the incoming tide, scraping the caked filth off the timbers, sprinkling the interior with vinegar, and putting in fresh ballast. It took a long time, and obviously could not be done, or even attempted, at sea.

Dirt and food stores encouraged rats and cockroaches. It was a rule of the sea that every ship should carry at least one cat. Cockroaches had to be stepped on; to this day the Royal Navy's slang name for the petty officer is "the crusher" because, first out of bed, he is the first to tread on anything crawling about the deck. As more ships sailed, their crews gradually realized that warmer weather brings out more insects. So, of course, did warmer conditions, such as the crowding together of passengers in the narrow spaces below decks.

• 14 •

One Richard Braithwaite, writing in 1631, described a sailor as an otter or amphibian whose familiarity with danger and death gave him "a kind of dissolute security against any encounter." He would appear particularly bold if fired with liquor, though he was not beyond praying in storms. His prayers, however, were those of a man unused to the practice. He could sleep anywhere, "as well on a Sack of Pumice as a pillow of down." He was "most constant to his shirt" and the rest of his infrequently washed clothes. Able to spin up a rope like a spider, down it like lightning, having seen death in so many shapes that nothing surprised him, though calm waters worried him by their infrequency, the sailor could not speak softly, for the sea spoke so loud. "He was never acquainted much with civility," declared Braithwaite; "the Sea has taught him other Rhetoric."

It is interesting to note the comment about prayer. Aware of their perilous calling, sailors were conscious of depending on the protection of heaven for safety. Prayers at sea were read at fixed times, usually by the master, unless the vessel carried a chaplain. Rules, drawn up systematically as late as the present century, prohibited blasphemy and cursing, so that God would not be provoked sufficiently to withdraw his interest in the welfare of a crew. In 1634 the goldsmith and business magnate of Boston, John Hull, told his ships' captains that he knew they would take care to have daily prayers on board, enforce Sunday observance, and suppress all profanity "that the Lord may delight to be with you." In the early days of sail, gambling and the telling of blue stories were officially forbidden for the same reason.

Superstitions proliferated, as they do still. (It is supposed lucky today to touch a sailor's collar.) Some communities insisted on having a burning torch carried through a newly built ship to drive evil spirits away; and if a baby that had died unbaptized were buried beneath a tree used for shipbuilding the baby's ghost, "the sweet little cherub that sits up aloft to keep watch for the life of poor Jack," would guard the crew from harm. Silver coins were set under the mainmast to guarantee protection, and it was asking for trouble to sail on a Friday. The custom of always boarding a ship from the right, or starboard, side dates back to the fishermen of Galilee. Printed pages must never be torn up or burned, because they might be out of a Bible. (This provides a dramatic moment in Stevenson's

Treasure Island.) Certain birds were luck-bringers and should be treated as such: witness the consternation among the crew when the Ancient Mariner shot the albatross.

Frobisher paid his sailors ten shillings a month, but it was customary for shipowners to provide some clothes as well as a little pay for their crews. Most of them brought on board loose coats with hoods, made of serge, the direct ancestor of the duffle coat, for use in wet or cold weather. Only at about the time the *Mayflower* was sailing did shipowners begin to arrange for spare clothing for the men; these garments were kept in boxes. Because cheap clothes for sailors were made in the county of Shropshire, still addressed by its Latinized abbreviation of Salop, these boxes were called slop chests, and they still are. Columbus discovered hammocks in the West Indies, but the Royal Navy did not adopt them for over a century, and then piecemeal, so it is impossible to assume that the *Mayflower* carried many, or any at all. Bunk beds existed for the officers and were built in the after part of the ship, as high up as possible. Ships that had carried cargo and were chartered for a voyage with passengers often had a few primitive cabins hastily built in between decks; headroom was low enough in all conscience without that, and the cabins let in water, but they permitted easier stowing of baggage and a tiny amount of privacy for the people crammed into them.

It was the duty of the ship's steward, or the cook if the ship did not have a steward on board, to present his account of food and drink consumed to the captain every week. One hazard of ship's housekeeping was that flour and ship's biscuit went moldy and produced weevils and maggots. As late as the time of Nelson it was a recognized sport for sailors to tap bits of biscuit on the table and see which walked away first. Rules notwithstanding, they would bet on it, as indeed on almost anything. One of Columbus's sons reported that many crew members waited for darkness to eat their porridge or biscuit, so that they need not see the weevils in it. Water seldom ran short on Atlantic crossings, because rain refilled the water barrels; but in any case no one drank water while the wine and beer supplies held out.

If a ship carried a marshal among her crew, his duties were disciplinary. If not, and the *Mayflower* did not, discipline was the responsibility of the master. Sometimes the master acted as pilot, but usually a pilot was specially appointed to deal with the navigation. Some ships had a surgeon, but more often his function was shared among any moderately competent people on board, so it was a matter of pure chance.

One absolutely essential petty officer was the boatswain, then, as now, referred to as the bosun. He passed on the master's orders to the right man at the right time and looked after the rigging. It was he who taught the ship's boys to tie knots. Another important person was the ship's carpenter, immemorially named Chips, who had to look after the woodwork of the vessel, repairing it and making sure that the planking was made properly watertight with pitch, and seeing that the decks were kept in workmanlike condition. This was not easy when passengers and their belongings were spilling into every available bit of deck space. Some sailors were detailed to swab, or clean, the ship; the youngest and most nimble were sent scurrying up the rigging, to lash or trim the sails.

Very important was the cooper, who was in charge of the barrels. Sometimes a sailmaker was numbered among the company, but many bosuns could patch or repair a sail, and as an extra safeguard they would see to it that this skill was passed on to some of the able seamen under their orders, along with care of the anchors and cables. Occasionally the carpenter took along a mate specifically known as the caulker, to keep the pumps going and oversee the watertight condition of the vessel; if not, he trained a mate to assist him from a likely member of the crew. Firewood, ship's lamps, and sand glasses came under the care of the steward.

The *Mayflower* crew totaled between twenty and thirty men. In addition to the pilot, John Clarke, a carpenter, a gunner, a bosun, a cook, and four quartermasters, there was Robert Coppin, the second mate, who had crossed the Atlantic once already; Andrew Williamson, referred to as the ship's merchant (today he would be the purser), who was reliable enough for Captain Standish to choose him on the first landing to accompany the captain ashore; John Parker; and one Jones, whose first name was perhaps Thomas. This has given rise to some later confusion as to whether the *Mayflower* master's name was Thomas or Christopher Jones: general opinion inclines toward the latter. There was a crew member called Leaver, first name unknown, who on January 12, 1621, led a party to rescue two Pilgrims who had been lost for several days in the forest where they had gone to look for thatch to roof their houses. There was Giles Heale, member of the Company of Barber Surgeons in London, where, after his apprenticeship, he became a freeman and licensed to practice in 1619, which indicates that he was still a very young man by modern standards. Then there was the master.

Captain Christopher Jones, born in 1570 at Harwich, son of Christopher and Sybil Jones, inherited from his father, who died when the boy was eight, a share in the ship *Marie Fortune,* which would come to him when he was eighteen. According to some accounts he began his seafaring life in the corsair *Lion,* sailing in the Mediterranean. His first command was in the *Falcon* and it is tempting, though unprofitable, to speculate whether Clarke sailed with him. On December 23, 1593, he married Sarah Twitt of Harwich, who died ten years later; within a few months he had remarried, his second wife being Josian, widow of Richard Grey of Harwich, who had been listed as a burgess in the town charter granted by James I. Since in 1606 and 1607 Jones was master of a ship named the *Josian,* it seems reasonable to suppose that Grey had been a shipowner. At some stage, presumably early in his career, Jones seems to have been accused of piracy, and released through the intervention of the Earl of Warwick.

The piracy story and the connection with Warwick has led some chroniclers to suggest that Jones was in the supposed plot worked out by Gorges with Warwick's knowledge to land the Pilgrims farther north than the Hudson River. Here they would be free of the Dutch, and the Adventurers could enjoy the plantation profits without interference. If the land was under the Plymouth Company's jurisdiction, so much the better. Weston's name was linked with this plot too. Other historians have suggested that the Dutch bribed Jones to keep away from the Hudson. But the majority incline to the view that the *Mayflower* was supposed to go, as the terms of her charter stated, to the Hudson River area, and that the landing at Cape Cod took place because Jones had to land where he could. Time was short, too, for arranging plots and bribes.

In 1609, as we have seen, Jones was master and quarter owner of the *Mayflower* (principal owner Thomas Goffe, Merchant Adventurer), and in 1610 or 1611 both Jones and the ship moved to the Port of London. Jones settled in the village of Rotherhithe near Southwark; the place was still rural enough for Samuel Pepys in the sixteen-fifties to mention his walks there to the Half-Way House, picking cowslips by the river on the way and once meeting a pretty girl in a lane. Rotherhithe was Jones's home for the remaining eleven or twelve years of his life, and he was buried there on March 5, 1622. By one of his wives, more likely Sarah, he had four sons, Roger, Christopher, Thomas, and John. When Goffe in consultation with Jones offered the *Mayflower* to Weston for the Pilgrims' crossing, the crew of some thirty-four members was complete.

The *Mayflower*'s charter stipulated that she was to make "the viage" as a colonist transport "from the City of London to the neighbourhood of the mouth of Hudsons River in the northern part of Virginia," calling at Southampton en route, and then return. It was perhaps the earliest transatlantic package deal, paid for as a lump sum. John Winthrop later noted, when ships were sailing far more regularly between England and New England, that passengers paid from four pounds to five pounds ten shillings for their own tickets and three pounds for every ton of goods; by 1650 the most luxurious terms cost two pounds three shillings for the crossing and four pounds eleven shillings and fourpence for cabin charges, making a total of £6. 14s. 4d.

· 15 ·

It was practical good sense for the two ships to meet as they did on July 26 at Southampton. Not only did this save the *Speedwell* the extra distance up the Thames estuary and back, but Southampton was a quiet provincial port where fewer people existed to ask awkward questions. After all, the Pilgrims had been stopped before.

In 1620 Southampton was a small walled town with only a few diminutive clusters of dwellings outside the Bargate and the East-gate. Because some people helped themselves to stones from the walls, which were two centuries old anyway, these needed expensive repair; James I had recently announced that he no longer intended to pay for the upkeep of Southampton Castle; and the citizens had handed to the town council a petition complaining that the pavements were crumbling dangerously and the streets were filthy. This means that both were appalling. All seventeenth-century towns had broken pavements and dirt lying about in heaps in the streets.

The little *Mayflower*, with *Speedwell*, one third of her size and smaller than a modern Thames barge, lay at anchor by the West Quay on the River Test. The quay as such exists no longer, for the original outline of the town has been blurred out of shape by building far inland and by the huge complex of docks spreading in a broad arrowhead between the two rivers, the Itchen and the Test.

The two groups of passengers, Leyden Pilgrims, London Pilgrims and others, met with delight, talking eagerly and warmly among themselves, until they stopped gossiping and began to discuss business. What was all this, they wanted to know, about changed conditions? What had happened about the terms to which they would not agree? Carver, appealed to first, said he had been in Southampton for some time and could not be expected to know what had been going on in London; Cushman said that he had followed his instructions to the letter, partly in order to be fair, partly from necessity, as otherwise it would have created a dreadful

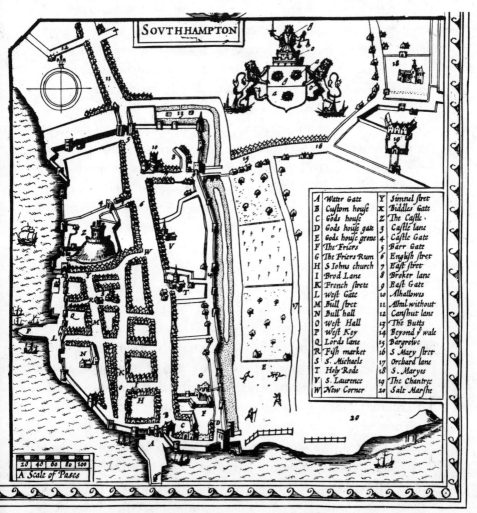

A	Water Gate	Y	Simnel ſtret
B	Cuſtom houſe	X	Biddles Gatt
C	Gods houſe	Z	The Caſtle
D	Gods houſe gate	3	Caſtle lane
E	Gods houſe grene	4	Caſtle Gate
F	The Friers	5	Barr Gate
G	The Friers Rum	6	Engliſh ſtret
H	S Iohns church	7	Eaſt ſtret
I	Brod Lane	8	Broker lane
K	French ſtrete	9	Eaſt Gate
L	Weſt Gate	10	Alhallowes
M	Bull ſtret	11	Alhal without
N	Bull hall	12	Carſhut lane
O	Weſt Hall	13	The Butts
P	Weſt Key	14	Beyond ẏ wale
Q	Lords lane	15	Bargrewe
R	Fiſh market	16	S Mary ſtret
S	S. Michaels	17	Orchard lane
T	Holy Rode	18	S. Maryes
V	S. Laurence	19	The Chantrie
W	New Corner	20	Salt Marſhe

John Speed's 1611 map of Southampton. The letter P marks the West
Quay, where *Mayflower* and *Speedwell* were anchored, and L marks the
West Gate. (BRITISH MUSEUM)

muddle. He had consulted his fellow agents, who approved all he did, and had arranged to receive the money in London and send it to Southampton to pay for the ships' stores. He had not much liked doing that (Weston never liked parting with money), and some of the provision merchants had been dubious, but that was the agreement, and far too short an interval had existed between chartering the *Mayflower* and sending off the *Speedwell* to notify Leyden. There had been delay enough already; no one wanted more.

Weston also had come down from London to see the two ships sail. He expected the Pilgrims to agree to his conditions of contract, but they proved unexpectedly recalcitrant, saying simply that they promised to agree to nothing without the consent of the Leyden congregation as a whole. Weston took offense at this and said that in that case they must stand on their own feet; he washed his hands of the whole business and was going back to London.

The Pilgrims now realized that in order to clear all their expenses they had to find a large sum of money—from £60 to £100—it is not clear which—and quickly. Weston, who would in the normal course have done this for them, had gone off in a huff, so they had to raise the money themselves. They did it by selling some of their surplus stock of butter—sixty to eighty firkins of it according to Bradford: this meant between 3360 and 4720 pounds. So the last debt was cleared, but to make everything absolutely plain to the Adventurers they wrote a letter, dated August 3.

They were sorry, they said, to have to write at all: they had rather expected that some, if not most, of the Adventurers would have come to Southampton to see them off. Since they could not talk together, they wanted the Adventurers to know why they had not consented to the agreement drawn up without their knowledge by Cushman. He should not have done it, however good his motives might have been. The main trouble was the old question about house and land property belonging to the Pilgrims absolutely. Cushman had given William Mullins a copy of the original agreement, to which they had all consented. People in both Leyden and London had invested money in this project. Let the Adventurers therefore think the matter over impartially, and see the justice of the Pilgrims' case, because they were set on going and were not intending to turn back now.

At the end of the letter came a comment on shortage of supplies, indicating that they had parted with too much.

> We are in such a strait at present, as we are forced to sell away £60 worth of our provisions to clear the haven, and withal to put ourselves upon great extremities, scarce having any butter, no oil, not a sole to mend a shoe, not every man a sword to his side, wanting many muskets, much armour, etc. And yet we are willing to expose ourselves to such eminent dangers as are like to ensue, and trust to the good providence of God. . . .

Two other letters arrived at the same time, both from Robinson, "in which," wrote Bradford, "the tender love and godly care of a true pastor appears." One was addressed to the company in general, and was his parting salute to them.

It was a thoughtful and influential letter. It opened by emphasizing that the writer was with them in spirit, though for a while he must postpone his actual joining with them. He had been more than willing to sail with the rest, and would have preferred to do so, but "by strong necessity" had felt it his duty to stay in Leyden. He was torn in two between what he ought to do and what he wanted to do. Since he could not go with his "loving and Christian friends" he had written this exhortation, and if they did not need one, it was still his pleasure to write.

It was proper, said Robinson, for them all to consider their sins and shortcomings every day. Sometimes God so arranged matters that his faithful had to pass through hard and dangerous experiences. When this happened, it prompted more careful examination of personal need for reform than usual. God was kind in this, for it was easy to forget or overlook some faults, and when one's own conscience was cleared by facing a considerable challenge one could go forward with a calm and comforting assurance that was the best of shields.

So the Pilgrims would be setting out in peace of mind with God. They must next make sure of feeling the same tranquil tolerance toward their fellow men, especially their associates. This meant watching particularly carefully not to give or take offense. (The example of Weston was of course by that time fresh in every mind.) In First Corinthians Paul had written that none of his work had been done in order to produce a specific reaction, so how much more did this apply to evil, which regarded neither the love of man nor the honor of God. And it was not enough to be so good that one never caused offense to others: the great thing was not to take offense at others' actions, for "how unperfect and lame is the work of grace" in any person who lacks charity to cover a multitude of sins; Peter put this very well. It was not just a matter of Christian behavior. Touchy people were commoner than offensive ones, and a lot more trouble, particularly in groups bound closely together in some enterprise or work.

The Pilgrims, Robinson pointed out, had to be very careful. They were not all familiar with one another's appearance, let alone character, virtues and faults alike. It was all too easy to misjudge the words and actions of comparative strangers. Such wrong judgments added fuel to the fire that must be diligently quenched all the time with brotherly tolerance. Impatient grumbling at others' shortcomings was only a short step from impatient grumbling at God, wondering why he had chosen to afflict them in some way, instead of recognizing his justice and wisdom in all matters.

They must also take care that whatever they did was aimed at promoting the general good. They were building God's new house in the wilderness; no house rose strongly, or stood firm, on a shaky foundation. When the building was solid and complete, there might be modifications or even changes, but in the early stages each man should treat his personal quirks of preference as he would deal with rebels against a noble state.

They were going to have to govern themselves, too, so in this important matter they should choose and elect the best among them as leaders. Those ought to be "such persons as do entirely love and will promote the common good" and then "in their lawful administrations" they should be honored and obeyed. Again, personal traits should not be made too much of, "like the foolish multitude who more honour the gay coat than either the virtuous mind of the man, or the glorious ordinance of the Lord." It was their own choice, anyway; no governors would be arbitrarily set over them. This part of the letter is said to have prompted the creation of the Mayflower Compact.

Robinson ended his wise and compassionate statement by saying that there were a lot more points he could make but he felt sure the Pilgrims would have thought of them already. He commended them to the loving and watchful care of the Lord "who hath made the heavens and the earth, the sea and all rivers of waters."

The second letter was short, and addressed to Carver personally. It was dated July 27, 1620, and included this sensitive comment:

> I have a true feeling of your perplexity of mind and toil of body, but I hope that you who have always been able so plentifully to administer comfort unto others in their trials, are so well furnished for yourself, as that far greater difficulties than you have yet undergone (though I conceive them to have been great enough) cannot oppress you.

He reminded Carver that he was traveling with "so many godly and wise brethren" who would help him to bear his burdens and would never doubt his good faith.

"Now," went on Robinson, "what shall I say or write unto you and your good wife my loving sister?" He wished them all possible good and blessing; he had written at length to the company because he had been unable to preach the farewell sermon; knowing they took no minister to the New World was a spur to impel him in coming out and joining them as soon as he could, which he would assuredly do. He ended with a simple but beautifully phrased prayer:

And the Lord in whom you trust and whom you serve even in this
business and journey, guide you with His hand, protect you with
His wing, and show you and us His salvation in the end, and bring
us in the meanwhile together in the place desired, if such be His
good will.

It was evidently not. This was the last letter Carver received
from his pastor.

· 16 ·

The company assembled to hear the letter read. It met with general
approval, and Bradford thought it bore fruit later in the lives of
many. Then they decided who should go on which ship, and held
their first election, to select a governor for each vessel, with assistants. This was not only sensible, as somebody had to be responsible
for managing the passengers' affairs, and perhaps the passengers
themselves, and for seeing to the stowing of the baggage and
provisions; but the two ships' masters had asked for this to be done.
Martin, who had squabbled with Carver and Cushman all along
over the vexed question of supplies, was elected governor of
Mayflower, with Cushman as his assistant. Most of the senior Leyden people stayed on the *Speedwell,* to give extra confidence to her
less experienced master, Captain Reynolds. He was anxious about
his cargo, believing it overweight, and *Speedwell* was trimmed twice
at the West Quay before she was ready to sail. One new member of
the company came aboard at the last minute, a young cooper called
John Alden, tall and fair-haired and powerfully built.

To get a ship under way in 1620 required a complicated ritual of
orders. The splendid *Complaint of Scotland,* supposed to date from
1548, describes what happened.

First the anchor, or anchors, had to be raised and secured. Light

in weight by modern standards, with poor-quality iron that made
snapping a risk and forced captains to carry spares, the seventeenth-century anchor was in shape almost exactly like the anchor
of today—curved, with flukes sometimes at right angles so that at
least one of them would bite, and with a straight stock. Hauled up
dripping on its tarred cable, its fixing in place gave the master his
cue to order "Two men above to the foretop to cut the ribbons and
let the foresail fall." The next order was: "Haul out the bowline.
Now hoist!" To the accompaniment of a chanty, the men hoisted
the main yard and sheeted home the mainsail. One chanty quoted in
the *Complaint* is worth noting for part of its refrain:

> Tell 'em all, tell 'em all,
> Gallowsbirds all, gallowsbirds all,
> Great and small, great and small,
> One and all, one and all . . .

which is very close indeed to that most popular of British military
songs of World War II, "Bless 'Em All."

The chanty rhythm for windlass and capstan is that of *Shenan-
doah*, and for halyards *Blow the Man Down*.

Then came a flood of orders: "Make fast the halyards—set your
topsails—haul your topsail sheets—veer your lifters and your topsail
braces—hoist the topsail higher—haul taut the topsail bowline—
hoist the mizzen and change it over to leeward—sway the sheets and
the belaying pins—haul the braces to the yard." Each order, given
by the master, was bawled by the appropriate officer to the crew.
The master then told the helmsman: "Mate, keep her full and by,
a-luff. . . . Come no higher. . . . Hold your tiller steady as you are. . . .
Steer from the tip of the helm thus and so," and the ship tacked
neatly to take, it would be hoped, the breeze.

Now the final orders: "Boy to the top, shake out the flag on the
topmast. Mariners, stand by your gear. Every quartermaster to his
own station."

With a favorable wind behind them, blowing from the north,

the two little ships went quietly down Southampton Water. In front of them lay the Isle of Wight and the tricky waters of the Channel. Commander Alan Villiers of the *Mayflower II* has well described *Mayflower* and *Speedwell* on that occasion as two tiny and undistinguished vessels carrying some of the bravest individuals who ever put to sea. Men and women of incredible fortitude, they were going to need it from the first moment.

PART TWO

A Hatful of Wind

· 1 ·

The North Atlantic is the smallest of the world's seven seas, taking up less than one tenth of the world's ocean area. Its average depth is just over two miles. It is the most used of waters, the most fought-over, has witnessed the most history. It is an evil-tempered ocean, boiling and thrashing at the rocky coasts of its loveliest islands (among them the Western Isles, Ireland, and England), dramatically spectacular off Land's End and the Lizard. It is myth-laden, a place of drowned Atlantis and Lyonesse, of violent storms, westerly gales piling up huge waves, easterly gales drenching everyone on board. Its winds and currents endlessly circle about the calm Sargasso Sea with its motionless golden weed, full of tiny crabs and sea horses, where ships could be trapped and slowly lost, giving rise to legends of monsters that swallowed them up. It has impenetrable white fogs. It has the becalming doldrums, where sailing ships can lie for weeks, eating up stores, through days of thick oily water with the sails banging against the masts and every deceptive cat's-paw hailed as precursor of a possible breeze. Early mapmakers drew it vaguely, shoving in islands where they liked the look of them. Other oceans have winds to go out with and winds to come back with, but the North Atlantic is not accommodating.

It can be beguilingly beautiful. On quiet summer days with a big steel liner driving placidly ahead across sparkling water, under a pale blue sky, steadily overhauling a vessel on the horizon, there is the endless therapeutic pleasure of leaning on the rail and watching the exquisite bow wave, or gazing out astern at the straight pastel line of the wake. Passengers, full of salt air and delicious food, go up in a lift and are conducted in groups onto the bridge, where the youngest or oldest lady present is invited to hold the wheel for a

91

minute and keep her eyes riveted to the ink line slowly tracing itself on a strip of graph paper to mark the course. In anything like decent weather the surrounding eight-mile circle of sea is dark green, with little washes of thin gray bubbles here and there. But it is still the ocean of the *Mary Celeste,* the *Titanic,* and the Battle of the Atlantic, and its devil's temper is never far below the surface. One night in 1946 (for example), the superb *Queen Mary* herself lay hove-to for half an hour, the first night out of Southampton, while a gale blew itself out; and four days later, dead on her time, slid toward landfall at Nova Scotia in a dense fog, her mighty siren booming regularly out, as the little pilot boat slipped like a wraith to the rendezvous, to bring her in to Halifax. Today even those who sail across alone in small yachts, taking weeks to do it, have accurate charts, two-way radio sets, courteous inquiries for their welfare from passing ships and aircraft; and, above all, every transatlantic traveler knows perfectly well that at the end of the voyage, however sick or frightened he has been, he will find food and beds and water and people.

In 1620 pilotage, the art of taking ships from port to port within sight of land or areas of soundings, was a comparatively sophisticated practice. Navigation, taking a ship outside both, was crude; grand navigation, involving the crossing of a full ocean, was chancier still. The master of an oceangoing vessel had a course of sorts to steer by, based on the sketchy maps of the period. It took little or no account of variations of season, gave a very rough idea of how long the voyage might last, and a vague guesswork description of the land he was aiming at; and of course he had such charts of his destination as happened to exist. He had to sail by deduced, or dead, reckoning, depending particularly on working out his speed. This was not difficult to do on a straight course with a following wind, as he could stream the log astern by its towline knotted at regular intervals and gauge his speed as the knots ran out. Bits of flotsam floating by helped too in judging how fast the ship was moving. But ships were blown off course, or sailed deliberately off in search of a better wind; so the master depended upon such aids to navigation as the compass, the traverse board, the quadrant, and the astrolabe.

Ships carried two compasses, one for the helmsman and one for the man conning the course. By 1620 they were fairly efficient. A round box held the compass card, which pivoted on a bent piece of magnetized iron: this had to be remagnetized at intervals with a lodestone, an operation equivalent to recharging a battery today. The box was held level against the roll and pitch of the vessel by balancing on brass gimbals, and had its own lamp to light it at night. The compass card, bearing on its surface a line representing the fore and aft line of the ship in motion, was divided into thirty-two points, four for each of the eight principal winds: ship apprentices were taught to say or box the compass by naming off the points. The shape they made on the card, like a many-petaled flower, caused the design to be named the compass rose.

The traverse board also carried a compass rose, with eight holes in each of the thirty-two radii of the circle. At the end of every half hour at sea, measured with a sandglass, the helmsman put a peg in the hole on the radius that matched the course, and transferred the result to a slate at the end of the four-hour watch, thus clearing the board for the next watch. The master calculated the distances and directions as best he could by this, bearing in mind that he believed a league to be a good distance for an hour's sailing and a degree on the map reasonable for one day.

The quadrant, a quarter circle divided into ninety degrees, with sights to align on a star and a plumbline to calculate the altitude where it cut the degree scale, gave the latitude, provided always that allowance was made for the circle of the polestar. The snag about the quadrant was that it had to be held in the hand, and the plumbline swung with the roll of the ship. The astrolabe, however, was hung up on a hook, and supplied a solidly carved map of the stars, a full circle of 360 degrees, and a rotating bar for plotting heights.

Charts of 1620 were, of course, principally for coastal waters, where distances between landmarks and soundings formed a spider's web of compass bearings. These charts were used with a pair of dividers and the recently invented parallel ruler. Naturally the vast bulk of the Atlantic was uncharted, but Captain Jones sailed with such maps of North America as were available, notably those of Cabot, Smith, Gosnold, Dermer, Pring, and Champlain.

The ship's company was divided, then as now, into watches, each one four hours long, though only two sets of men operated all of them. Half-hour sandglasses, turned with the appropriate chant by a ship's boy, told the time. Midnight was calculated by an instrument called the nocturnal, a circular card with a hole in the middle for finding the polestar, and a movable pointer to fix on the brightest star of the Polaris guards. The rim of the card bore the marks for midnight on every day in the year.

The helmsman, standing aft at the heavy tiller, could see neither sky nor sails for the floor of the quarterdeck just above his head, so the officer of the watch, whose duty it was to con the course above him, had to shout down his orders through a hatch. If the ship had a whipstaff, which the *Mayflower* had, the helmsman could steer from the upper level. The whipstaff was a lever on the quarterdeck attached to the tiller below, but it was limited in movement and useless in heavy weather. The small rudder ports, openings in the hull where the tiller was fastened to the rudder, were replacing the big tiller ports in newly built ships, but even these let in a good deal of water so that the helmsman and his assistants were wet through in a following sea, a problem unsolved until the development of the ship's wheel a century later.

Lookouts, positioned well forward and as high as possible, kept their eyes not only on the horizon and the surrounding water but also on the trim of the ship and the quantity of sail, both of which had to be constantly adjusted in difficult winds. The rigging was another problem, as it was made of hemp, which stretched when it was new yet rapidly tightened when wet and slackened when dry. Painting the ship was not the everlasting task it later became, but the wooden construction had to be treated with pitch to keep it watertight, and there were always places with actual or potential leaks to search out and repair. Pumping out, cleaning, and scraping kept the crew busy when they were not trimming the balance of the vessel, raising or lowering the sails, attending to the treacherous rigging, or helping to hang on to the tiller in a heavy sea, which might go on for hours at a stretch and often did.

Built in by the tiller were shelves and lockers to hold the charts and the traverse board. The sailors' chests were lashed into place on the main deck against the bulwarks. Often the men slept by their chests, when the weather permitted, lying on deck wrapped in a blanket or an old piece of sail. The low-cut middle or waist of the ship, often very wet, usually had long strips of canvas known as waistcloths fixed along either side: these kept some of the water off and helped, if necessary during a sea fight, to repel boarders. Also in the waist were lashed and stowed the smaller ship's boats; if the ship carried a pinnace, or longboat, or shallop, it would probably be towed, and consequently often lost at sea. The longboats were sometimes referred to as "gundelows"—it is strange to find the early version of that charmingly evocative word *gondola* used in this connection. The *Mayflower,* as we know, did not tow her shallop. Boats were of course of the greatest importance in New England, where no quays, wharves, or slipways yet existed, and where it was essential not only to land people and supplies from anchorages but also to explore narrow twisting rivers.

The mainmast rose out of the waist, in the center of the ship. In a rack around it were the belaying pins that secured the running rigging; these were of exactly the same design as those of today. Nearby stood the capstan, crude by modern standards, with its wooden handspikes to wind up the anchor. Weighing anchor was a laborious job; so was the cumbersome business of hoisting the main yard, the big spar that crossed the mainmast and held up the great mainsail. This spar was normally lowered while the ship was in harbor. The long, heavy spar was hauled up on ropes called halyards through large blocks of hardwood at the masthead, blocks which, according to Dr. J. H. Parry, were virtually the only labor-saving devices on board, unless there might be a second capstan to aid the operation. Not for more than half a century would the drumhead capstan, familiar in scores of seafaring pictures, evolve. The *Mayflower* capstan was the usual square-headed wooden spindle of the time, set upright in its bearing socket, and held from walking back, if the crew's hands released it, by a special hawser called a voyol, a stout rope with nipper ropes spliced on it at intervals.

One absolutely essential piece of equipment was the lead and line for taking soundings. It served, in the opaque and often fog-bound Atlantic waters, to give warning in plenty of time of a ship's nearness to the coast. The line was normally two hundred fathoms long, marked with knots at twenty and then at every ten fathoms, and the lead tied on the end of it weighed fourteen pounds. Tallow was placed in a hollow of the lead, so that bits of shells, sand or mud on the sea-bed could stick to it and be identified as characteristic of one area or another. To take full soundings, the line was arranged along the deck on the leeward side in regular coils, a man stationed by each, and as his coil ran out he called to alert the next man. The last man reported the number of fathoms of depth, or the slightly forbidding result of "no bottom." For soundings in shallower shoal water a thicker line, twenty fathoms long, and a seven-pound weight of lead were used. Soundings were, and still are, basic essential precautions in sailing, and masters like Captain Jones took them automatically, finding familiar patterns showing time after time in waters where they had sailed before, making it easier to plot and identify their position.

Pilot books, known as *rutters* (a corruption of the French word *routier),* gave soundings wherever possible, standardizing distances during the sixteenth century into leagues or miles. All rutters reminded pilots to transfer all their information to the ship's chart, which they called the card, and to "prick the card" (mark the chart specially) for every noon position. It was possible in those days to estimate latitude, however roughly, but longitude was a matter of guesswork until the invention of the chronometer a century later. The *Mayflower* pilot, like his fellows, just guessed his speed. It was easier to navigate in the open sea, clear of obstacles, where the only real problems arose from wind and weather; anywhere off the coast of western Europe within soundings was, and indeed still is, treacherous in the extreme. It is here, says Professor Samuel Eliot Morison, that a ship's captain, poring night and day over his chart and rutter, shouts at his crew and may even aim a kick at the ship's cat.

One William Bourne, setting on paper in 1574 his recommendations for oceangoing masters, said that they must be good coasters, knowing every place by sight. This was particularly important in the difficult English Channel. The Cornish and Breton coasts, the jaws of the Channel, are full of hazards to shipping: if one passes safely between the Eddystone shoals and the Casquets of the Channel Isles, there are still the dangers off the Lizard, Land's End, and the Isles of Scilly, with all their swirling currents and multitude of rocks, before a vessel can run clear into the open sea. The risks are naturally greater for ships that depend on wind and water alone to drive them forward. It is all too easy to be crowded too close to the shore for comfort: passing into the drag of a big sea crashing over a reef they can, given a touch of luck and a quick response to clear orders, rise on a wave crest, hang apparently poised for an endless instant above the reef, then claw past, shaking the water from the scuppers, while the wind slams into the canvas like a fist. The southwest Channel waters can fling rocks weighing half a ton with contemptuous ease. On stormy nights with a deafening gale throwing up a mist of sand and spindrift against the black cliffs, sailing may well be said to separate the men from the boys. Even in sunny weather, when the water is pale green streaked with purple, there is a heavy swell. At one moment a boat is on top of a hill of sea, with the gray-brown cliffs, deeply clefted with black, patchwork fields, and blue sky visible for miles; at the next it is low in a green valley of rushing water, shut out from everything else. Then there are the sudden, silent fogs, when ships must feel their way forward in a pearl-gray emptiness of damp chill air where anything may lurk unseen. In the seventeenth century buoys were few and lighthouses fewer. Only dim little local lights here and there glimmered uncertainly from the coast by night. Where a lighthouse did exist (like

the coal-fire beacon on St. Agnes, the only light in the Scillies), it
was thought wasteful to set it going on a clear night, especially if the
moon was shining, and rain or sleet would extinguish the fire. The
law did not yet require vessels to carry running lights, but they were
supposed to have a lantern in a bucket which should be lit if they
were likely to meet other shipping. It is easy to see why masters
preferred to begin a voyage from England in the moon's first
quarter, so that they might have moonshine, as well as stars, to light
the way for them to clear the Channel.

· 2 ·

Whether Reynolds realized it fully or not, *Speedwell* was overmasted for her size and carrying a tremendous press of sail. The two
ships were still traveling level with the coast of Devon when he
signaled *Mayflower* to heave to. It was Tuesday, August 8; the wind
had been dead ahead for them to beat down the Channel on Saturday, and had turned baffling on Sunday. It was what an experienced
seaman would call a bit of a blow, nothing much: certainly nothing
compared with what they would be sure to meet in mid-Atlantic.
Jones listened to what Reynolds had to say, which was that the
Speedwell was leaking to the extent that he dared not go on until she
was examined and repaired. Jones thought it over. The apprehensive twittering among some of the passengers, the critical comments of others, may be imagined. At length Jones unwillingly
agreed, and they decided to put in to Dartmouth. The wind turned
disobliging, and it was not until Saturday, a week after setting out
from Southampton, that they came into the lee of Start Point,
turned below the Mewstone, and headed into the exquisite estuary
of the River Dart.

Sheltered by hills thick with trees and framed by the red,
yellow, and green quilt of the summer fields, Dartmouth is still a
most beautiful place. The two crews had little leisure to observe this

just then, occupied as they were with the task of having *Speedwell* thoroughly searched and mended, "to their great charge and loss of time and a fair wind," noted Bradford.

Cushman, fuming at the delay, wrote a letter to his friend Edward Southworth, a member of the Leyden congregation who did not emigrate. The letter, dated August 17, was addressed to Southworth at Heneage House, Duke's Place, London—a warren of tenements in Aldgate that had for years housed nonconformists. The opening was pessimistic: "Loving Friend . . . whom in this world I never look to see again." Cushman felt ill, as though crushed by a weight of lead, and was obviously apprehensive in the highest degree.

So far, he said, the voyage had been as full of crosses as the passengers of bad temper. They should have been halfway to Virginia by now. They had a week of fair weather at Southampton, waiting for *Speedwell* to be made ready; here they were again "in as fair a wind as can blow" for probably eight days, and the wind might well turn before that. They were eating up the stores, and if the crossing was a long one they might well land with less than a month's supply.

Certainly *Speedwell* had leaked very badly. If she had stayed on her course a few hours longer, she would probably have sunk. "Now she is as open and leaky as a sieve; and there was a board a man might have pulled off with his fingers, two foot long, where the water came in as at a mole hole."

But, went on Cushman, there were other troubles too. One of the worst was the behavior of Martin. He was proving difficult in so many ways. Having spent nearly seven hundred pounds at Southampton in getting supplies, Martin now refused to submit his accounts. He neither could nor would: they were ungrateful for all he had done, and suspicious in asking questions. He refused to let anyone go ashore, in case they ran away, and treated the passengers very badly, speaking to them with scornful contempt. In their distress they appealed to Cushman, who could make no impression on Martin:

If I speak to him, he flies in my face as mutinous, and saith no complaints shall be heard or received but by himself, and saith they are froward and waspish, discontented people, and I do ill to hear them. . . . He was not beholden to the merchants for a pin, they were bloodsuckers, and I know not what. Simple man, he indeed never made any conditions with the merchants, nor ever spake with them. But did all that money fly to Hampton, or was it his own? Who will go and lay out money so rashly and lavishly as he did, and never know how he comes by it or on what conditions?

Cushman, who had been very close to quitting altogether at Southampton, referred again to the unagreed conditions, which had made Weston so angry. All this dissension would bring ruin; the company lacked resolute leaders and strong self-discipline. He and a companion, William King, had wondered which of them would feed the fishes first. He expressed his despair in a memorable sentence: "Friend, if ever we make a plantation, God works a miracle."

All seemed well on the morning of Wednesday, August 23, and the two ships set off again. With a fine fair wind they made good progress down the Channel, successfully clearing Land's End and thus having the worst of the journey behind them. It was still possible at this point to have made a good transatlantic run in fairly quick time, for summer was not yet over, though a touch of tarnish was beginning to show in the trees, and the air bit a little sharper at night. But the wretched Reynolds found that he was again in trouble. Exactly where the ships were when he signaled for another conference is uncertain. They were undoubtedly clear of Land's End, but Bradford's estimate of over a hundred leagues—three hundred miles—is too far to fit the dates. Captain John Smith, commenting two years later on the business, wrote that Reynolds spoke the *Mayflower* on the Thursday, that is one day out from Dartmouth. The two ships hove to, and this time the principal passengers as well as the masters and carpenters joined in the somewhat acrimonious consultation. It clearly spread over into the following day, but at some moment on Friday, August 25, Jones announced that they had better put back to the nearest port and settle the question once and for all. With the wind on the starboard quarter they did so, and on Sunday the *Mayflower* led the *Speedwell* in between Mount Batten and Mount Edgcumbe, under the Hoe, past Fisher's Nose crowned by the new fort built by Drake and commanded by Gorges, to anchorage in Plymouth. The Pilgrims were there for ten days.

The old fort still stood by the harbor entrance, but had been converted to a military store. Here was the Barbican, the local watergate, where a chain fixed to a winch could be run across the entrance to keep out hostile ships. A short pier stuck out there, with new stone steps down to the water, and then came the causeway and the quay built in 1570. New houses, brightly painted, with typical overhanging upper stories, lined the quay and the newly laid out little streets linking the port with the town. One street here was built by one John Sparke, who had sailed with John Hawkins and had been the first to write a description of tobacco and potatoes; it was called New Street, and number thirty-two, which still stands, was named London House. It is assumed to have been the Plymouth office of the London Company for the western plantations.

The rest of the west and north harbor was lined with warehouses, except for a building known as Island House and one that contained Hawker's wine cellars. In both of these some of the Pilgrims are supposed to have slept for a few nights; many had to come ashore for *Speedwell* to be reexamined, and if she was beached in the east harbor Hawker's would have been the nearest building. Likewise, if *Mayflower* was anchored below the castle, Island House stood close by. Many friendly people came to watch, talk, and offer hospitality; Plymouth already knew a good deal about the New World. Indians, including Princess Pocahontas, and Negroes were familiar sights in the port; New England fish, Virginia tobacco, well-known commodities.

In order to visit the harbor today, travelers must get out of the train or detour their cars and buses, but even to one who simply passes through, especially by rail, Plymouth is superb. Not that it is a particularly beautiful town: indeed in some ways it is frankly ugly. But the setting is tremendous. Working around clockwise, from Maker heights above Cremyll on the Cornish shore behind Rame Head, the Sound lies placidly blue between bare Mount Batten and leafy Mount Edgcumbe. The Breakwater and Drake's Island stand gray upon the blue. Four estuaries gleam in the sun: Tamar, winding away past Saltash, leaving the St. Germans river wandering among trees, Tavy, past Tamerton Foliot and the windy spaces of Roborough Down, and Plym, slanting out of the Cattewater to the east, the whole horizon framed in hills—the green, gray, brown of Cornwall, the deepening lush green and softer outlines of Devon. And in the center, between the Hamoaze and Millbrook Lake, the Three Towns—Plymouth, Stonehouse, and Devonport—go sprawling and soaring over their headlands, dipping and rising, fringed as they have been for centuries with the masts of shipping. Crossing the Saltash Bridges—either of them, for they run close and parallel—is maddening for the traveler who naturally wants to look in both directions at once: north to the tors and the curving hills, south to the water scattered with vessels. He who explores on foot will find the great artificial frontage of the Hoe impressive from a distance, cluttered with monuments at close quarters: here, after all, Drake apparently played bowls when the Armada was sighted, and his braggadocio statue, bulging with puffed sleeve and breeches and muscle, looks out with upcurled beard toward the slim pencil of the Eddystone lighthouse on the horizon. But it is down at the Barbican that the stone gateway stands, overlooking Sutton Pool, with the words on the pavement carved before it: *Mayflower 1620.*

· 3 ·

Now it was that *Speedwell* backed out, and in so doing made the legend possible. Twin achievements, for some reason, never quite catch world imagination as single ones do. (Compare, for example,

Alcock and Brown with Lindbergh.) Reynolds and his crew had been engaged to work for a year in the plantation. Some historians, including Bradford, believe that they wanted to withdraw; some even see the whole thing as an elaborate plot. It appears rather more likely that those who did not go had simply seized the opportunity. If so, it was not a bad thing: "the great design" was not one for any hesitant or doubting person, and the withdrawal of *Speedwell* can be interpreted as a timely weeding out.

Mayflower carried the greater part of the stores, too: it was so very possible for the two ships to be separated at sea, and if that happened, would not the *Speedwell* face starvation? Any ship that was overmasted and carrying in consequence too much sail would open her seams in the full ocean. Bradford himself pointed this out.

> No special leak could be found, but it was judged to be the general weakness of the ship, and that she would not prove sufficient for the voyage. Upon which it was resolved to dismiss her and part of the company, and proceed with the other ship. . . . And thus, like Gideon's army, this small number was divided, as if the Lord by this work of His providence thought these few too many for the great work He had to do.

It took days to transfer stores and passengers aboard the *Mayflower*. During this time, other changes were made. On Friday, September 1, John Carver was elected governor in place of Martin: a distinct change for the better, if Cushman's comment was anything to go by:

> The sailors also are so offended at his ignorant boldness in riddling and controlling in things he knows not what belongs to, as that some threaten to mischief him. But at least this cometh of it, that he makes himself a scorn and laughing-stock unto them.

Cushman himself, and his seasick companion William King, gave up at this point, and decided not to go. So did his wife, Mary Singleton Cushman, and Dr. Thomas Blossom and his son, and Anne Heilsdon Blossom, whom he had married in Cambridge on

November 10, 1605. The *Speedwell* was to go back to London as soon as Reynolds could make the journey, taking the Cushmans, the Blossoms, and "others, in regard of their own weakness and charge of many young children" who "were thought least useful and most unfit to bear the brunt of this hard adventure." Most of those who went back, said Bradford, "were for the most part such as were willing to do so, either out of some discontent or fear they conceived of the ill success of the voyage, seeing so many crosses befall, and the year time so far spent."

This was a major hazard. The summer was over, the stormy autumn starting, and it was not the practice to make the crossing westward in that part of the year. For the Atlantic, it was usual to go out in spring, back in autumn. Although for a century fishing vessels had gone to the Grand Banks, only Gosnold so far had sailed the northern route to New England, and he had done it in summer weather. Now it was late, perhaps too late.

But *Mayflower* was not turning back now. Toward the rim of the habitable globe, with no return ticket for her passengers, she was setting out. Edward Winslow, after the last sad parting at the Barbican, noted the facts very simply:

> Wednesday, the sixth of September, the wind coming east-north-west, a fine small gale, we loosed from Plymouth, having been kindly entertained and courteously used by divers friends there dwelling. . . .

His wind is a bit peculiar, but the idea is plain. It had all been a matter of chance in so many ways. If one detail had altered, it might have been so different. The possibilities are legion, the speculation unlimited and fruitless. For now everything had fallen into place —Leyden, London, Southampton, Dartmouth, Plymouth. Crew and passengers alike had automatically put their trust in God, and they were asking a great deal of him. The fine small gale caught the sails, curving them out: the tiny ship, carrying what might be described as an enormous postdated weight of responsibility, bobbed away down Channel: and *Mayflower* was a legend.

• 4 •

There were two ways in which it was, in time, considered proper and sensible to sail across the Atlantic. One was to go by the trade winds, heading south to the Azores and then west—the Columbus route. The other was to avoid the Gulf Stream by going north first, roughly in the direction of Greenland, and then let the Arctic current carry the ship on—the fishers' route. The southern way was longer, but sunnier: the northern was rougher, but shorter. For both it was essential to get a good offing well clear of Biscay, so that one would not risk being pulled too close to the very rocky and dangerous coast of Finisterre. Captain Jones may or may not have met Bartholomew Gosnold, but he had certainly met captains who had sailed to the Grand Banks. He knew—it is obvious because he got there—how to manage his ship across the trackless ocean, and only a brave, tough, careful, and prudent master could have done it.

The secret of a sailing ship, as Stuart Upham told Warwick Charlton on *Mayflower II,* is rhythm, operating through the rigging to the sails, spars, and hull, blending smoothly to give the ship a hatful of wind. Without wind a vessel can barely hold her own against a tide. It has been known to take weeks to clear the Channel. If a ship is taken aback with the wind on the wrong side of the sails there is nothing that can be done but to haul them all around, a most laborious task taking at least half an hour, to wear the ship through a full circle back on her course. In a dead calm, with a heavy swell, spars and rigging dry out and become brittle enough to crack: a stern test of shipbuilding. Shortness, width, and a high superstructure in proportion make a ship like *Mayflower* difficult to maneuver and fatiguing to steer.

The actual voyage occupies fewer than seven hundred words of Bradford's journal, yet it took nine and a half weeks—sixty-seven days. Sixty-seven days of pitching, rolling, and swaying, two thirds of it through storms and squalls. From the beginning many passengers were seasick. From this fact sprang one event that in retrospect seems ironic. One young crew member made fun of the sick people. He was a conceited fellow, strong, lively, and vigorous, extremely talkative, and peppered his speech with bad language. Swinging cheerfully up and down the ship, stepping over and around the crammed men, women, and children, he cracked jokes all the time, telling them that at this rate half of them would never survive the crossing. He would heave them overboard all right, funerals at sea were nothing to him, and when they were gone he could help himself to their belongings. Some gently remonstrated with him as best they could: but it only made him laugh and curse more enthusiastically. One grinning face is more than enough for anyone suffering from that most wretched of maladies; and it speaks volumes for the self-control of the Pilgrims that somebody did not kill him.

Fate, however, saved them the trouble. Before the voyage was half over, the young man fell ill, and actually died, in what Bradford calls a desperate manner, though he did not say what the illness was. Considering the date, it might have been almost anything: but since it was an isolated case it would not have been infectious. Perhaps a perforated appendix? At any rate, it was the joker who was discarded; and Bradford's calm comment was inevitable: "Thus his curses light on his own head, and it was an astonishment to all his fellows for they noted it to be the just hand of God upon him." One can readily imagine the frisson of superstitious horror that ran through the crew, and the complacent comments of the passengers, at this neat providential sign, as if God, losing patience, had swatted a troublesome fly.

The ship was wet—Upham thought there could not have been a dry bone on board—and cold. She was cramped, too, badly ventilated, unlit below decks, none too lavishly provisioned, reeking of vomit and bilge. Commander Villiers, wondering what the Pilgrims did to pass the time, answered his own question from personal experience by saying that their main occupation was simply survival. Packed in as they were, every operation took a long time: cooking their own meals in twos and threes and fours, the smoke

from their little braziers blowing into their faces, keeping an eye on
the children so that they neither fell over the side nor got under the
sailors' feet unendurably, trying to make themselves comfortable
enough to snatch an hour or two of sleep below decks, where it was
not always possible even to stretch out—these framed their days.
Days of wrestling with private terrors, with personal sickness and
discomfort (how did the women and girls manage when they had
their periods, for example?), of endless speculation about how long
this was going on and what they would find when at last the blessed
land appeared, about what was happening to the friends they had
left behind them. Nights of wind and rain and mountainous seas, the
sea so wide and their boat so small. So very small. And always there
was the noise—the wind whistling and screaming in the rigging, the
slam of the sails, the creak of the timbers, the eternal wash of water
thudding against the side or crashing over the bowsprit, as the little
Mayflower tossed and plunged on the great Atlantic billows.

At first the weather was good. But then came the crosswinds
and the "many fierce storms with which the ship was shrewdly
shaken," in Bradford's excellent phrase. The upper works sprang
leaks which had to be repaired: hardened down with a caulking iron,
packed with a thread of oakum, and then painted with pitch, which
acted as a glue. In storms there is only one thing for a sailing ship to
do: she must hull, that is, heave to, lower all sails, and allow herself
to drift with the wind, not attempting to fight against it. In a really
big sea the *Mayflower* would float like a cork. Before storms there
would be a period of calm, perhaps a dead calm, with the canvas
aimlessly flapping and banging and the crew peering anxiously for
any sign of wind. Under a windless sky they would have recourse to
the ancient superstitions: to whistle for a wind (this is referred to in
Treasure Island), to set one's cap for a wind like King Erik of
Sweden, to stick a knife in the mainmast. If after seven days none of
these had produced the desired result, a member of the crew must
crawl out along the mainstay and tie a boot to it: that had never been
known to fail.

It was easy to see a storm or a squall coming. If it was going to be big, stormy petrels would appear, ominously circling: they can smell a storm miles off. The air might grow heavy, then in the distance a zigzag of lightning and a dull rumble of thunder as the clouds massed up announced the approach. Frantic activity to lower the heavy sails. Long before they were out of the way the sea would be confused and angry, clawing at the vessel; thick dark-green water poured over the sides, washing across the deck and crashing over the bowsprit. If the spritsail had not already been taken in, now was the time to do it, and quickly, before the bowsprit could get carried away. Men crawled out to perform this task, drenched to the skin on the slippery wood, as the ship lurched up and down great hills of water and the wind roared everywhere with deafening force. In the dark it was worse—a black sea heaving and thrashing under a heavy black sky, and the ship tossing and rolling under her bare poles, riding it out as best she could, while the passengers lay in the noisy darkness and wondered fearfully whether every stomach-shaking wrench would be their last.

In one storm young John Howland had a lucky escape. He had come "upon some occasion" on deck above the gratings, when the *Mayflower* pitched particularly violently and he was swept over-board. By great good luck he caught hold of the topsail halyards, which hung over the side, and managed to cling on, although he went down a long way. He was seen, and several men rushed to the side and began to haul on the rope. As the *Mayflower* righted herself, they pulled him up; one of them reached over with a boathook, and he was tugged aboard, dripping and spewing up water, breathless on to the deck. He was "something ill with it" but recovered, as Bradford was happy to record, and lived to eighty (he was twenty-seven at this time).

One mishap occurred which might have had fatal consequences. A main beam amidships bent under the strain of the storm and cracked. At once the crew began to mutter among themselves as to whether *Mayflower* could survive the voyage; the Pilgrims' leaders, hearing this, consulted Jones and his officers. There was much argument all over the ship, because the sailors wished to do their duty, yet they naturally wanted to live to sail another day; but two points decided the issue. They were more than halfway there, and felt, like Macbeth, that "returning were as tedious as go o'er." Also Jones and his chief assistants affirmed stoutly that the ship was strong and firm under water. Now it was that the "iron jack scrue" proved a lifesaver. This would raise the beam into place, and Jones and the carpenter could set a post under it "firm in the lower deck and otherwise bound" and the damage would be made good. Good enough to reach land safely, anyway. The iron screw, brought from Leyden, was probably part of the printing press; it is not easy to determine why the Pilgrims had brought it all that way with them, but it was exceedingly fortunate that they did.

In addition, said Jones, the decks and upper works could be recaulked after a fashion. The water could not be completely kept out, but there would be no great danger, provided that the ship did not carry too great a press of sail. "So they committed themselves to the will of God," wrote Bradford, "and resolved to proceed."

So *Mayflower* rolled and pitched and wallowed along, day after endless day, always in the center of the surrounding circle of sea, and when the sun came out the passengers could try to dry their clothes and bedding a little; and perhaps for some of them the seasickness would not be quite so bad. They calculated the food very carefully. Usually there were three meat days and four fish days a week on board. Two thirds of a codfish a day for four men, two three-pound pieces of salt beef or pork per man are quantities quoted, the meat representing a week's supply. A pound of biscuit, a gallon of drink each day, with a quarter of a pound of butter and half a pound of cheese, allocated to each person, and three pints of peas between eight people. It sounds a lot, but the Jacobeans ate bigger quantities than we do.

The gratings above which Howland went when he was swept over the side covered the main hatch, and allowed a little light, some cold fresh air, and a good deal of water to penetrate to the men, women, and children packed below among their belongings. One or two makeshift cabins had been wedged in (Captain Smith refers to people lying wet in their cabins between decks), but the entire vessel was so crowded that Captain Jones would barely have had the space to spread a chart. Not that he would need one for much of the voyage. Yet he had to work out his dead reckoning, and take his noon and midnight sightings as best he could. The crew were as wet as the rest, and the less experienced, tugging and pulling at the ropes for long stretches, got sea sores on their hands and wrists, difficult to heal and smarting under the lash of the salt.

During the first part of the crossing they were able to see the harvest moon, big and yellow, swinging up slowly into the deep-blue sky and making a broad silver-gilt track across the water. But for much of the later, and longer, part they passed days and nights without a glimpse of sun or star. The visibility was down to half a mile: taking sights and trying to fix a position or plot a course was impossible.

The wind screamed malignantly, tossing the *Mayflower* with terrifying persistence. That was the worst of it: it never let up. Most of the people on board had never imagined such weather possible, though those who had made the villainous two-week crossing of the North Sea with the Dutchman, having survived that, no doubt helped to comfort the rest. But it was all so exhausting: the wet cold, chilling to the bone, feet squelching inside soaked boots, hair dripping inside collars, water running down faces, tasting like tears, and all the time the heart quailing as *Mayflower* balanced uneasily before lurching sideways down a hill of sea that crashed into her, while the wind howled out of the black night or the dim gray wilderness that could hardly be called day. Frightening on deck, it was little relief below, where water washed about everywhere, and foul smells reeked up among the huddled people crammed among their belongings, tied in a makeshift way into place and always shaking loose, and it was so hard to sleep, yet every ragged nerve cried out for rest.

In the middle of all this, Elizabeth Hopkins had her baby. No date is given: but it was fairly late on in the voyage, for the one birth and the one death among the passengers happened close together, and the death was shortly before they sighted land. The Hopkins family consisted then of six members, Stephen Hopkins, a lay reader, aged thirty-five or thirty-nine (one account gives his date of birth as October 29, 1581), Giles aged fifteen, Constanta aged eleven, Damaris aged five or six, Elizabeth, and now the new boy, appropriately named Oceanus. One account says that Elizabeth married Stephen on February 19, 1617, in which case she would of course have been his second wife and Oceanus her first baby: but other books do not mention this.

The death was of young William Butten, Dr. Fuller's manservant. Bradford reports the fact without further detail. The significant thing is that it was the only death among the passengers, just as the "profane young man" was the only crew fatality. Despite the terrible conditions of the voyage, the people did survive.

Exactly when William Butten died is not known, but there was as short a delay as possible always between a death and a burial at sea, and somehow his body was committed to the deep on Tuesday, November 7. The weather was, mercifully, easing by this time, and the very next day, ironically enough, signs that land could not be far off became visible. The smell of the air subtly changed. Bits of driftwood floated by. Birds circled mewing above. Jones began to take soundings, and slowly a current of optimism, half fearful as yet, began to stir throughout the *Mayflower.* All Wednesday and Thursday this continued, while the wind fell slacker and the ship crept forward, and passengers fell into exhausted sleep from which they twitched awake wondering whether the storm would pounce again. It had been so long that they could not now believe it: surely soon the struggle would begin all over again. But Friday's light moved up the sky, inch by inch, and the lookout shouted the words so long awaited and so often utterly despaired of: "Land ho!"

Yes, there it was—a low outline on the dim horizon, dark and silent in the chill thin air of a November dawn, but land unmistakably. Be sure that everyone who could stand had a look, peering ahead to catch a glimpse, and excitedly voicing their thankfulness that the long ordeal was as good as over. It did not look very welcoming: not a glimmer of light to be seen anywhere, no sign of another vessel, no man-made landmark of any description. But it was land: they could step onto it, stand still, stand upright, walk steadily. Bradford noted with typical lack of dramatics: "They were not a little joyful."

What they were looking at, straining their eyes through the steel-gray dawn light, was, Jones calculated, Cape Cod. This meant that they had made their landfall much too far to the north: they ought to be a lot nearer the Hudson River. As soon as there could be no doubt, he consulted Carver and others. They ought to start where they were supposed to: they must tack about and stand for the southward, which was perfectly practicable, as it was going to be a fine day, and the wind was slight, but blowing from the northeast.

The senior passengers agreed, and *Mayflower* turned. Within a few hours, however, she was in trouble. She met the heavy breakers and dangerous shoal water of Pollock Rip, below Monomoy Island. This is an area treated very respectfully by modern sailors with every mechanical aid: Jones hesitated. The wind slackened and the sea still boiled; Jones decided to put back, and the Pilgrims, thankful at the prospect of escaping from that perilous place before nightfall, hastened to agree.

Mayflower dragged herself free of the Rip, and slowly stood north again, patiently pulling along parallel with the low wooded shoreline. Saturday morning before dawn found her back at the long crooked finger of Cape Cod, very close to the coast, edging around what is now Race Point. As the sun came up, *Mayflower* felt the water fall calm under her keel. She nosed her way forward to a suitable anchorage. There was no lack of such: Winslow commented that there was a fine open harbor where a thousand sail could ride in safety. It was just inside the northernmost hook of the Cape. The last sails were lowered, the anchors dropped; in a kind of bellowing silence the Pilgrims realized that it was all over, storm and terror and doubt; they had done it, they had arrived, weary, apprehensive, but alive, in the New World.

· 5 ·

Bradford's summing up at this moment, one of the big historical moments as everyone senses them, is worth looking at in some detail.

> But here I cannot but stay and make a pause, and stand half amazed at this poor people's present condition; and so I think will the reader, too, when he well considers the same. Being thus passed the vast ocean, and a sea of troubles before in their preparation (as may be remembered by that which went before), they had now no friends to welcome them nor inns to entertain or refresh their weatherbeaten bodies; no houses or much less towns to repair to, to seek for succour. . . . And for the season it was winter, and they that know the winters of that country know them to be sharp and violent, and subject to cruel and fierce storms, dangerous to travel to known places, much more to search an unknown coast. Besides, what could they see but a hideous and desolate wilderness, full of wild beasts and wild men—and what multitudes there might be of them they knew not. Neither could they, as it were, go up to the top of Pisgah to view from this wilderness a more goodly country to feed their hopes; for which way soever they turned their eyes (save upward to the heavens) they could have little solace or content in respect of any outward objects. For summer being done, all things stand upon them with a weatherbeaten face, and the whole country, full of woods and thickets, represented a wild and savage hue.

All things stand upon them with a weatherbeaten face. . . . This magnificent passage states the voyagers' condition very simply. Behind them lay the wide Atlantic that they had just spent sixty-seven days crossing. On the far side of it were their friends and relations, loving and anxious, certainly, but helpless at that distance, and the Adventurers, offended by the failure to agree to all the conditions. In front was who knew what? A silent, empty, inhospitable vista that showed no immediate comfort and almost certainly concealed menacing unknown hazards. *Mayflower,* familiar and sheltering, was there; but she had to travel home, so they must settle quickly. Jones must make certain that he had enough food and drink on board for the passage back. He might feel compelled to sail away at any time, leaving them marooned, and he could hardly be blamed for that. How long then would it be before another ship came?

"What could now sustain them," commented Bradford, "but the Spirit of God and His grace?" Certainly the first emotion was one of thanksgiving. This buoyed them up. Some of the passengers had been grumbling, and, realizing that the landing was at a place where the writ of the charter did not run, believed it possible that the Pilgrims had no legal right in it. These mutterers were heard to say that no one had any power to command them here, and that when they got ashore they would "use their own liberty." The leaders' answer was sensible, prompt, and impressive. They called a general meeting in the crowded main room of the *Mayflower,* and drew up an agreement for every head of a household to sign. In this document they bound themselves to create a civil body politic, to make laws, and to elect officers to administer the government of the new colony.

This document is known as the *Mayflower* Compact. Forty-one men signed it, every man of adult age with the possible exceptions of several indentured servants and apprentices. The Compact was brought to light in 1802 by John Quincy Adams, future sixth President, who described it as

> the first example in modern times of a social compact or system of government instituted by voluntary agreement conformable to the laws of nature, by men of equal rights and about to establish their community in a new country.

The rights were not completely equal in practice, but one can see what Adams meant.

Having drawn up the Compact, the signers elected John Carver

IN YE NAME OF GOD, AMEN.

We whofe names are underwritten, the loyal fubjects of our dread fovereigne Lord, King James, by ye grace of God, of Great Britaine, France and Ireland, King, defender of ye faith, etc., haveing undertaken for ye glory of God and advancement of ye Chriftian faith, and honour of our King and countrie, a voyage to plant ye firft Colonie in ye Northerne parts of Virginia, doe by thefe prefents folemnly, and mutualy, in ye prefence of God, and of one another, covenant and combine ourfelves togeather into a civil body politik for our better ordering and prefervation and furtherance of ye end aforefaid, and by vertue hearof to enacte, conftitute and frame fuch juft and equal lawes, ordinances, acts, conftitutions and offices from time to time, as fhall be thought moft meete and convenient for ye generall good of ye Colonie, unto which we promife all due fubmiffion and obedience. In witnes whereof we have hereunder fubfcribed our names at Cape-Codd ye 11 of November, in ye year of ye raigne of our fovereigne Lord, King James of England, France and Ireland, ye eighteenth, and of Scotland ye fiftiefourth. Ano Dom. 1620.

1. John Carver,
2. William Bradford,
3. Edward Winslow,
4. William Brewster.
5. Isaac Allerton,
6. Myles Standish,
7. John Alden,
8. Samuel Fuller,
9. Christopher Martin,
10. William Mullins,
11. William White,
12. Richard Warren,
13. John Howland,
14. Stephen Hopkins,
15. Edward Tilley,
16. John Tilley,
17. Francis Cooke,
18. Thomas Rogers,
19. Thomas Tinker.
20. John Rigdale,
21. Edward Fuller,
22. John Turner,
23. Francis Eaton,
24. James Chilton,
25. John Crackston,
26. John Billington,
27. Moses Fletcher,
28. John Goodman,
29. Degory Priest,
30. Thomas Williams,
31. Gilbert Winslow,
32. Edmund Margeson,
33. Peter Brown,
34. Richard Britteridge,
35. George Soule,
36. Richard Clarke,
37. Richard Gardiner,
38. John Allerton,
39. Thomas English,
40. Edward Dotey,
41. Edward Lister,

MAYFLOWER COMPACT

as their first governor, and the meeting ended, having achieved a
notable success: that of bracing everyone to the first duties. Sixteen
men volunteered to go ashore and have a look around. They took
the longboat.

The shoregoing party did not stay very long, but brought back
a mixed report. Miles of trees stretched down to the water's edge
in places: oaks, pines, juniper, sassafras, "and other sweet
woods"—they brought back some juniper for firewood. They said
that the sandhills were "much like the Downs in Holland but much
better and all wooded." Some places were swampy, edged by tall
cedars and fine red maples, and they had noticed ash, birch, and
walnut trees. They had seen no living thing, no sign of habitation,
and had found no sweet water, but had probed the ground and found
it "a spit's depth excellent black earth."

Sunday was the first complete day in the new colony, but it was
still Sunday, and the full observation was meticulously kept:
preaching, psalms, prayer, and meditation. But Monday, November 13, saw work begin in earnest. Sentries were put out, the
women went ashore and started washing. They used the nearest
suitable place—an oval pond less than a mile long, where the water
was brackish, but it was an unutterable relief to stand on land again
and to refresh the caked and dirty clothes that had offended the
senses for so long. The children and dogs, likewise released, ran
about on the sands, shouting with pleasure after having been
cooped up for all those weeks. No doubt the cats and pet birds, all of
which arrived alive, felt relief in their own way.

Some of the men, exploring on the beach, found clams and
mussels. The clams, locally termed littleneck and cherrystone
clams, are a great delicacy, but the unfortunate Pilgrims, who had
never seen them before and did not know how to eat them, were so
delighted to find the first fresh food they had tasted for over nine
weeks that they made themselves sick. Not until they learned better
from the Indians did they have a kindlier experience of one of New
England's most characteristic dishes.

Looking about them at the wintry bay, with its panorama of

wild wood, rock, dune, and scrub, it seemed that the first job to be done was to put the shallop in order, ready for the exploration they must do. The shallop was accordingly lifted out in pieces, and examined by the carpenters. It was going to take a long time to set right, battered as it was by the long crossing. A few volunteers offered to take a look around on foot, particularly toward the south, where they could see what looked like a river mouth. Sixteen men were mustered for this exploration, armed with muskets five feet long. These muskets had a smooth bore, about .75, and the loading was a cumbersome business. Black powder was poured down the muzzle, tamped, and wadded, a lead ball dropped in and rammed with a thick pad. Fine-grain powder tipped on to the flashpan was lit by a small match (a kind of flint and steel to strike sparks) pressed down as part of the hammer and released by the trigger with a tongue of flame a yard long, a loud crack, and a cloud of smoke. One of the sixteen was put in charge of the party: Captain Miles Standish, now starting a career of nearly forty years as military commander for the Pilgrims.

Standish, then thirty-six, was a short man (Thomas Morton derisively nicknamed him Captain Shrimp) with reddish hair and complexion and a hot temper (Winslow described him as "an easily kindled little chimney"). He had served as a soldier of fortune in the Low Countries. He came originally from Duxbury in Lancashire, and was selected by Carver and Cushman, perhaps through Weston, to go in the *Mayflower* as military adviser. His fifteen included Carver and Bradford, Edward Winslow, John and Edward Tilley, Howland, Warren, Hopkins, Edward Doty, the seamen English and Ely, and four of the *Mayflower* crew—Clarke, Coppin, the master gunner, and one of his assistants. They set out on the morning of Wednesday, November 15.

At first they walked along the beach, roughly northeast. When they had gone about a mile, they stood still, staring, for there were people—five or six Indians, with a dog, coming toward them. The Indians stopped too, hesitated, consulted rapidly, turned, and ran into the woods. Standish and his men promptly gave chase, hoping to speak with the Indians and find out if they were part of a bigger group: it was rather a foolhardy thing to do. Nothing came of it, however: the Indians, seeing the English come on, ran away along the sands as fast as they could, rapidly dwindling out of sight. The English followed the tracks in the sand, but saw no more of them.

The tracks led them on for several miles, and it was beginning to get dark, so the party camped for the night, setting out sentinels, who reported no disturbance. In the morning the party went on, still hoping to find an Indian village. They found a wide creek, from which they turned, and entered the woods, guessing the Indians had gone that way. Here, however, they felt acutely uncomfortable. They were parched with thirst, and the woods were full of dense thorny thickets that tore their clothes and wrenched at their armor. The tracks had, of course, vanished utterly. At last they found water, at the spot called today Pilgrim Spring, the first New England water they had tasted. Bradford wryly commented that this was "now in great thirst as pleasant unto them as wine or beer had been in foretimes."

Knowing that they were on a neck of land, for water was visible on both sides at times, they went on, much refreshed now, and came out on the beach at the other side. They found a pond of clear fresh water, and, nearby, a broad stretch of open ground where corn had been planted. Some shallow mounds intrigued them. They dug into one and found, to their horror, bones, old arrows, and a bow: it was hateful to think that they had violated a warrior's grave (or that of anybody else), for this was both sacrilegious and unlucky. So they smoothed it reverently back again, and went on.

The next thing they discovered was new stubble, and the remains of a house—planks and "a great kettle"—and heaps of sand. These they explored. They found a number of fine baskets full of corn, some in ears, all good, of various colors: a most encouraging sight. They filled the old kettle and their pockets with it, promising to repay the Indians for it later. Not far off was the river they had hoped to find, opening in two arms "with a high cliff of sand in the entrance" and wide enough to admit the shallop comfortably. This was the Pamet River, and the place where the corn was dug up is still called Corn Hill.

They went as fast as they could along the dunes back to the *Mayflower,* having stayed away as long as they had intended, and eagerly showed the corn to the rest of the party. Once in sight of the ship they shot off their muskets as a signal, the longboat picked them up, and Jones and Carver hurried down the beach from the ship to meet them. Everyone was delighted to see them safely back, and to examine the tangible guarantee of survival they carried. The *Mayflower* company had increased by one in their absence: Susanna White had had her baby, a boy, named Peregrine. A suitable choice: it means a pilgrim.

It was another ten days before the shallop was ready, and when it was, Jones said he would like to lead the second exploratory party himself. Some thirty men went with him, and the shallop felt her way cautiously around to the Pamet River. The weather turned nasty—a strong wind, snow settling six inches deep, and a piercingly cold night. Some of the party waded ashore, thereby (according to Winslow and Bradford) "taking the original of their death here." The river mouth proved to be swampy and tidal, fit for boats but not for ships, and the party walked up and down the wearying shallow snow-covered indentations of the land toward Corn Hill. They found two typical Nauset wigwams, built of arched boughs interwoven into a framework covered with woven mats. In these were tools and utensils, but no people. Apparently the half dozen with the dog had reported the arrival of the *Mayflower* locally, and the Indians had gone into hiding until they could find out whether the strangers were friendly.

Jones's party found more corn, and some beans of various colors. They brought away about ten bushels of corn, and a bag of beans, again promising among themselves to pay for it whenever they met the Indians to whom it belonged. (Indeed they did so some six months later.) They were particularly thankful to have found this supply, as this was seed corn which they could plant for the coming year. They went back to the ship, having taken two days for this expedition, from Tuesday, November 28, to Thursday, November 30.

The virtues of Indian corn were already well known to settlers in the New World. Word had spread from explorers in the Caribbean and the Carolinas, as well as from the north, that it produced two good harvests a year, from which wholesome bread and good-quality biscuit could be made, dressed in various ways with milk: the ancestor, no doubt, of that great American export the breakfast cereal. The Spaniards had found that an excellent drink could be created from the juice of green corn mixed with chocolate and spices; the English in the Caribbean roasted green ears of corn on charcoal fires; the Indians in the Carolinas dried the ripe corn and pounded it to a powder which they put in leather bags when traveling. They mixed it with water in the palms of their hands and ate the result: in this way they could keep going for several days. It was, of course, made into cakes to feed cattle in the West.

On the Wednesday night, they camped out in the rain, building a good fire and setting up a screen against the wind. Three men at a time kept watch throughout the night, each one "standing when his turn came while five or six inches of match were burning." They did not, however, go to bed hungry, having shot three fat geese and six ducks, which they devoured "with soldiers' stomachs" because they had not eaten much all day.

Edward Winslow later wrote a precise description of some of the things they had seen. He said that when they opened the grave

we found first a mat, and under that a fair bow, and there another mat, and under that a board about three-quarters of a yard long finely carved and painted, with three tines or broaches on the top like a crown. Also between the mats we found bowls, trays, dishes and such like trinkets. At length we came to a fair new mat, and under that two bundles, the one bigger, the other less. We opened the greater and found in it a great quantity of fine and perfect red powder, and in it the bones and skull of a man. The skull had fine yellow hair on it, and some of the flesh unconsumed. There were bound up with it a knife, a pack-needle, and two or three old iron things. It was bound up in a sailor's canvas cassock and a pair of cloth breeches. The red powder was a kind of embalmment and yielded a strong, but not offensive, smell. It was fine as any flour. We opened the less bundle likewise and found of the same powder in it, and the bones and head of a little child. About the legs and other parts of it were bound strings and bracelets of fine white beads. There was also by it a little bow about three-quarters of a yard long, and some other odd knacks.

He pictured the wigwams exactly too:

They were made with long young sapling trees, bended and both ends stuck in the ground. They were made round like an arbour, and covered down to the ground with thick and well wrought mats, and the door was not over a yard high, made of a mat to open. The chimney was a wide open hole in the top, for which they had a mat to cover it when they pleased. One might stand and go upright in them. In the midst of them were four little trunches knocked into the ground and small sticks laid over, on which they hung their pots and what they had to seethe. Round about the fire they lay on mats which are their beds. The houses were double matted, for as they were matted without so were they within, with newer and fairer mats.

Among other objects inside the wigwams were wooden bowls, trays, dishes, earthenware pots, baskets made of crab shells, and other baskets of different sizes and degrees of fineness, some of them "curiously wrought with black and white, in pretty works." There were deer feet and deer heads, one of them quite fresh, harts' horns and eagles' claws, dried acorns, pieces of fish one of which was broiled herring, tobacco seed, other unfamiliar seeds, and a little silk grass.

There was plenty of game in the woods, and they found an Indian trap:

As we wandered, we came to a tree where a young sapling was

bowed down over a bow, and some acorns strewed underneath. Stephen Hopkins said, It had been to catch some deer. So as we were looking at it, William Bradford being in the rear, when he came, looked also upon it. And as he went about, it gave a sudden jerk up and he was immediately caught by the leg. It was a very pretty device, made with a rope of their own making, and having a noose as artificially made as any roper in England can make, and as like ours as can be, which we brought away with us.

They saw three bucks, "but we had rather have had one of them," and three pairs of partridges, as well as great flocks of wild geese and ducks by the creek. These rose fluttering in a cloud as the strangers approached. There were whales in the bay, too:

There was one once, when the sun shone warm, came and lay above water as if she had been dead for a good while together, within half a musket shot of the ship. At which two were prepared to shoot to see whether she would stir or no. He that gave fire first, his musket flew in pieces, both stock and barrel. Yet thanks be to God neither he nor any man else was hurt with it, though many were there about. But when the whale saw her time, she gave a snuff and away! If we had instruments and means to take them, we might have made a very rich return. . . .

But the required "instruments" were lacking, they were sorry to say. Jones, and Clarke, and other crew members experienced in fishing, declared that they could make three or four thousand pounds in whale oil, and suggested trying the following winter, because it was probably better here than in Greenland.

· 6 ·

This was all very well, but the need to make some kind of proper settlement was pressing. The cold bit to the bone: winter was upon them with all its rigor. Going ashore meant wading knee-deep at least, often thigh-deep, and clothes took so long to dry out that almost everyone was perpetually coughing and streaming with colds. If this went on long, they would grow dangerously weak. Storms were ferocious enough to make surveying risky: not only men but the precious boats might be lost. Supplies of food and drink were diminishing daily, and the *Mayflower* had to have enough left to get home with; once she was gone, they would have no lodging other than whatever they managed to build.

Discussion about where to settle was long and profound. Three possibilities lay before them. They could build on the Pamet River, which was nearby, and where they had already explored; they could go up to the northern headland, the future Cape Ann; or they could cross the bay to a place Robert Coppin knew about, that he had visited before, to which he could pilot them. It would, they thought, be wise to take a look at it before deciding.

First, however, they had another shore expedition where they were. Before this party set out the whole company had a narrow escape. Young Francis Billington, fidgeting about for something to amuse himself with in his father's cabin, seemed to think that something was necessary to liven things up. He tried his hand at making small noisy fireworks, known as squibs. The cabin was between decks, with plenty of people close by, flints and iron tools lying handy, and a little barrel of gunpowder, half full, standing open. Some of the gunpowder was spilled about the floor. In the four-foot space beside the bed the fourteen-year-old scientist cheerfully fired off a couple of muskets and a fowling-piece charge. Why he did not succeed in blowing up the *Mayflower* no one will ever know; but providentially no harm was done (perhaps the powder was damp) and the ship was undamaged. Not a soul was scratched: Master Francis emerged without so much as a singe, except, of course, for the spiritual scorching he no doubt received from the alarmed and protesting grown-ups, who clearly saw that Satan finds some mischief still for idle hands to do.

The carpenter had been slow, but he was careful, and the next day, Wednesday, December 6, a party set off in the reconstituted shallop. Standish, Carver, Howland, Bradford, Hopkins, Doty, Winslow, John and Edward Tilley, Warren, Clarke, the master gunner, and three crew members—the same people as on the first expedition. It was piercingly cold: the spray froze on their coats. The shallop moved down the deep bay, reaching the area of present-day Eastham in the early evening. As they drew near the shore they saw ten or twelve Indians very busy about something. They were, in fact, cutting up a large fish: the remains of three great stranded blackfish, with flesh two inches thick, lay there next morning.

The Pilgrims kept a cautious distance. They landed some way off, not without difficulty as the wide flat sands stretched out so far, and camped for the night. They hurriedly roughed up a screen of logs and branches, set out their sentinel, and saw in the distance the glow of the Indians' fire. They built up their own fire, and lay around it, and went wearily to sleep.

In the morning they divided into two groups, one to take the shallop along the shore, the other to explore on foot. It was a long, tiring day. The walking party found the remains of the fish, but no Indians; nor did they find a suitable place to build. They covered a good deal of ground up and down, and when the sun grew low in the sky, they hurried out of the woods to signal the shallop, which came up into Herring Creek. It was a relief to be all together again after the day's separation; and as usual they built their screen, logs, stakes, and pine boughs as tall as a man, left open to leeward, and made their fire. The sentinel took up his position, the rest lay down to sleep.

About midnight they started into wakefulness. A wild howling noise and the voice of the sentinel shouting "Arm! arm!" jerked them out of their uneasy slumber. They scrambled up, pulled the guns out from inside their coats, where they had wrapped them up against the damp and possible surprise, and fired off a couple. The howling stopped. One of the sailors said it was probably wolves: he had heard that sound once before, in Newfoundland. The men went back to rest, but were up again by five in the morning, in order to catch the tide to take them back.

First, of course, they said their prayers, and then began to get breakfast ready. The sky was slowly lightening, so it seemed sensible to start carrying things down to the shallop. A slight difference of opinion arose, as Bradford noted.

> Some said it was not best to carry the arms down, others said they would be the readier . . . but some three or four would not carry theirs till they went themselves. Yet as it fell out, the water being not high enough, they laid them down on the bank side and came up to breakfast.

Suddenly the same howling noise burst out again, though with varied notes in it this time, and one man came running in past the barricade, shouting: "Men, Indians, Indians!" At the same moment, arrows whizzed and twanged among them. In the wild scramble for the guns, two of the shallop party who had held onto their muskets fired them off, and two others stood to arms at the entrance, under orders (presumably from Captain Standish) not to fire until they could aim properly. The first pair frantically reloaded, while the rest, wearing their armor and carrying cutlasses, dashed down to the creek to fetch their own weapons.

This move made the attackers shout more ferociously than ever as they circled about the screen within bowshot distance. One big Indian stood behind a tree and shot three arrows; in reply the defenders fired three times at him—he was within half a musket shot—and once the ball splintered the tree trunk at the level of his head, whereupon he let out "an extraordinary shriek" and retired. Meanwhile a flurry of shots had dispersed the rest, and silence fell as the smoke slowly cleared.

Leaving some of the party to guard the shallop, the rest gave chase for about a quarter of a mile, shouting once or twice and firing a few shots, more to show they were not afraid than for any other reason. The Indians vanished into the woods, and the defenders came back to assess the damage.

It was not much. They found some arrows sticking in the barricade, some in the men's coats hanging there, and more arrows on the ground, almost covered with leaves. They picked up all they could see, and examined them. Some had brass tips, others harts' horn or eagles' claw heads. (Later on they sent them back to England as a curiosity.) Characteristically the party then knelt down and gave thanks for their deliverance. They named the place First Encounter, a brave and confident choice, and set off in the shallop to look for a good harbor.

None appeared. After a while Robert Coppin said again that he remembered, from his previous visit, a likely spot, not too far off to reach before dark. This was encouraging, because the weather was worsening: sleet fell, the wind rose, and the water grew choppy. The rudder broke, and it took the maximum effort of two men laboring at the oars to keep going in the right direction. Coppin told them to keep their spirits up, for he could see the harbor ahead. The wind howled and the sea ran high, so they worked as hard as they could to get into safe waters while it was still possible to see where they were going. It was almost a disaster: the mast broke into three pieces and the sail fell overboard, so that for a few terrifying minutes it looked as if they would be wrecked. But they managed to wrench the shallop into quieter water, where they could take breath and look about them in the gathering gloom.

Coppin instantly realized that he had made a mistake. He said, according to Bradford, "The Lord be merciful unto them for his eyes never saw that place before, and he and the master's mate would have run her ashore in a cove full of breakers before the wind." One valiant sailor, who was steering, told them: "If you are men, row like fury and put about, or we shall all be cast away—there's a fair sound before us," and this they managed to do, weathering Saquish Head and getting into the lee of a small island.

Contrary opinions exist about precisely what Coppin's mistake was. Gershom Bradford, formerly of the U.S. Hydrographic Survey, believed that the storm blew from the northeast, so the shallop passed between Browns Bank and Long Beach, and the cove full of breakers was Warrens Cove. Professor Morison, however, thought that the wind was blowing from the southeast, and that Coppin mistook the Gurnet for Saquish Head and Saquish for Goose Point. Both, though, agree that it was Saquish Head the shallop pulled around, encouraged by the sailor at the oars, and certainly it was not until morning that the party realized that the land in whose shelter they stood was an island.

When they came to a stop in calm water, they were divided in opinion as to what was the best thing to do. Some thought they ought to stay on board in case there were Indians about. Others were so cold and wet that they could not bear the idea. These stepped ashore, and with a good deal of trouble made a fire, where the rest were glad to join them about midnight, for the wind veered around to the northwest and it froze hard.

Next morning, Saturday, December 9, dawned fine, sunny, and calm. Thankfully the party observed that they were on an island clear of Indians, where they could dry out, clean their weapons, and rest. They stayed there all that day and the next, for of course the next day was Sunday, and they kept that as always. They named the place Clarke's Island, after John Clarke, the mate of the *Mayflower*. On Monday morning they cleared up, stacked everything on board, and took the shallop into the wide harbor nearby. Sounding it, they found it fit for *Mayflower* to ride at anchor. Eventually they landed, somewhere between what is now called Captain's Hill and the spot named Plymouth Rock.

· 7 ·

History has heavily overdramatized this first landing. The moment when the Pilgrims first set foot in Plymouth was on the morning of Monday, December 11, they landed from the shallop, the party numbered sixteen men, and no one else was present or visible. It was an entirely unspectacular occasion. They were there on business, to see if this looked like a good place for a colony. Apparently it did. They found little running brooks, cornfields, which proved the ground could be cultivated, and a sheltered situation; Bradford said of it:

> a place (as they supposed) fit for situation. At least it was the best they could find, and the season and their present necessity made them glad to accept of it.

It was not ideal. No big river led into the hinterland, no deepwater harbor existed as it did farther north in Massachusetts Bay, and much of the local soil was exhausted by previous Indian cultivation; but they were not to know that, nor were they in a position to be too fussy about their future place of settlement. They simply took a look, decided "this will have to do," and, getting back on board, took the shallop across to the *Mayflower*, where they reported that they had found a suitable site.

Heartily relieved at this news, everyone busily made ready to sail. Jones weighed anchor on the morning of Friday, December 15, and crossed the bay. Some six miles offshore the wind went against them, and all that night they lay hove-to, while the gale blew itself out. On Saturday morning the wind was with them, and *Mayflower* came safely to anchor in Plymouth harbor.

She arrived one passenger short. When the shallop party returned on Monday evening or Tuesday morning (no one says which it was) they were met with the sad news that Dorothy Bradford was dead. She had apparently fallen overboard, and was drowned. Bradford refers to her as his "dearest consort" but makes only the briefest reference to her death; this has given rise to the theory that, faced with the desolate prospect of her surroundings, she had chosen to commit suicide. Then the most sinful of acts, it could explain Bradford's reticence; but then he is always reluctant to write much about himself.

The reader must draw his own conclusions. If Dorothy Bradford's courage had quailed during the long days in Provincetown Harbor, it is hard to blame her.

· 8 ·

Again, history has tried to dress up the landing at Plymouth in lively colors. One reads of Priscilla Mullins jumping lightheartedly on to the Rock, of the elders stepping ashore and sinking to their knees, picking up handfuls of earth, making grandiloquent speeches. The reality is more prosaic, and better. The first thing they did was to have a close look at the area, discussing where was the best spot to start building. They had another good look around, debating the rival merits of Clarke's Island, the nearby river which they named Jones River after the master of the *Mayflower* (this would be the site of present-day Kingston), or Plymouth itself. Plymouth won for three good reasons. A lot of the land was cleared already. The hill now known as Burial Hill was ideally placed to build a fort commanding a clear view of the country all around. The Town Brook was found to be a stream of sweet water. That settled it. The colony would be built here, and it would be named New Plymouth, after the port from which they had sailed. It was proper to give the place an English name: Bradford had crystallized the basic idea in a noble sentence:

> May not and ought not the children of these fathers rightly say:
> our fathers were Englishmen which came over the great ocean,
> and were ready to perish in this wilderness.

They were utterly ignorant about the land they had come to. Stephen Hopkins had voyaged to Virginia, Jones and Clarke had crossed the Atlantic, Coppin had entered Cape Cod Bay; but the rest had known only England and the Netherlands. They had arrived at the most difficult season, badly equipped by colonial standards and far from help. They had four things going for them: courage, faith, endurance, and good sense. As a result, they show up better than any other group of settlers, so that by any standards the *Mayflower* voyage remains a magnificent achievement.

Mercy Otis Warren, born in 1728 at Barnstable, Massachusetts, who lived for many years in Plymouth, wrote:

> The first emigrations to North America were not composed of a strolling banditti of rude nations, like the people of most other colonies in the history of the world. The early settlers in the newly discovered continent were as far advanced in civilisation, policy, and manners; in their ideas of government, the nature of compacts, and the bands of civil union, as any of their neighbours at that period among the most polished nations of Europe. . . . Learning was cultivated, knowledge disseminated, politeness and morals improved, and valour and patriotism cherished, in proportion to the rapidity of the population.

· 9 ·

The Pilgrims did everything in order. First they formally chose John Carver, as "a godly man and highly approved among them," as governor of the colony. It was essential to work within a legal framework, because their charter applied to Virginia, and they were in New England. Actually, by the terms of the charter, they had the right to form their own government, but they were a naturally orderly people and proceeded in a naturally orderly fashion.

Discussions about law and order, civil and military, went on in the first days in the intervals of unloading all the cargo into a common store protected from the weather, a long job in rain, sleet, and snow, with only the three boats, and sickness spreading menacingly among the company. They had to row backward and forward about a mile and a half, for the comparative shallowness of Plymouth Harbor forced *Mayflower* to anchor that distance off shore. Burial Hill, referred to by the Pilgrims as Fort Hill or the Mount, was to hold a kind of gun platform, with the cannon mounted on it. They made a start on the first cottages, one-room frame houses with roofs of rough thatch. Lots measuring eight feet by forty-nine and a half, a curiously narrow shape, were mapped out and drawn for, one per person, so that a family of six would take six of them. The only people not included in the draw were Governor Carver, who was given a large corner site, and Captain Standish, who appropriately received a plot next to the future fort.

It was of course impossible to manage everything without somebody starting to grumble. Various people muttered among themselves, others spoke out rebelliously about the division of lots and the order in which buildings were set up, but Carver and his particular adherents smoothed matters over by firm, patient justice and equable attitude. The common dwelling house was built first, and most of the company spent the worst part of the winter in it, though it was only twenty feet square, with a few window spaces covered with oiled paper. The rest lived in dugouts, covered by turf roofs resting on wooden posts.

Nine days after the landing was Christmas Day, not observed as a religious festival, but marked all the same:

> Monday the twenty-fifth being Christmas Day, we began to drink water aboard. But at night the master caused us to have some beer. And so on board we had divers times, now and then, some beer. But on shore none at all.

The following Thursday, December 28, the layout of the town was fixed, lots measured out, and work started on the fort. It was decided to build the town in the shape of a cross, with two intersecting streets, to make defense easier. The hill commanded a wide view across the surrounding plain and the bay right across to Cape Cod. Nineteen houses were planned, single men asked to join families so that fewer houses would be needed. Of Indians there was no sign, except on Wednesday, January 3, when a thatch-gathering party saw smoke in the distance. From members who went scouting around, reports came in of hopeful supplies: wildfowl were abundant, crab, lobster, cod, turbot, herring, and skate, fine big mussels, all obviously plentiful in season. And as for vegetation:

Two or three great oaks, but not very thick. Pines, walnut, beech, ash, birch, hazel, holly, asp, sassafras in abundance, and vines everywhere. Cherry trees, plum trees and many others which we knew not. Many kinds of herbs we found here in winter, as strawberry leaves innumerable, sorrel, yarrow, carvel, brook-lime, liverwort, watercresses, great store of leeks and onions, and an excellent strong kind of flax or hemp. Here are sand and gravel and excellent clay, no better in the world, excellent for pots, and will wash like soap, and great store of stone, though somewhat soft, and the best water that ever we drank.

But it was winter, and the kindly fruits of the earth were not yet growing. Illness and death began to creep among the little company. It was a slightly milder winter than the average, but the settlers were lowered in stamina after the long voyage, were still crowded together, and lacked fresh vegetables and fruit. Scurvy spread, chills turned to pneumonia. Six died in December, eight in January, seventeen in February, thirteen in March: nearly half the total of passengers, while the *Mayflower* crew lost almost half its number. Digerie Priest died on New Year's Day, Christopher Martin a week later. Many of those who did not die fell ill. Peter Browne and John Goodman went with their dogs to collect reeds for thatching; the dogs scented a deer and followed the scent into the woods, the men followed in hope of fresh meat, and got lost. They wandered all night in the forest, cold and frightened, hearing noises like wolves howling. A search party went out but found no trace. Men and dogs got back next day, but Goodman's shoes had to be cut from his frostbitten feet, and he died within a few days. Browne and the two dogs survived.

On January 14 the common-house thatch caught fire. Inside, among the sick, stood several barrels of gunpowder, some of them open. The sick people struggled up and managed to move the barrels outside, though quite a quantity of clothing was burned. Bradford, who had collapsed while working, was among the sick at this point, and so was Governor Carver.

Bradford wrote about this sad time that

there was but six or seven sound persons who to their great commendations be it spoken, spared no pains night nor day, but with abundance of toil and hazard of their own health, fetched them wood, made them fires, dressed them meat, made their beds, washed their loathsome clothes, clothed and unclothed them. In a word, did all the homely and necessary offices for them which dainty and queasy stomachs cannot endure to hear named; and all this willingly and cheerfully, without any grudging in the least, showing herein their true love unto their friends and brethren; a rare example and worthy to be remembered.

Two of these helpers were the elderly Brewster and Captain Standish, who worked unremittingly among the sick, escaping illness themselves, though Rose Standish died. Brewster not only spent hours in the community house among the close-packed beds: he worked on the land and acted as minister, preaching twice every Sunday to the comfort and edification of his hearers. Bradford said that he did more in that first year than many a man with a good income (the more money a man had the better life he was supposed to lead) accomplished in a lifetime of service.

Apprehensive of Indians as they were, the settlers did not want anyone to realize how weak and reduced in number they were. They took every precaution, burying the dead by night and making the graves flat so that nothing revealed their dwindling company. The ground chosen was named Coles Hill.

Indians were seen from time to time, always at a distance: Captain Jones spotted two on Clarke's Island; one man, out after duck and concealed in the reeds, saw a file of them moving toward Plymouth. He wriggled clear, dodged back, and gave the alarm to others working at the edge of the woods. These dropped their tools and rushed back to fetch their guns; when they came back the Indians had gone, and the tools as well. Other tools vanished while their owners were having their midday meal. After that a stricter watch was kept, and the guns set ready all the time, which was something of a job as the rain and cold had put the weapons "out of temper."

Food consisted mainly of corn bread, wildfowl, and shellfish. One sailor picked up a live herring on the beach, and gave it to Jones for his supper, but the party did not have suitable hooks to catch small fish. On January 8 Jones, with several crew members, took a cod and three seals. On the same day young Francis Billington climbed a tree and saw in the distance what he thought was "a great sea"—it proved to be a lake and is still called Billington's Sea. On February 9 Jones shot five wild geese and then found a dead deer, killed by an arrow, partly consumed by wolves. It was on Friday, February 16, that the file of a dozen Indians stole the tools, and on Saturday the company met to elect Standish as their commander for defense.

Those who fell sick on board the *Mayflower* were brought ashore, in order, according to Bradford, that those remaining could have more beer. The sick were given water. Bradford himself asked for a small mug of beer, and received the curt reply: "If you were my own father you shouldn't have any"—it is not clear who said that. Perhaps it was Jones: for Bradford went on to note that as so many of the ship's company had died, including the boatswain, the gunner, three of the four quartermasters, and the cook, "the Master was something strucken and sent to the sick ashore and told the Governor he should send for beer for them that had need of it, though he drunk water homeward bound."

Some of those suffering in their illness began to turn against their friends and even their families. One lay cursing his wife, saying that if it had not been for her he would never have set out on this unlucky voyage, and complaining about his ungrateful friends: he had done all sorts of things for them, including spending money on them, and now they were tired of him and unwilling to help him in his need. One man told a comrade that he would leave him all his belongings if only he would help him now; the comrade fetched a little spice and made "a mess of meat once or twice" for the sick man, but when the patient did not obligingly die soon the comrade told the others that he was a cheat and a rogue and he would see him choked before he made any more food for him: "yet the poor fellow died before morning." The boatswain, until he too was struck down, cursed and scoffed freely at the passengers: he was a conceited young man. But he experienced a change of heart when the very people to whom he had been so disagreeable tended him faithfully when he lay sick: "Oh, you, I now see, show your love like Christians indeed one to another, but we let one another lie and die like dogs," he said to them. According to Bradford it was the crew members who were more callous: boon companions in drinking and jollity deserted one another when the illness caught them, the healthy ones stating openly that they were not going to risk their lives and court infection by coming to help in the close cabins: those mortally ill could be left to die. The Pilgrims still living on board toiled ceaselessly among the sick, however, which made a few of the hardhearted crew think again.

The worst was over (though of course no one realized it yet) when an extraordinary event took place. Almost at the moment when Standish was elected and had decided to have the big guns mounted on the hill, an Indian approached. Not skulking, like the others, not staying at a distance, but boldly walking up to the settlement. He spoke to them in English.

· 10 ·

It was broken English, but they could understand it. His first word—a most incongruous one in that spot and under those conditions—was "Welcome." He said his name was Samoset and that he was a stranger in that region himself. He came from Maine—Pemaquid Point actually—where he had met Englishmen from the fishing vessels. He could name some of them; they had taught him to speak English. He was, in fact, an Algonquin sagamore, and he had seen the English ships fishing off Monhegan Island. It was, he said, a day's sail if the wind was right, and five days overland, from Plymouth. He asked for a drink of beer.

The Pilgrims did better than that. They gave him gin with a biscuit, butter and cheese, pudding, and a piece of mallard: all of which he liked very much, recognizing each as English victuals.

The Pilgrims were embarrassed by Samoset's appearance. A tall upright man, with black hair short in front and long at the back, clean-shaven, carrying a bow and two arrows one of which was unheaded, he wore nothing but "a leather about his waist with a fringe about a span long or a little more," and the wind was beginning to rise a little. So they put one of the red-laced horseman's coats on him, and felt better. They found him "free in speech, so far as he could express his mind, and of seemly carriage."

Samoset gave them plenty of information. The local tribe was friendly. The immediate surroundings, the small area of Patuxet, the Indian name for Plymouth, was shunned by them ever since, four years ago, a great plague had carried off all the inhabitants. The Indians who had stolen the tools and fired the arrows were of the Nauset tribe, about a hundred strong, who eight months earlier had killed three Englishmen and only just failed to slaughter two more, who had managed to get away to Monhegan. These English had belonged to Sir Ferdinando Gorges' expedition. Samoset referred to the Pilgrims' November brush with the Nausets as a "huggerie" and told them that a certain Captain Thomas Hunt had started trading with the Indians. Hunt deceived them into thinking he meant no harm, captured twenty Patuxets and seven Nausets, took them to Spain and sold them as slaves for a clear profit of twenty pounds a head. Samoset told the Pilgrims much about the surrounding country, who lived there, how many, how powerful, what the chiefs' names were. The great local chief, or sachem, was Massasoit; one day they could meet him, and another Indian too, named Squanto, who spoke better English than Samoset did.

Samoset clearly assumed that he was going to stay the night. The conversation had lasted all afternoon, and the Pilgrims grew slightly apprehensive when their guest showed no signs of departure. Perhaps, they thought, it would be safest to let him sleep on board the *Mayflower*. Samoset did not mind in the least, and stepped on board the shallop, but the tide was out and the wind high, which meant that if the shallop rowed out to *Mayflower* she could not get back. Accordingly they lodged Samoset in Stephen Hopkins' house, and in the morning they gave him a knife, a ring, and a bracelet. In return he promised to do his best to start up fur trading for the settlers, and to see that they got their tools back. He did both, bringing five Indians carrying deer and beaver skins and the missing tools. It was unfortunately Sunday, and of course no Pilgrim could trade on that day. The Indians were asked to come again later, and went away, except for Samoset, who stayed till the Wednesday, enjoying the English food and companionship. No Indians, with or without furs, had appeared by then, so Samoset went off to look for them.

The Pilgrims had already begun to see to their defenses. On Wednesday, February 21, Jones, with a work party from his crew, came ashore with one of the heavy minions and helped the stronger settlers to drag it by main force up the hill. Then they brought up the other minion, which was already on the beach, one of the sakers, and two of the smaller cannon. All five guns were mounted and set ready, facing the likeliest directions of possible approach.

The house building had been going on all this while, with its accompanying ground clearing, and planting had begun. Winslow noted that on Wednesday, March 7, a fine day but cold with a chilling east wind, the Pilgrims sowed seed, mainly peas and beans. The sowing went on all the more cheerfully because the previous Saturday had revealed the first signs of spring. The wind blew from the south, the day opened misty, and the sun came out and felt faintly warm. By noon the woods rang with birdsong. Winslow recorded:

> At one of the clock it thundered which was the first we heard in that country. It was of strong and great claps but short. But after an hour it rained very sadly till midnight.

When Samoset left to seek out his companions, the settlers brought the last of their stores ashore and stowed them in the repaired community house. The women and children who had been sleeping on board the *Mayflower* came ashore too. Standish started drilling those men who in his opinion would be the most use from a military standpoint.

When Samoset returned, which he did very soon, he did not come alone. With him appeared, on the little hill fronting the fort, a company of sixty impressive-looking Indians escorting the chief, Massasoit himself, and his brother Quadequina. After a short consultation among the Pilgrim leaders, Edward Winslow advanced to greet him, the first ambassador's function of many in his life. Winslow presented Massasoit with a pair of knives, a ring, biscuits and butter, and "a pot of strong water," and gave Quadequina a knife and "a jewel to hang in his ear." Massasoit wanted to trade at once for Winslow's armor and sword, to which he had taken an enormous fancy, but Winslow diplomatically diverted the chief's attention with a long, imposing speech, in which he said on no grounds whatever that King James of England was anxious to make an alliance with this powerful sachem. Exactly how this was interpreted to Massasoit is hard to determine, but in the friendliest way he arranged to go with twenty of his warriors to speak to Governor Carver, prudently leaving Winslow as a kind of hostage on the hill with the rest of the escort.

All the Indians were tall, and reminded the English of Gypsies, with their faces boldly painted, some in black, some in red, some in yellow and white, decorated with crosses "and other Antick works." The chief's own face was painted a subdued shade of mulberry, well suited to his grave and dignified manner and sparing speech. A deerskin was fastened over one shoulder, and a long chain of white bone beads lay around his neck; from it a knife hung down in front, and a small leather tobacco pouch at the back.

The Pilgrims received Massasoit with bows and smiles, and conducted him to one of the partly finished houses, where they spread out a green rug and three or four cushions for him to sit on. With a pleasing touch of ceremony the drum and the trumpet heralded the governor's arrival, and a few of Standish's musketeers, headed by Williamson, escorted Carver into the chief's presence. Both men bowed courteously, Carver kissed the chief's hand, and Massasoit embraced Carver rather in the manner of a French general or Russian leader greeting a gallant officer. They sat down, the governor called for strong water, and drank Massasoit's health; replying, the chief took a draft big enough to make his eyes water, which made him sweat profusely.

The real fruit of this meeting was a treaty drawn up on the spot. It was of cardinal importance because it ensured the Pilgrims' survival; Massasoit, followed in time by his sons, kept it for over fifty years, in spite of occasional rocky episodes. The six main points were: that no Indian should harm a settler, that if any did so the offender should be sent to the Plantation to be punished, that anything stolen from either side should be sent back or replaced, that each would help the other if attacked, that Massasoit would let his neighboring tribes know about the treaty, and that any of his braves visiting the Plantation should approach unarmed.

The principal interpreter through all this was the famous Squanto, whose life story was fantastic enough for any tale of wild adventure.

One Captain George Weymouth, exploring the coast of Maine in 1605 on behalf of the Adventurers, had taken Squanto back to England with him; that was how he had come to learn English. In 1614 he had returned across the Atlantic as interpreter to Captain John Smith. One of Smith's ships was commanded by John Hunt (not to be confused with Captain Thomas Hunt), who persuaded Squanto and nineteen other Indians to come aboard; he promptly hijacked them and took them to Spain, where he sold them in the Málaga slave market for twenty pounds each. Some of them went as slaves to North Africa, and were presumably never heard of again; others, including Squanto, entered religious houses as servants, where they were probably treated better. The valiant Squanto somehow got away, and reached London, where he lodged for a time in Cornhill with a merchant called John Slaney. Slaney lent him to Captain John Mason as guide-interpreter for a voyage to

Newfoundland; in 1619 Mason lent him to Captain John Dermer, who was setting out to explore the New England coast. Dermer dropped Squanto at Patuxet, or perhaps Squanto jumped ship there: it was the place his people came from. He found nothing left of them but bones: the Indians of Patuxet had all died of the plague two years before. Dermer died of arrow wounds on Martha's Vineyard early in 1620; Squanto, roaming upcountry looking for friendly shelter, threw in his lot with Massasoit.

After all his experiences it seems astonishing that Squanto was willing to go anywhere near a paleface ever again, but he proved to be worth his weight in gold to the Plantation. He told the Pilgrims where to find the best fish and how to catch them; where to plant corn and how to fertilize it; he guided and piloted many of their first expeditions, and, in fact, stayed with them for the rest of his life. Massasoit's statue stands in Plymouth today, but perhaps it ought properly to be Squanto's, for the debt owed to him by the United States is incalculable.

· 11 ·

Now it was clear that the worst was over. The sick were on the mend; the Indians were met and pacified; the settlement was taking shape. The weather had turned and spring was showing in green buds and scattered flowers. The count of survivors showed distressing gaps: the three Tinkers, the three Turners, both the Rigdales, and all the Tilleys except Elizabeth, aged thirteen, were dead; so was Mary Norris Allerton after giving birth to a stillborn child. Richard Britteridge, Richard Clarke, John Crackston the elder, Sarah Eaton, Moses Fletcher, Ann and Edward Fuller, John Goodman, William Holbeck, John Hooke, Edward Margerson, Digerie Priest, Thomas Rogers, Elias Story, Rose Standish, Edward Thomson, William White, Thomas Williams, and Elizabeth Barker Winslow were all dead, reducing the original Leyden members to thirty. Of the rest, Robert Carter, James and Susanna

Chilton, John Langemore, Christopher and Marie Prower Martin, three of the four More children, three of the Mullins family, leaving only young Priscilla, and Solomon Prower were dead too. So was the mid-Atlantic baby, Oceanus Hopkins. This left twenty-four. Fifty-four persons, twenty-one of them under sixteen, were left to start the process that created the United States of America.

· 12 ·

They were morally equipped to do it. It is true that several of the little company returned to England later, or went away elsewhere, but not one of them left on the *Mayflower,* and as far as the historian can tell, no one asked to go. Those first dreadful months, packed with terror, disease, death, discomfort, and privation, had not daunted them. They had come and they intended to remain. Commander Villiers thought that they had the hearts of lions, and indeed it does seem so. "Friend, if ever we make a plantation, God works a miracle." It looked remarkably as though he had.

PART THREE

Establishment

On Thursday, April 5, 1621, the *Mayflower* sailed for home. She carried no passengers, and was manned by a crew at only half strength. She carried no cargo, either, for the Pilgrims had not yet cut timber enough for themselves, had not got their fishing going, and had not collected enough furs to make a bale worth taking. The ship made a good, fast run, arriving in the Thames estuary on Saturday, May 5, and docking in the Pool of London the day after, a voyage of thirty-one days.

When the *Mayflower* dipped below the horizon on that April Thursday the Plymouth Plantation had to stand for better or worse on its own feet. Their nearest European neighbors were five hundred miles away in either direction, the French in Nova Scotia and the English in Virginia. Now there was no question about it, they had to survive and make good.

Corn planting, directed by Squanto, who showed them the best method, went on briskly. The settlers sowed some English wheat and peas, which did not grow, but the lifesaving maize did. By mid-April, Squanto said, there would be fish in the Town Brook, and he was right. House building went steadily on. The place was beginning to look like a settlement. Friendly Indians drifted in all the time, and were rather a nuisance, but the planters put up with them because it helped to keep the peace. When the herring swarmed up the brook they were caught in the fish traps Squanto supervised, sometimes as many as ten thousand fish being taken in one tide. These were used to fertilize the young corn. When the leaves of the white oak were as large as a mouse's ear, said Squanto, corn must be planted in little mounds three or four feet apart, three herring to a mound, set heads to middle around a few seeds, which would eventually be thinned to the strongest plant. More than ninety-six thousand mounds requiring forty tons of herring were prepared on twenty acres of ground cleared and dug over.

Herring, of course, were not the only seafood available. There were eels, oysters and clams, lobster and cod, and the striped bass of which William Wood wrote: "Though men are often wearied with other fish yet they are never with bass." Yet it was only slowly that the planters grew accustomed to fresh fish rather than salt, or expanded their preferred staple diet of bread, cheese, dried peas and beans, oatmeal, and salt beef or pork to include the native delicacies of New England: duck, turkey, partridge, deer, and the proliferating berries at first unfamiliar. One criticism leveled justly at the English for centuries has been their unwillingness to try new foodstuffs, and in this respect the Pilgrims were typical, going hungry out of what seems sheer cussedness and almost preferring to starve in the midst of plenty rather than to experiment with the strange but kindly fruits of the earth.

One day soon after the departure of the *Mayflower,* Governor Carver came in from the fields complaining of a headache. He lay down upon his bed and appeared to fall asleep, but within a few hours it was found that he had sunk into a coma. He never woke again: within a day or two he was dead. He was the same age as Brewster: fifty-four. The sorrowful Pilgrims buried him "in the best manner they could, with some volleys of shot by all that bore arms." Carver's widow, Catherine White Leggatt Carver, outlived him by less than six weeks. Bradford described her as only a weak woman, but whether he meant that her health was delicate, or that she had died of a broken heart, as the more romantically disposed historians suggest, is not certain.

Bradford, then thirty-one, was elected governor to fill Carver's place, with Isaac Allerton, thirty-four, as his assistant. With Standish, thirty-six, as military commander, Edward Winslow, twenty-five, as Indian ambassador, and Stephen Hopkins, thirty-five, as foremost among assistants in general activities, the temporal leadership rested in vigorous younger hands. Spiritual head of the colony was William Brewster. One of the marked strokes of luck that operated for the Pilgrims was the quality of their leaders: of these six men only one proved to be an unfortunate choice, a very good proportion indeed for a newborn colonial settlement.

On May 12 there occurred the first wedding in the Plantation. Winslow, who had been a widower for six weeks, married Susanna White, widowed during the winter. It was a civil marriage in accordance with "the laudable custom of the Low Countries" and Bradford was the officiating magistrate. No one commented on the haste of the wedding; such quick remarriages were quite normal.

By that time, although many difficulties remained, survival was virtually certain. There had been mistakes: Captain John Smith, with the natural dryness of the experienced man whose proffered advice had been rejected, thought they could have managed better:

> At the first landing at Cape Cod, being a hundred passengers besides twenty they had left behind at Plymouth, for want of good take-heed, thinking to find all things better than I advised them, spent six or seven weeks in wandering up and down in frost and snow, wind and rain, among the woods, creeks, and swamps. Forty of them died and threescore were left in most miserable estate at New Plymouth where their ship left them, and but nine leagues by sea from where they landed.

· 2 ·

The visiting Indians were eating up the Plantation stores at an alarming rate, and the Pilgrims thought they had better send a deputation to Massasoit politely requesting him to do what he could to curtail this dropping in and out. They chose Winslow and Hopkins to go, with Squanto as guide, to Massasoit's headquarters, about forty miles away. Everywhere along the route the Englishmen were welcomed and admired, and in one small Indian camp they performed a valuable service by shooting some crows that were eating the crops. The smoke, noise, and fairly accurate marksmanship of the muskets deeply impressed the Indians, though none seemed anxious to handle the guns for themselves.

The whole territory was littered with skulls and bones, relics of the great plague three years before, when so many Indians had died that their comrades were unable to bury them, and abandoned fields that had once borne maize lay on all sides. The three travelers fed well at each stopping place on fish and roast crab, but when they reached Massasoit they found him short of supplies. He made them welcome, however, with long cordial speeches in which he declared himself King James's man and promised that his people would pester the colonists no longer. Winslow gave him one of the laced red coats, which delighted the chief, and a copper chain. This, Winslow explained, was for any messenger of Massasoit's to wear, and would be accepted as the chief's own warrant by any settler. Winslow also said that he was empowered to pay for the corn the Pilgrims had taken in the first days if Massasoit could trace the Indians to whom it had belonged.

Massasoit provided his visitors with a bed made of planks raised about twelve inches off the floor and covered with a thin mat, but two of his personal aides shared it with them, squashing them up most uncomfortably. There were fleas and lice, too, and clouds of mosquitoes, and the Indians had the disturbing habit of singing themselves to sleep, so the night's rest that Winslow and Hopkins experienced was a good deal more tiring than the forty miles had been that they had walked to reach it.

Next day they demonstrated their muskets again, and sat down to eat at one o'clock. The meal was scriptural: two fish, like bream but tastier, and three times the size, shared among forty people. It was hardly surprising that after the scanty food and restless slumbers when the three set out to walk back they felt doubtful whether they could manage the distance. Morsels of fish and mouthfuls of water sustained them on the journey home, but they found an Indian along the way and sent him ahead to ask for a meal to be made ready so that they could fall to the minute they arrived. They staggered into Plymouth weary, wet, and footsore, but thankful to be safely back with their mission accomplished.

Within a day or two of their return young John Billington went off into the woods to have a look around. When he did not reappear, a search party took the shallop and went off to find him. A messenger from Massasoit signaled the shallop to say that the boy was not far from Corn Hill near Cape Cod; he had apparently been found and passed on from one tiny Indian outpost to another. The shallop put in at Cummaquid, near the wrist of the Cape, where they were warmly welcomed by the local sachem, Iyanough. A gentle-mannered, personable young man still in his twenties, "indeed, not like a savage save for his attire," Iyanough invited the shallop party ashore to eat with him and his men. He had news of the missing boy, and, sure enough, after sunset a stately Nauset sachem named Aspinet arrived, with a great train of warriors, "and brought the boy with him, one bearing him through the water. There he delivered us the boy, behung with beads, and made peace with us, we bestowing a knife on him and likewise on another that first entertained the boy and brought him thither."

The shallop party went away, but shortly afterward came back to repay the Indians for the corn as they had promised. Iyanough was as friendly as ever, helping his men to carry water to the boat, while the squaws joined hands and danced and sang. The Indians showed the party every kindness, and Iyanough himself took "a bracelet" from about his own neck and hung it upon one of the Englishmen. "His entertainment," reported Winslow, "was answerable to his parts, and his cheer plentiful and various."

Soon after that another Indian came to live in the colony. This was one Hobamock, or Hobomok (the spelling varies), a member of Massasoit's council of braves, who traveled up from the chief's camp at what is today Barrington, Rhode Island, to Plymouth. He was a fine, strong fellow, well thought of by other Indians, for he held the rank of *pinese:* bravest and strongest in the tribe with an arduous and lengthy training in his youth. Supposedly great in both courage and wisdom, discreet, courteous, and humane, he could reputedly endure hardship above the common, and lived under the special protection of the gods. He could, they said, not be wounded in battle. For that reason such a warrior would readily chase almost a hundred others, secure in the knowledge that they thought it fatal to stand in his way.

In time Hobamock became Standish's man as Squanto was Bradford's. The two were rather jealous of each other, and the Pilgrims did not try to discourage this, feeling that it would keep the pair of them on their toes. Very early after Hobamock's arrival the two got involved in a fracas which might have had dangerous consequences. They had been on an expedition to promote trade between planters and tribes and were on their way back when, at the Indian settlement of Namasket (today Middleborough), four-teen miles west of Plymouth, they met one Corbitant, a quarrel-some sachem who hated the English invaders, or at least had the reputation of doing so. Corbitant drew a knife and threatened to stab Hobamock, who nimbly dodged him and ran off; as he went he heard Corbitant shouting that if he could kill Squanto the English would have lost their tongue.

Not waiting to see whether or not Corbitant carried out this threat, Hobamock ran all the way back like Pheidippides of Mar-athon, burst into the settlement streaming with sweat, and told Bradford what had happened. He sounded highly dramatic, but Bradford's reaction was cool and practical. He consulted his chief helpers and they decided something must be done: if their mes-sengers could not travel in safety the whole enterprise was in danger. No Indians would take their part, fetch and carry news, interpret for them, or assist them, and the Indians in a body might turn against the colony and wipe it out.

Accordingly Standish was asked to pick a squad of fourteen armed men and go to Namasket to find out what had actually taken place. If on arrival they found Squanto was dead, they were to seize Corbitant and cut off his head, but harm no one else: justice must be seen to be done. Hobamock would guide them to the place during the night. This was done, and the attacking party surrounded Corbitant's house. They fired their muskets into the air, which had the desired effect of cowing the village into quivering silence, and Standish went into the house to look for Corbitant. He was not there. Several Indians made a dash for the woods, three were wounded by musket shots from Standish's men, and Squanto appeared, unharmed, bringing with him some trembling braves who offered the best provisions they had. Standish accepted this peace offering, Hobamock explained why they were there, and the search for Corbitant was called off. The party went back to Plymouth, taking Squanto and the three wounded men with them. At the Plantation the wounds were dressed and the three Indians went back to Namasket as soon as they were well enough to travel.

This all happened in mid-August, and during the following month various sachems congratulated the planters on their firm handling of the affair, a number of them sent envoys to offer friendship (some from as far away as Capawack, or Martha's Vineyard), and were somewhat quaintly proclaimed loyal subjects of James I. Corbitant himself offered peace through the mediation of Massasoit, but understandably was, as Bradford put it, "shy to come near them a long while after."

On September 18 Squanto went as guide-interpreter with a party ten strong in the shallop to explore Massachusetts Bay. On the way they named several places, which still bear their names today. One headland, in a graceful compliment to the Indian, was called Squantum, the islands at the bay entrance were called the Brewsters, and the long sandy spit to the South Point was named Point Allerton. In the bay they landed at what within nine years would be Boston Harbor. The local chief told them that the raiding Tarentine Indians were a source of great trouble: they were the Norsemen of New England, who preferred to steal their neighbors' corn instead of growing their own. The Pilgrims persuaded the chief to make the same kind of alliance with them for mutual protection as the others had done. The squaws, they noticed, all wore magnificent beaver wraps; Squanto wanted these removed at musket point, but the Pilgrims wanted to establish peaceful trade, not a reign of terror. They offered to make a deal, and proffered trinkets; the women at once stripped off their wraps, beneath which they wore very little, accepted the beads cheerfully in exchange, and then modestly tied boughs around themselves, being, as Winslow noted, more easily embarrassed than some Englishwomen he could mention.

On detail of particular interest was recorded by Bradford:

> They returned in safety and brought home a good quantity of beaver, and made report of the place, wishing that they had been there seated. But it seems the Lord, who assigns to all men the bounds of their habitations, had appointed it for another use.

Boston's subsequent size, prominence, and prosperity shows how right they were, but the grass is always greener on the other side of the fence and there could have been no Boston as we know it without Plymouth.

Now it was autumn, and the Pilgrims had almost completed their first year. Shaky and uncertain as the colony had often been, frighteningly reduced in numbers, yet it had survived, and there was even a small harvest to gather in before the winter. They did not lack provisions. Fish and fowl in plenty, including wild turkeys, venison, a peck of meal and a peck of corn a week for each person, fruit for stewing and making wine, victualed the people, restored to health through the warm summer days and with eleven good houses now completed. Truly they had much to be thankful for. It seemed to them appropriate to express this gratitude in some way, and a special celebration was arranged.

> The harvest being gotten in, our Governor sent four men on fowling, that so we might after a more special manner rejoice together, after we had gathered the fruit of our labours. They four in one day killed as much fowl as, with a little help beside, served the Company almost a week. At which time, amongst other recreations, we exercised our arms, many of the Indians

coming amongst us, and amongst the rest their greatest king, Massasoit, with some ninety men, whom for three days we entertained and feasted. And they went out and killed five deer which they brought to the planatation and bestowed on our Governor and upon the Captain and others.

In addition to the military review, the Pilgrims played games of chance and skill, and the Indians danced for them. They all enjoyed roast duck and goose, eels, clams and other shellfish, leeks, watercress "and other salad herbs," wild plums, dried berries, white bread and corn bread, white and red wine. They certainly ate roast turkey, but not, that first time, cranberry sauce. It is not clear precisely when the Thanksgiving took place. It was at some date between the beginning of October and the first week of November. The fixing of the last Thursday in November for it had to wait two hundred and forty-two years, until Abraham Lincoln settled it in 1863, close upon the day when he attended the ceremony of dedication at Gettysburg. But Thanksgiving was definitely over, and normal daily work had resumed in Plymouth, by November 10. Something exciting happened that day. A ship of fifty-five tons appeared over the empty horizon, drew nearer, and anchored in the harbor.

· 3 ·

It is not difficult to imagine with what feelings the settlers saw the *Fortune* sail in. Their first contact with England for sixty-two weeks, just over fourteen months! And some new recruits to the colony were on board, too, new vigorous hands to help those who had battled it out alone for so long. Among the thirty-five passengers were some who did not stay: William Beale, William Corner, a sailor aged twenty-four called Benedict Morgan, Augustine (or Austin) Nicolas, William Pitt, an armorer from the London district of St. Peter ad Vincula, and James Steward. But others came to settle and settle they did: John Adams, a carpenter aged twenty-five or -six or maybe thirty-one (three dates of birth are variously attributed to him), with his wife Ellen; William Bassett, just twenty-one, gunsmith and metalworker; Clement Briggs and Robert Hicks, fellmongers in their late twenties from Southwark; Stephen Deane, miller, who had six years to wait before marrying Elizabeth Ring from Leyden; Philip de la Noye from Leyden, aged sixteen; Thomas and Elizabeth Hayward Flavel and their daughter Susan; Thomas Morton, aged thirty-two; Moses Simonson of Leyden; William Tench; John Cannon; William Wright, aged thirty-three. There was the Palmer family, headed by forty-one-year-old William Palmer, a nailer, his wife Frances, his son William, and two daughters, Anne and Rebecca. William Ford, a leather dresser of Southwark, had set out, but died on the voyage. Mrs. Martha Ford and six-year-old William came ashore, and "the goodwife Ford was delivered of a son the first night she landed, and both of them are very well," noted Winslow. Two years later Martha Ford married Peter Browne of the *Mayflower*.

Two brothers had arrived, William and Edward Hilton. Edward, a freeman of the London Fishmongers' Guild, had left behind him a wife and two small children, William, aged four, and Mary, aged two. There was a yeoman called Hugh Stacey and a young man named Edward Bumpus. But there were four others whom the planters were particularly delighted to see.

One was Jonathan Brewster, now twenty-eight and recently a widower, the eldest son of William Brewster. One was Thomas Prence, future governor, then just turned twenty-one, son of a carriage builder. And there was Robert Cushman himself, with his son Thomas, then a lad of fourteen.

Captain Thomas Barton of the *Fortune* reported that on first sighting Cape Cod, deserted and barren in the autumn chill, his passengers had voiced doubts and fears, wondering what would become of them if the *Mayflower* party had died of hunger or in an Indian massacre. There was no way of knowing just where they were, what condition they were in, what had happened to them. The *Fortune* was in a bad way, too, with just enough food on board to reach Virginia, barring accidents:

> There was not so much as biscuit bread, or any other victuals for them, neither had they any bedding, nor pot nor pan to dress any meat in, nor over many clothes, for many of them had brushed away [sold to get extra money in a hurry] their coats and cloaks at Plymouth as they came.

There were "some Birching Lane suits" on board (this seems to mean a kind of cheap ready-made garment from the street of that name in London) and these were hastily unpacked and distributed among the needy passengers. The *Fortune* had set out in July, making a voyage that had lasted even longer than that of the *Mayflower,* and carried no supplementary stores for the Plantation. What she did carry was a bad-tempered letter from Weston, dated from London on July 6, addressed to the late Governor John Carver, complaining about the original delays in getting the *Mayflower* off, and then sending her back to England without a cargo. How were the Adventurers to recover their investment at that rate? Weston pointed out that he had never dared to tell them about the disputes over conditions laid down in the charter, and was glad he had not done so, because if he had they would not have advanced a halfpenny. He had to keep putting the Adventurers off with promising speeches. Would the Pilgrims be good enough to copy out the terms of the agreement if they meant in good faith to carry them out, sign them, send full accounts of their expenses and a cargo of tradable goods as well to keep their creditors quiet, and address any other questions to Cushman? He wrote sharply:

> That you sent no lading in the ship is wonderful, and worthily distasted. I know your weakness was the cause of it, and I believe more weakness of judgment than weakness of hands. A quarter of the time you spent in discoursing, arguing and consulting would have done much more; but that is past. . . .

Before signing himself their very loving friend, he added the words: "I pray write instantly for Mr Robinson to come to you."

The charter brought over by Cushman was the so-called Peirce Patent of June 1. It allocated a hundred acres of land to each colonist in "any uninhabited place" with freedom to fish and trade, and 1500 acres in addition for each Adventurer. It started that after a proper survey made within seven years the charter would be replaced by a fresh one setting out precise boundaries and governing rights, but in the meantime all laws made by the undertakers, planters, and their associates would be considered legal. The charter thus confirmed the *Mayflower* Compact.

Bradford wrote a quietly dignified reply to Weston, opening with the news of Carver's death. Of Carver he wrote:

> He needs not my apology; for his care and pains was so great for the common good, both ours and yours, as that therewith (it is thought) he oppressed himself and shortened his days; of whose loss we cannot sufficiently complain.

He acknowledged Weston's expenses, and went on to comment on what those first months had really been like:

> She lay five weeks at Cape Cod whilst with many a weary step (after a long journey) and the endurance of many a hard brunt, we sought out in the foul winter a place of habitation. Then we went in so tedious a time to make provision to shelter us and our goods; about which labour, many of our arms and legs can tell us to this day, we were not negligent. But it pleased God to visit us then with death daily, and with so general a disease that the living were scarce able to bury the dead, and the well not in any measure sufficient to tend the sick. And now to be so greatly blamed for not freighting the ship doth indeed go near us and much discourage us.

He somewhat ambiguously added that the Pilgrims were prepared to put up with this rebuke patiently "till God send us wiser men." One criticism did escape him:

They which told you we spent so much time in discoursing and consulting, etc., their hearts can tell their tongues they lie. They cared not, so they might salve their own sores, how they wounded others. Indeed, it is our calamity that we are, beyond expectation, yoked with some ill-conditioned people who will never do good, but corrupt and abuse others.

The *Fortune* did not stay very long: two weeks according to Bradford, a month according to Captain John Smith, who gave the sailing date as December 13. The passengers were suitably distributed among the *Mayflower* households for the time being. Cushman had come to bring his son and see for himself how they were all getting on, never intending to stay. He was returning on the *Fortune,* leaving his young son in the colony. On December 12 he preached a sermon. The text of it was later published in London under a resounding title:

A Sermon preached at Plymouth in New England in an Assembly of His Majesties faithful Subjects there inhabiting, together with a Preface Showing the state of the Country and Condition of the Savages.

Cushman took his text from First Corinthians: "Let no man seek his own but every man another's wealth." To hear him speak on the dangers of selfishness the Pilgrims packed the community house and listened enthralled as he exclaimed:

Why wouldst thou have thy particular portion? Because thou thinkest to live better than thy neighbour and scornest to live as meanly as he? But who, I pray, brought this particularising into the world? Did not Satan, who was not content to keep that equal state with his fellows, but would set his throne above the stars? Nothing in the world doth more resemble heavenly happiness than for men to live as one, being of one heart and one soul; nor does anything more resemble hellish horror than for every man to shift for himself, for if it be a good word and practice thus to affect particulars, *mine* and *thine,* then it should be best also for God to provide one heaven for thee and another for thy neighbour.

The published version was addressed to his loving friends the Adventurers for New England, "together with all well-willers and well-wishers thereunto." Its second edition was published in Boston in 1724, and its third in Plymouth in 1785.

The *Fortune* was loaded with a cargo estimated to be worth nearly five hundred pounds: "good clapboard as full as she could stow" and two hogsheads of beaver and otter skins. What the Pilgrims meant by clapboard, apparently, was oak staves. As the ship sailed away, the governor and Allerton began to take an inventory of all their stores, in order to calculate how they might best be shared out among the newly swollen total of residents. It seemed prudent to put the whole Plantation on half allowance, which ought to last them for six months, well past the second winter, and this was done.

The *Fortune* did not live up to her name. She reached the Channel safely, but was stopped and boarded by a French pirate ship, which escorted her to the French coast. There the cargo was removed, along with everything of value that the pirates could lay their hands on, including most of the passengers' clothes. Left with only what they stood up in, they were set free to go on to London.

The pirates were not interested in Cushman's papers. He was able to keep the signed charter, and the letter to Weston, and, most important of all though it did not seem so at the time, a bundle of manuscript written by Bradford and Winslow describing their experiences in the Plantation up to then. He took it to a London printer, who published it in 1622 under the title *A Relation or Journal of the Beginnings and Proceedings of the English Plantation settled at Plymouth, New England.* The authors' names did not appear on the title page, but that of G. Mourt did. Who G. Mourt was—the printer, or George Morton, who crossed to Plymouth later, or someone else—has never been known. But the name's existence

explains why this great document has been referred to ever since by
the slightly puzzling title of *Mourt's Relation.*

One basic document in *Mourt's Relation* is a letter written by
Winslow, dated December 11, 1621, and obviously designed to
encourage people to come to New England. It contains the only
account ever found of the first Thanksgiving, and goes on to
present a quite idyllic picture of the settlement:

> We have found the Indians very faithful in their covenant of
> peace with us, very loving and ready to pleasure us. We often go
> to them, and they come to us; some of us have been fifty miles by
> land in the country with them, the occasions and relations where-
> of you shall understand by our general and more full declaration
> of such things as are worth the noting. Yea, it hath pleased God
> so to possess the Indians with a fear of us, and love unto us, that
> not only the greatest king amongst them, called Massasoit, but
> also all the princes and peoples round about us, have either made
> suit unto us or been glad of any occasion to make peace with us,
> so that seven of them at once have sent their messengers to us to
> that end. Yea, an isle at sea, which we never saw, hath also,
> together with the former, yielded willingly to be under the
> protection and subjects to our Sovereign Lord King James, so
> that there is now great peace among the Indians themselves,
> which was not formerly, neither would have been but for us. And
> we for our parts walk as peaceably and safely in the wood as in the
> highways in England. We entertain them familiarly in our
> houses, and they as friendly bestowing their venison on us. They
> are a people without any religion or knowledge of any God, yet
> very trusty, quick of apprehension, ripe-witted, just. The men
> and women go naked, only a skin about their middles.
>
> For the temper of the air, here it agreeth well with that in
> England, and if there be any difference at all, this is somewhat
> hotter in summer. Some think it to be colder in winter, but I
> cannot out of experience so say; the air is very clear and not
> foggy, as hath been reported. I never in my life remember a more

seasonable year than we have here enjoyed, and if we have once but kine, horses, and sheep, I make no question but men might live as contented here as in any part of the world. For fish and fowl, we have great abundance; fresh cod in the summer is but coarse meat with us; our bay is full of lobsters all the summer and affordeth variety of other fish; in September we can take a hogshead of eels in a night, with small labour, and can dig them out of their beds all the winter. We have mussels and others at our doors. Oysters we have none near, but we can have them brought by the Indians when we will. All the springtime the earth sendeth forth naturally very good sallet herbs. Here are grapes, white and red, and very sweet and strong also; straw-berries, gooseberries, raspas, etc.; plums of three sorts, with black and red being almost as good as a damson; abundance of roses, white, red, and damask, single, but very sweet indeed. The country wanteth only industrious men to employ, for it would grieve your hearts if, as I, you had seen so many miles together by goodly rivers uninhabited, and withal to consider those parts of the world wherein you live to be even greatly burdened with abundance of people.

Having pictured the Earthly Paradise, Winslow went on to tell prospective planters what sensible precautions they should take and what supplies to bring.

Be careful to have a very good bread-room to put your biscuits in. Let your cask for beer and water be iron-bound for the first tire if not more; let not your meat be dry-salted—none can better do it than the sailors. Let your meal be so hard trod in your cask that you shall need an adze or hatchet to work it out with. Trust not too much on us for corn at this time, for by reason of this last company that came, depending wholly upon us, we shall have little enough till harvest; be careful to come by some of your meal to spend by the way—it will much refresh you. Build your cabins as open as you can, and bring good store of clothes and bedding with you. Bring every man a musket or fowling-piece; let your piece be long in the barrel, and fear not the weight of it, for most of our shooting is from stands. Bring juice of lemons, and take it fasting; it is of good use. For hot waters, aniseed water is the best, but use it sparingly. If you bring any thing for comfort in the country, butter or sallet oil, or both, is very good. Our Indian corn, even the coarsest, maketh as pleasant meat as rice, therefore spare that unless to spend by the way. Bring paper and linseed oil for your windows, with cotton yarn for your lamps. Let your shot be most for big fowls, and bring store of powder and shot.

Cushman appended an essay to this, using scriptural texts and references to prove that men did not always have to live their lives out in the place where they were born. It was lawful for them to live among the heathen if they brought the true gospel to give these benighted souls. In the wilderness, "a drop of the knowledge of Christ is most precious." It was the duty of settlers to minister to the Indians and to convert them.

He, like Winslow, emphasized that there was peace and plenty in the New World, unlike the Old World, where opportunity was all too often restricted. Each man in Europe had to fight for a living in competition with his neighbor, instead of sharing with him in the overflowing bounty of a new place.

There is such pressing and oppressing in town and country about farms, trades, traffic, etc., so as a man can hardly set up a trade but he shall pull down two of his neighbours. The rent-taker lives on sweet morsels, but the rent-payer eats a dry crust, often with watery eyes; and it is nothing to say what one in a hundred hath, but what the bulk, body, and communalty hath—which, I warrant you, is short enough. Multitudes get their means by prating, and so do numbers more by begging. Neither come these straits upon men always through intemperancy, ill husbandry, indiscretion, etc., as some think; but even the most wise, sober, and discreet men go often to the wall when they have done their best. Let us not thus oppress, straiten, and afflict one another, seeing that there is a spacious land, the way to which is through the sea.

· 4 ·

Not long after the *Fortune* departed, the Narragansett Indians, the People of the Small Point, rivals of Massasoit's men and sworn enemies of immigrants, who like all the tribes of the region had heard that new settlers had come in, decided to issue a challenge to what they piously hoped was a small weak band huddled in Plymouth. In January they sent a brave to present the guard with a bundle of arrows wrapped in a snakeskin. When Squanto saw it, he explained that it was a threatening challenge, and, after consultation, Bradford sent the snakeskin back, filled with powder and shot, and a message saying that if the Indians wanted war they could start when it suited them; the colonists were neither frightened nor unprepared, and their consciences were clear as they had done the Indians no harm.

The snakeskin reached the sachem who had sent it, a Narragansett pleasantly named Canonicus, and, according to Winslow, the Pilgrims' stalwart reply scared him. "He dared not touch the snake-skin, nor would he suffer it to stay in his house or country, and at length having been posted from place to place a long time it came back to Plymouth unopened." By that time the Pilgrims had looked to their defenses. They set to work to finish the palisade enclosing the settlement. Between eight and eleven feet high, almost a mile around, from the community house along the edge of the brook, past the burial ground and around the other side, it was strong and solid, with lockable gates at three suitable points. Sentries were posted every night, and, when it seemed prudent, in the daytime as well. Standish divided the men into four squadrons, each with a commanding officer—Bradford, Allerton, Winslow, and Hopkins—and announced fixed stations to which everyone must go as soon as the alarm was sounded. Some men were told off as special fire guards, armed, and under orders to deal with any fire started by the Indians. "This," said Bradford, "was accomplished very cheerfully, and the town impaled round by the beginning of March, in which every family had a pretty garden plot secured." By this he did not mean a flower garden, but simply that each piece of dwelling land was neatly fenced off from its neighbors. The gates were at the north, south, and east ends of the two streets.

The fact that the defense works were cheerfully finished shows that the new settlers bore no malice for having their games stopped on Christmas Day. Bradford had treated it, of course, as a normal working session, but the *Fortune* arrivals demurred, saying it went against their principles. Bradford, always sympathetic in matters of conscience, told them he would not press the question, but hoped they would learn better in time, and led his own men off to work as usual. When they came back at noon, they found the newcomers playing games in the street:

> some pitching the bar, and some at stool-ball and such like sports. So he [Bradford] went to them and took away their implements and told them that was against *his* conscience, that they should play and others work. If they made the keeping of it a matter of devotion, let them keep their houses; but there should be no gaming or revelling in the streets. Since which time nothing hath been attempted that way, at least openly.

Bradford was not really angry: he saw the funny side, for he described it as an event "rather of mirth than of weight." The Pilgrims were unwilling to stay inside their palisade too much. Apart from having to find supplies of food and skins, it would look bad if they appeared willing to live on the defensive. Toward the end of March, therefore, the shallop was made ready to take a trip along the coast to find more beaver and promote trade. Before the expedition, numbering ten men, could set out, Hobamock started issuing sinister warnings. He believed that a plot was forming among the Narragansetts backed by the Massachusetts to attack the Plantation; Corbitant had allied himself with Massasoit; Squanto himself was involved, for Hobamock had seen him whispering with Indians in the woods. The shallop party set out anyway, taking both Squanto and Hobamock with them as a precaution.

They had not been gone long when an Indian of Squanto's family ran up "in seeming great fear" and reported that a big Narragansett force with Corbitant "and he thought also Massasoit" were advancing against the town. He had managed to get away to warn Bradford, but they were hard behind him. Bradford ordered the guard out to their stations, and fired off a couple of cannon to recall the shallop. It was a calm day and the boat could not be far off. The party heard the shots and came back, and the watch stood to their posts all that night, but nothing happened. Hobamock said he was sure Massasoit was loyal to the treaty, so Bradford suggested that Hobamock's wife could go to Massasoit's camp under pretext of a normal friendly visit and see what was going on.

All was peace. But the reason for the visit leaked out, and Massasoit was furious to think that anyone could doubt his honor. He sent a group of envoys to Plymouth, demanding Squanto, whose fault it was. Squanto had apparently been taking protection bribes from the Indians, telling them he could set the Pilgrims against anybody he liked, and that the Pilgrims kept the plague buried in the ground with their gunpowder barrels and could send it at will against anyone.

Bradford was now in an acute dilemma. The colony depended for its very life upon Massasoit's good will, yet Squanto was so useful in so many ways that he hated the thought of giving the Indian up. Massasoit unwittingly delayed Bradford's decision by offering a good supply of beaver in exchange for Squanto, which enabled Bradford to reply that Englishmen did not trade in men's lives. If a man deserved to die, that was one thing: accepting payment in a matter of justice was quite another. Squanto, faced by Bradford with the whole question, said he would leave the answer to the governor.

Pure coincidence worthy of a Western film saved Squanto. At the precise moment when Bradford had decided to hand over the Indian to be judged by his peers, a boat was seen off the shore. It crossed the harbor and disappeared behind a nearby headland. Rumors of possibly hostile French vessels in the vicinity, originating possibly from the Indians, had been circulating for some time, so Bradford said that this was a matter so urgent that the question of Squanto would have to wait until they had investigated. The embassy, "mad with rage and impatient at delay," went off "in great heat." Massasoit, determined come what might to stick closely to the colonists, took no further action; the Pilgrims decided that the best course would be to make "good use of the emulation that grew between Hobamock and him [Squanto], which made them carry more squarely." Bradford kept an eye on Squanto, Standish on Hobamock, "by which they had better intelligence, and made them both more diligent."

But meanwhile, what of the strange vessel? It proved to be English: the shallop from a ship called *Sparrow,* sent out to fish along the Maine coast by Weston, who was attempting in this way to recoup some of the money he said he had advanced to the Pilgrims. The *Sparrow* had been up at Damaris Cove, one of thirty to forty English ships among three to four hundred from various European countries. Seven men came to Plymouth in the shallop, intending to stay: one of them, Phineas Pratt, aged thirty-two, actually did so in time, and eight years later married Mary Priest, daughter of the dead Digerie, who arrived in the colony in 1623.

The seven men delivered a letter from Weston, brought over by Captain Rodgers of the *Sparrow,* which was, according to Bradford, "tedious and impertinent." It was dated January 12, so was over four months old by now, and was again addressed to Carver. In it Weston said he was expecting the *Fortune* any day, but in the meantime he and John Beauchamp had bought the *Sparrow* and were sending her out at once, partly to help make money, partly "to uphold the Plantation" (Bradford scribbled irritably by the word *uphold:* "I know not which way"). He had asked the other Adventurers to send men and provisions, but they would do nothing until they heard good news of the colony. "So faithful, constant and careful of your good are your old and honest friends," wrote Weston sardonically, "that if they hear not from you, they are like to send you no supply."

Weston asked the Pilgrims to look after the newcomers, to lend or sell them seed corn, to supply them with salt until a salt pan could be set up "in one of the little islands in your bay," to help prepare a cargo of timber for the *Sparrow* to take back quickly, and to make the seven welcome. "I find the general so backward" [meaning that he found most of the non-Pilgrims so reluctant to get things done], he wrote, "and your friends at Leyden so cold, that I fear you must stand on your legs and trust (as they say) to God and yourselves."

Enclosed with this was another short note, still addressed to Carver, and dated January 17, reporting a division of opinion among the Adventurers. Some wanted to back out altogether, others to put up only one third of the amount originally agreed. Another letter, signed by nine other Adventurers, said the same; Bradford, wondering what exactly this meant, did not make these letters public, but showed them cautiously to a few trustworthy friends, who concluded, with him, that it looked as though the Adventurers were splitting up, and that Weston was trying to ensure his own profit at all costs.

The seven new passengers were temporarily housed and fed with fair shares of what the Pilgrims themselves had, but it was too late in the year for them to plant corn, and there were no signs of the promised salt pan either, so Weston's requests had to go unmet.

The colony did get hold of a few supplies, however: the *Sparrow* carried a letter from Captain John Huddleston, of whom they had heard before, fishing in Maine, which opened promisingly:

> Friends, countrymen and neighbours: I salute you and wish you
> all health and happiness in the Lord.

It reported a massacre in Virginia, where 347 settlers had been killed by Indians, and warned Plymouth: "Happy is he whom other men's harms do make beware." Winslow took the shallop up to Huddleston's fishing grounds and asked whether the helpful Captain could spare any supplies. He gave them what he could, and sent Winslow with a letter of introduction to all the other English fishing captains in the area, who, between them, loaded the shallop to the gunwales. Huddleston's ship was the *Bona Nova,* two hundred tons, and the Virginia Company considered him "one of the sufficientest masters" ever to sail to the Maine coast.

While Winslow was away, work on the fort went steadily on. Its full construction took ten months, but that included the colony's meetinghouse, so it was usable for defense long before that. Built of "good timber, both strong and comely," it had a flat roof and battlements. The guns were set on the roof, and a permanent watch kept there. A few settlers saw no great need for it:

> Amongst us divers seeing the work prove tedious, would have dissuaded from proceeding, flattering themselves with peace and security, and accounting it rather a work of superfluity and vainglory than of simple necessity. The devil will cause reasonable men to reason against their own safety.

About the last day of June two more ships arrived: the hundred-ton *Charity* and the tiny thirty-ton *Swan,* which had taken two months to make the crossing. No supplies came with these ships either, but some sixty men, intended by Weston to set up a new plantation as Wessagusset (the present Weymouth), about twenty-five miles north of Plymouth. One man on board was Weston's son Andrew, then a young man in his twenties. The colony was expected to feed and house these newcomers temporarily until they were ready to start the new settlement. They were, Bradford noted, not the right sort of people at all to suit the Pilgrims: "an unruly company and had no good government over them." The *Swan* was supposed to go on to Virginia, and indeed arrived there a year later.

There were more letters from Weston, dated April 10; he reported the safe arrival of the *Fortune* after her French detour (which had taken place at the Ile de Dieu on the west coast, where the French seized goods worth £450, and had stingily fed the hijacked English for two weeks on "lights, livers and entrails"). Weston announced that he had sold out to the Adventurers, "so I am quit of you, and you of me for that matter."

Bradford's comment was heartfelt and typical.

Mr Weston, who had made that large promise . . . that if all the
rest should fall off, yet he would never quit the business but stick
to them . . . all proved but wind, for he was the first and only man
that forsook them, and that before he so much as heard of the
return of this ship, or knew what was done. . . . Thus all their
hopes in regard of Mr. Weston were laid in the dust; and all his
promised help turned into empty advice.

The advice was to do as Weston had done, and break off the
Adventurers' contract. There was a little cloak-and-dagger work
going on, too, for Weston wrote, not without relish:

I desired divers of the Adventurers, as Mr Peirce, Mr Greene
and others, if they had anything to send you, either victuals or
letters, to send them by these ships; and, marvelling that they
sent not so much as a letter, I asked our passengers what letters
they had, and with some difficulty one of them told me he had
one, which was delivered to him with great charge of secrecy, and
for more security to buy a pair of new shoes and sew it between
the soles for fear of intercepting. I, taking the letter, wondering
what mystery might be in it, broke it open and found this
treacherous letter subscribed by the hands of Mr Pickering and
Mr Greene.

The treacherous letter stated bluntly that the Adventurers
were very glad to be rid of Weston. He thought himself above the
rest, would not allow letters from anyone else to be sent in his ships,
was acting in contempt of the rest in making out expeditions on his
own account, and intended to come over himself to take all the
trading goods he could lay his hands on and keep the profit. He was
sending his son Andrew, "a heady young man and violent, and set
against you there and the company here," to see what he could find
out on Weston's behalf. (Andrew Weston, who went back to
England in the *Charity*, took with him a young Indian, the son of a
Massachusetts sachem, and the Council for New England ordered
the boy to be sent back to his father by the first available ship. The

authorities in England seem to have seen through the Westons very early.) The letter, signed by Edward Pickering and William Greene, bore a disarming postscript:

> I pray conceal both the writing and delivery of this letter, but make the best use of it. We hope to set forth a ship ourselves within this month.

Robert Cushman sent a letter too, commenting on the hard experience in France, outlining Weston's plans, and pointing out uncompromisingly that the newcomers in the three ships were "no men for us; wherefore I pray you entertain them not, neither exchange man for man with them, except it be some of your worst." He added cautiously: "If they borrow anything of you, let them leave a good pawn."

William Trevor, the young indentured sailor who had gone over on the *Mayflower* on the understanding that he could return after a year, had traveled back with Cushman on board the *Fortune*, and was now describing to everybody he met all over London the richness and beauty of parts of New England that he had never seen. This would give a false impression to others coming over, who in any case were unlikely to deal sensibly or fairly with the Indians. But two things were happier: "We are about to recover our losses in France. Our friends at Leyden are well and will come to you as many as can this time."

On the back of Cushman's letter John Peirce had scrawled a hasty note, endorsing what Cushman had written.

> As for Mr Weston's company, I think them so base in condition (for the most part) as in all appearance not fit for an honest man's company; I wish they prove otherwise.

All this gave the leaders in Plymouth plenty to think about. The *Swan* sailed up from Virginia at the end of the summer, and took Weston's planters on to Wessagusset; except for the men who had succumbed to sickness and were left to the mercy of the colonists until they were strong enough to leave. Plymouth, naturally, wanted to be rid of them, so everyone did his best to set them on their feet.

The corn harvest was thin, partly because the settlers had not yet perfected the knack of growing the corn in the Indian style, partly because some of Weston's men and some of the less upright Plymouth men had picked it surreptitiously before it was ripe. Those caught doing this were beaten, but many stole undetected; and a fresh stock of seed corn was not easy to come by, for it could be obtained only from the Indians, and the planters had run out of trading goods.

But the Pilgrims' special providence did not fail them. Thomas Jones, commanding the sixty-ton *Discovery*, employed by the Virginia Company, called at Plymouth on his way home. He had been told to move up the coast, sounding it and finding out suitable harbors. On board was a good stock of beads and knives, which he sold to the Pilgrims, charging a high rate, but supplying a most urgent want as they were running short of trading goods. He beat them down to three shillings a pound for beaver (later it fetched at least twenty), but the Plantation was once again in a position to trade for corn and furs, so the colonists did not make any objection.

Going home as a passenger on the *Discovery* was one John Pory, a learned graduate of Caius College, Cambridge, friend of the great Hakluyt and former secretary to the governor in Virginia. He was deeply impressed by what he saw in Plymouth, praised them for their good sense, warm hospitality, military readiness, and possession of good books. He wrote a charming thank-you letter, dated August 28, in which he said that in his quick visit he had forgotten to ask William Brewster to lend him, for agreeable reading on the voyage home, Henry Ainsworth's *Annotations upon the Fourth Book of Moses, called Numbers,* published three years earlier in London. He signed the letter "Your unfeigned and firm friend," which was true, for, as Bradford put it, Pory on returning to England "did this poor Plantation much credit amongst those of no mean rank."

Appeals came at intervals from Weston's badly organized men for goods, help in trading, general assistance, to all of which Bradford replied politely but firmly that he would sell them what he could spare when he was able, but all the same he and the rest of the colony felt perturbed by complaints that Weston's men were stealing corn from the Indians. This would jeopardize the safety of any English people in the territory, and when a request came from the Wessagusset leader, John Sanders, for help in taking a hogshead of corn by force, Bradford replied that on no account should they do any such thing. Some of Weston's men were so incensed by this that they told the Indians that Bradford was coming to take the corn away himself, which had disagreeable consequences later.

Bradford was certainly going to get corn, but in his usual lawful, sensible manner. Standish, with Squanto of course as guide-interpreter, was to have led the party, but there was a delay in starting out because of bad winds, and before the shallop could move he had fallen ill. Bradford therefore led the party himself. They had trouble off Cape Cod, encountering heavy shoal water which Squanto was not skillful enough to navigate. Unwilling to risk their lives in the treacherous currents of Pollock Rip and Monomoy, Bradford suggested that they should put in to Manamoyick Bay, near the site of the present-day town of Chatham. No Indians appeared, but the party knew there were some near by, so Squanto was sent to flush them out of the woods, persuade them that the visitors were friendly, and bring them along to trade. He did this, as Winslow noted:

> They came welcoming our Governor according to their savage manner, refreshing them very well with store of venison and other victuals which they brought to them in great abundance.

The Indians were shy at first, and for a few days kept nervously going and coming and shifting their huts from one place to another, but realized in the end that the Englishmen meant them no harm, and provided eight hogsheads of corn and beans.

Just as this transaction was concluded, Squanto fell ill. He developed symptoms of fever, and his nose bled freely, a certain sign of death according to Indian belief. Within a day or two he did die, after bequeathing his possessions to various English settlers he particularly liked, and, rather pathetically, asking Bradford to pray for him so that he could be sure to go "to the Englishman's God in Heaven." The Pilgrims sincerely regretted his loss, as well they might, for he had been a godsend to them in many ways and had made a marked difference in their struggle for survival. But the worst of that struggle was over now; Squanto had accomplished his essential work.

The shallop managed to get back around the Cape, crossed to the future Boston Harbor, where no corn could be found, and then went back to the inner coast of the Cape near First Encounter. Here the Pilgrims bought some corn from their stately acquaintance Aspinet, and went on to Mattakeeset, where a stiff gale from the north cast the shallop so far up the beach that they could not refloat her. They therefore piled the corn and beans into a mound, covered it, left it to be collected later, and went back to Plymouth on foot, a distance of forty to fifty miles. Everywhere Bradford received respectful greetings from all the Indians they met. The total quantity of corn and beans collected from place to place was about twenty-seven hogsheads, and as soon as the party reached Plymouth Bradford "took a few men and went to the inland places to get what he could" in addition, arranging to bring these stocks home in the spring. Winslow commented sturdily that to anyone who criticized his reports of a land of plenty during the rationed periods

> I answer, Everything must be expected in its proper season. No man, as one saith, will go into the orchard in winter, to gather cherries.... Only men of discontented passions and humours with their mouths full of clamours complain of having to drink water. How could anyone be so simple as to conceive that the fountains should stream forth wine or beer, and the woods and rivers be like butchers' shops and fishmongers' stalls, where they might have things taken to their hand?

In January 1623 Standish, in a suspicious frame of mind about

Indian dealings in general, led a group to Mattakeeset to fetch back the refloated shallop and the corn and beans from the covered mound. All were found intact. On this trip they met Aspinet again. He greeted Standish with deep bows, as Squanto had taught him to do, and by licking the captain's hand from wrist to fingertips, but he overdid it somewhat as the English had a struggle not to burst out laughing. He fed them on delicious corn bread, and next morning Standish led his party on to Cummaquid. Here a blizzard caught them, and they spent the night in the open boat frozen fast in the harbor. At dawn Iyanough's braves saw them and brought them to thaw out in their huts. Iyanough showed them how scrupulously his men had guarded the corn and beans, and his men helped to load them on board the shallop.

All was peace, apparently, but just as the Pilgrims were making ready to leave, Standish missed a few trinkets that he had brought along to trade with. He flew into a rage, marched up and threw a ring of armed men around the sachem's crowded lodge, and demanded the return of the beads, saying that if they were not instantly returned he would order his men to attack. Iyanough peaceably suggested that the beads had merely been mislaid, "desiring him to search whether they were not about the boat": in other words, he played for time to give the thief the chance of unobtrusively slipping the trinkets back. A man was sent to look and sure enough the beads were found "lying openly upon the boat's cuddy." There is no doubt that Standish thought it was a put-up job, but today it seems an unnecessary fuss to make about a few cheap ornaments, in view of Iyanough's gentle attitude and the way his men had guarded the food supplies and the shallop.

This was not the end of Standish's suspicions. One Pamet Indian came along "very affable, courteous, and loving, especially towards the Captain" and showing every sign of affection in order, Standish believed, to disguise the fact that "he had now entered into confederacy with the rest." Standish was so sure that the Pamet was going to murder him if he got the chance that he spent the whole night pacing up and down in front of the fire.

The Indians on both these trips had in fact been generous, providing more for the Pilgrims than they could well spare, because they planted comparatively little until they had English hoes to make the operation easier. It was worrying in the light of this generosity to hear that Weston's men were dangerously tilting the balance of trade in the bay by overpaying for what corn they could find, giving as much for a quart as the Pilgrims would have paid for a beaver skin.

· 5 ·

Weston's men had managed badly. They had started off far better supplied than the *Mayflower*'s passengers had been: yet they had wasted much of their stock, spending lavishly whenever they had any money or wampum, not budgeting, and generally living in a loose, unplanned style. Tales of their shiftless folly filtered through to Plymouth: Indians and Pilgrim traders heard of it from other Indians and traders. John Sanders was reputed to be keeping Indian mistresses; others, when they felt the pinch of poverty, started selling their clothes and bedding; others even went so far as to work for the Indians, chopping wood or fetching water for a capful of corn. Some stole, as Bradford had already recorded. Matters went from bad to worse. One man, gathering shellfish, "was so weak that he stuck fast in the mud and was found dead in the place." In the end the settlement broke up, going off in ones and twos and threes along the shore and into the woods, where they eked out a miserable existence on clams and what Bradford called ground nuts. It is one of the many ironies of history that the area of Boston, so eminent among the cities of America, had so sorry a first settlement.

Seeing the palefaces reduced to this way of life, lower than peasants, the local Indians grew scornful. Bradford wrote:

Many times as they lay thus scattered abroad and had set on a pot with ground nuts or shellfish, when it was ready the Indians would come and eat it up; and when night came, whereas some of them had a sorry blanket or such like to lap themselves in, the Indians would take it and let the other lie all night in the cold.

At one time, in order to placate the Indians, Weston's men actually hanged one of their number who was an irredeemable thief. A peculiar rumor spread about this, that what they had in fact done was to hang a sick man who was shortly going to die anyway. The story reached England, where Samuel Hudibras Butler put it into his great satiric poem. Many writers lumped New England settlers together under a common title of Puritans: Butler wrote, out of ignorance or malice, one cannot be sure which, as though it happened in Plymouth. A good cobbler had killed an Indian

> Not out of *Malice* but mere *Zeal*,
> Because he was an *Infidel*.

The local chief Tottipottymoy demanded the cobbler's death, but the Pilgrims thought him too useful to die, and on the principle of better hang wrong fellow than no fellow

> to do
> The Indian *Hoghan-Moghgan* too
> Impartial Justice, in his stead did
> Hang an old *Weaver* that was Bed-rid.

Thus, said Butler, preserving their religious beliefs:

> Our *Brethren* of *New-England* use
> Choice *Malefactors* to excuse,
> And Hang the *Guiltless* in their stead,
> Of whom the *Churches* have less need.

The bad conduct and reputation of Weston's men was doing the Pilgrims real harm, apart from Butler's fun, which was hardly taken seriously even at the time. If one settlement could destroy itself, so could others: Indians who feared or resented the incursion of the English into their territory (as well they might, because in time it led to their own virtual extinction) began to plot a rising. At one

time, when Standish was visiting a "grave sachem" named Canicum, a Massachusetts Indian called Wituwamat appeared, described by Winslow as

> a notable insulting villain, one who had frequently imbrued his
> hands in the blood of English and French and had oft boasted of
> his own valour, especially because as he said they died crying,
> making sour faces more like children than men.

Wituwamat had apparently come to recruit warriors to join in an
attack on Weston's men. Standish made no comment, but was
watchful and guarded, and "treasured up his anger" against the
"insulting villain."

But Massasoit was still loyal. A message reached Plymouth that
he was very ill indeed, probably dying, and Bradford's response was
to send Winslow with Hobamock and John Hampden, "a gentleman of London supplied with some cordials to administer" to the
sick chief. On the way they heard that Massasoit was dead, but they
went on, anxious to show their willingness to help and thinking it
only prudent to meet the new chief. Their journey lay along forest
tracks on which they stumbled in the dark, and the chief's lodge was
so crammed with people when they reached it that they could
scarcely squeeze in. A mob of chanting braves, "making such a
hellish noise as it distempered us that were well," ringed Massasoit's bed, on which he lay with squaws rubbing his arms and legs
and the medicine men noisily calling out spells. The chief was alive,
but unable to see; told that Winslow was there, he uttered faintly:
"Oh, Winslow, I shall never see thee again." Winslow discovered
that Massasoit had been constipated for five days after a bout of
gorging and that he had not slept for over forty-eight hours. The
chief's face and mouth were swollen and his tongue badly furred.
Winslow slipped "some conserve" into Massasoit's mouth on the
point of a knife, gave him sips of fruit juice, and followed it up with
a broth made of corn, strawberry leaves, and sassafras root. The
chief drank a bowlful and asked for more with a duck or a goose in
it. Winslow promptly shot a mallard and shoved it into the pot. Not

waiting for the new broth to be skimmed to take off the fat, Massasoit gulped down a bowl of it and vomited violently. His nose bled, but at last he was purged. Winslow washed him, he slept for eight hours, and within a couple of days he was on his feet again, shaky but saved. Now, he declared, he realized that the English were his loving friends; never would he forget their kindness.

Corbitant was present, in a far more accommodating frame of mind this time, and he fed the three guests lavishly and gave them room for the night. He proved to be a very pleasant fellow, "full of merry jests and squibs, and never better pleased than when the like are returned again upon him." After one meal, a long religious discussion developed: Winslow said he was not afraid to come among the Indians, because "where true love is there is no fear." Corbitant asked, rather pointedly:

> But if your love be such and bring forth such fruits, how cometh
> it to pass that when we visit Patuxet, you stand upon your guard
> with the mouths of your pieces towards us?

To which Winslow gravely replied that it was "the most honourable and respectful entertainment we can give you." Corbitant's answer was frank: "I like not such salutations."

Corbitant asked why the Pilgrims said grace both before and after meals. Winslow expounded and commented a little, but made no attempt to convert Corbitant, sensibly believing in letting well enough alone. They discussed the Ten Commandments. Corbitant liked most of them, but did not care much for the seventh, in which, he said, there were many inconveniences. In these conversations they were still using interpreters, but by now both could understand a few words here and there.

Before the three visitors left for Plymouth, Massasoit gave details of the proposed Indian attack on Weston's men and named seven tribes implicated in the plot. If the rising took place, he warned them, the attackers intended to come on to Plymouth afterward, so he begged Winslow to tell Bradford to stop the insurrection at the source.

This news naturally threw the colony into a whirl of defensive discussion and plans. Their apprehensions were reinforced by the unexpected arrival of Phineas Pratt with a small pack on his back. He had managed to get to Plymouth from Wessagusset, though he had not had the slightest idea of the way, and had gone off course several times, which was a good thing as the Indians had been after him. Pratt's advice was simple: he dared not stay with the Pilgrims, because from what he had been able to observe, they would all be knocked on the head shortly, unless they did the sensible thing and left.

Soon afterward, one Indian who had been chasing Pratt came through Plymouth "still pretending friendship." Taking no chances, Bradford lodged him in the fort, chaining him to a post where he would have to be content to remain until Standish got back from Wessagusset.

For as soon as Pratt had delivered his warning, Standish had set out for Wessagusset with eight assistants in a boat, sailed up to the site of Weston's plantation, and boarded Weston's ship, the *Swan*, riding at anchor in the harbor. It was silent and deserted. He fired off a musket or two and some of Weston's men straggled down to the beach. They spoke boldly: they had no need to mount a guard on the *Swan*, the Indians were friendly, they lived in the area quite safely without so much as a sword or a gun between them. Standish went on to see if he could find someone in some sort of authority to warn: these feckless people must be made to see reason. He found Sanders' chief assistant and disclosed to him the details of the rising as far as he knew them. One Indian appeared, carrying furs: Standish traded with him in his smoothest manner, though the choleric little captain was not as good at this as Winslow was. The Indian told his companions later that he could see the anger in Standish's heart by the look in his eyes. A powerful Indian named Pecksuot came up with a group of braves who stood about sharpening their knives in a menacing fashion. Pecksuot told Standish: "You may be a great captain, but you are a little man. I am not a great chief yet I am a man of great strength and courage." Standish, noting with grim relish that one of the knife-sharpeners was Wituwamat, whom he had never trusted, did nothing hastily, but next day he cornered Pecksuot, Wituwamat, a third brave, and an Indian youth in a hut, shut the door, gave the word to his men, grabbed Pecksuot's knife from its sheath at his throat, and after a sharp struggle killed him. The others dispatched Wituwamat and the third Indian, after a tremendous fight; Standish said it was incredible how many wounds they took in silence and how valiantly they fought to the last gasp. The young one was hanged.

Standish ordered every Indian in the settlement killed, but all except two had melted into the woods. The nine men marched out after them; the Indians withdrew from tree to tree, firing arrows, and Hobamock chased after them so fast that the other eight could not keep up. The Indians, shouting defiance, took refuge in a wooded swamp; Standish, prudently halting on the firm ground, roared at their leader to come out and fight like a man. This belligerent invitation was not accepted.

Standish went back into the settlement and confronted the chastened remnant of Weston's men. He told them that they could come to Plymouth if they wished, but to everyone's relief they refused, saying that they would prefer to take the *Swan*, sail up into Maine, and make passage home with the English fishing boats, if they heard nothing from Weston in time. They asked for corn, which Standish got for them from local Indians, leaving himself barely enough to get home with, and saw them off. When the *Swan* was out in the bay and making sail to the northeastward, Standish returned to Plymouth, bringing back "not the worth of a penny of anything that was theirs" but carrying Wituwamat's head, which, like those of executed felons in England, he stuck on a spike at the fort. The Pilgrims welcomed him with pleasure, but a rebuke came later from John Robinson at Leyden, who wrote that it was not pleasing to God to terrorize poor barbarous people, and telling the leaders to consider "the disposition of your Captain, whom I love" because "there may be wanting that tenderness of the life of man which is meet." Of course, Standish was a soldier, not a Pilgrim, and this kind of behavior was customary at the time.

The rout at Wessagusset had terrorized the Indians: many in

settlements all over New England left their homes and were seen running about like men distracted, or sheltering in swamps and thickets. A plague spread, killing, among others, the three chiefs whose attitudes had made Standish suspicious. The long decline of the New England Indians, partly from disease, partly from being killed off, which was to reduce them to a handful by the time of the War of Independence compared with the many thousands who had stood so proudly before, was by now visible. Among those who died were Canicum, Aspinet, and Iyanough.

Weston himself abruptly turned up, a very different man in appearance from the flourishing colonial planner they had last seen going off in a huff at Southampton. He had sailed across in a fishing vessel, under an assumed name, possibly to dodge his creditors, pretending to be a blacksmith of all incongruous pursuits, expecting to find a workable new command at Wessagusset. In the fishing grounds he heard of "the ruin and dissolution of his colony," whereupon he borrowed a shallop and went with one or two men to see for himself. Clumsy seamanship caused the wreck of the shallop in a bay between the Merrimac River and Piscataqua, site of a settlement later called Strawberry Bank and today the town of Portsmouth, New Hampshire. Weston just contrived to struggle ashore, where he fell into the hands of Indians, who promptly took all his belongings and clothes except for his shirt. He reached Piscataqua, borrowed a suit of clothes, and found his way to Plymouth. Bradford commented sorrowfully:

> A strange alteration there was in him, to such as had seen and known him in his former flourishing condition; so uncertain are the mutable things of this unstable world. And yet men set their hearts upon them, though they daily see the vanity thereof.

In Plymouth, Weston poured out all his festering grievances, and they were many, embracing most of the people he had ever met, but he was as full of specious promises as always. There was a ship coming, with good stores, and Plymouth should have whatever they needed; meanwhile, could he borrow some beaver to tide him over? The Pilgrims did not believe a word of this, but could not help feeling sorry for Weston, remembering that he had helped them in the past, however tiresome he had been since. They said that he could see for himself that they were poor, and short of supplies, and he knew perfectly well that they were still under contract to the Adventurers. They needed every scrap of beaver to get food and clothes, and if the colony knew they had given any skins to Weston there would be a mutiny; but they would do their best for him and let him have some skins, as long as the whole business was kept secret.

The best they could do was quite impressive: they let Weston have a hundred beaver skins, weighing 170 pounds, for which of course he never paid. They helped him when all the world failed him, as Bradford stated: for with his skins to sell he returned to the fishing fleet, provisioned his small ship, refitted himself and his men, and laid the foundations for the rest of his career. Like all persons of fluctuating fortunes forced to ask for aid in days of crisis, he remembered his benefactors with undying hatred, losing no chance of speaking or acting with hostility and spite against the Pilgrims. "But," wrote Bradford with calm assurance, "his malice could not prevail."

· 6 ·

It was in the spring and summer of 1623 that the pure communism that had ruled the Plantation until then was modified somewhat. The Separatists were often referred to as Saints, but some of the planters were not saintly enough to be free from the taint of self-interest, and grumbled a good deal about working only for the common good and not for a little private profit. Many of the strong young men objected to toiling for other men's families with no special reward; and they also pointed out that weak old people needed less food and drink than vigorous younger ones did. Elders disliked holding equal rights with their juniors, and some husbands complained that their wives were expected to cook meals and wash clothes for other men. More strikingly, revealing a trend that has made America the paradise of women that it has seemed for generations to women in other countries, the wives themselves said it was a kind of slavery.

Land was therefore reassigned in proportion to the size of each household, a tax levied to maintain the fishing and any community expenses, and apart from that each family might now keep what it produced. A better spirit was immediately apparent:

> It made all hands very industrious, so as much more corn was planted than otherwise would have been. The women now went willingly into the field, and took their little ones with them to set corn, which before would allege weakness and inability. . . .

Supplies were still short. Often people would go to bed not knowing where their next day's food was coming from. The prayer to give us this day our daily bread was never uttered more heartily than in Plymouth. Bradford drew comfort from other men's sufferings, reading Peter Martyr's *De Novo Orbe*, in which the writer described the Spanish colonists' starving time, when they eked out the parched grain by eating dogs, toads, and dead men: "from these extremities the Lord in His goodness kept His people." But Bradford did not fail to note that the Spaniards had won through in the end, and if the Lord could do this for Catholics, how much more would he do it for his true elect? Not that it was easy for him in Plymouth:

> They having but one boat left and she not over-well fitted, they were divided into several companies, six or seven to a gang or company, and so went out, with a net they had bought, to take bass and such like fish by course, every company knowing their turn. No sooner was the boat discharged of what she brought, but the next company took her and went out with her. Neither did they return till they had caught something, though it were five or six days before, for they knew there was nothing at home, and to

go home empty would be a great discouragement to the rest. Yea, they strive who should do best. If she stayed long or got little, then all went to seeking of shellfish, which at low water they digged out of the sands. And this was their living in the summer time, till God send them better; and in winter they were helped with ground nuts and fowl. Also in the summer they got now and then a deer, for one or two of the fittest was appointed to range the woods for that end, and what was got that way was divided amongst them.

Every morning the sentry pacing his watch at the fort would look out for signs of a ship, but the Plantation had no idea when to expect one. John Peirce had taken the *Paragon* to sea in December 1622 on behalf of the Adventurers, but within two weeks brought her back "being dangerously leaked and bruised with tempestuous storms," spent a hundred pounds on a refit lasting more than six weeks, during which the passengers had to be housed and fed, reloaded the ship, took on more people "and those not very good," and set off again in March. He was the man who had drawn up the two original Pilgrim charters, and he had a third on him, obtained from the Council for New England on the highly plausible grounds of the settlement's survival. He planned to keep this third charter for his own profit, acting as overall landlord in Plymouth. "But the Lord marvellously crossed him," said Bradford. Halfway over the storms were so violent that he ordered the *Paragon* to turn back, with the 109 people on board. The storms raged for two weeks, but a few days were particularly bad. The mast was cut down, the roundhouse and upperworks carried away, the helmsman had to be lashed to the tiller to keep from being swept overboard;

> the seas did so over-rake them, as many times those upon the deck knew not whether they were within board or without; and once she was so foundered in the sea as they all thought she would never rise again. But yet the Lord preserved them and brought them at last safe to Portsmouth, to the wonder of all men that saw what a case she was in, and heard what they had endured.

The facts all came out with the *Paragon*'s return. On the grounds of all the trouble it had cost him, Peirce demanded £500 from the Pilgrims for the charter, ten times the amount he had paid for it, and the Adventurers faced bills totaling £640 in addition for passenger charges and cargo.

But a ship did appear off Plymouth at the end of June. It was the *Plantation*, built at Whitby for the Council for New England at a price of £1250. Sir Ferdinando Gorges, one of the prime movers in the building, had obtained a land grant covering the area between the Merrimac and Kennebec Rivers, and had persuaded the Council to issue a proclamation "prohibiting interloping and disorderly trading" to New England. A copy of this proclamation was brought out by the captain of the *Plantation*, Francis West, brother of Lord de la Warr, who was empowered as a judge of admiralty to license fishing vessels and to take possession of an island called Mount Mansell. Captain West reported that the fishermen were stubborn fellows who refused to pay for licenses. They were strongly backed up by their shipowners, who complained to Parliament and wrung from that august body an order that all fishing should be free.

West presented himself at Plymouth as admiral of New England, and said he could sell the Pilgrims two hogsheads of peas at nine pounds each. This seemed extortionate: so he reduced the cost to eight. At the same time he wanted to buy beaver "at an under rate." The Pilgrims refused, saying that "they had lived so long without, and would do still, rather than give so unreasonably."

West told them that he had spoken a ship at sea, coming to Plymouth with passengers:

> and they marvelled she was not arrived, fearing some miscarriage; for they lost her in a storm that fell shortly after they had been aboard. Which relation filled them full of fear, yet mixed with hope.

The ship was the *Anne*, one hundred and forty tons, commanded by Captain William Peirce, perhaps a connection of the unscrupulous John, and one of the most highly esteemed of Atlantic masters.

The *Anne* had sailed in company with the forty-four-ton *Little James,* but they had parted company in the storm. The *Anne* came in about two weeks after the disgruntled West had taken the *Plantation* on to Virginia, and the *Little James* staggered in ten days after that, a fine new ship destined to stay in the colony, but shaken by the crossing. Between them they brought eighty-seven settlers, twenty-nine of them from Leyden, including Mary and Sarah Priest, Mrs. Samuel Fuller, Fear and Patience Brewster, Thomas Morton, Jr., with his uncle and aunt, George and Juliana Carpenter Morton, Sarah Allerton Vincent Priest with her third husband Cuthbert Godbertson, a Leyden hatmaker, and Alice Carpenter Southworth with her sons Constant, aged eight, and Thomas, aged six. There was also a girl called Barbara, who married Miles Standish. According to some historians she was the sister of Rose Standish, and if so it meant that Standish was entirely unconcerned with the Table of Kindred and Affinity and the taboo against marrying one's deceased wife's sister or husband's brother, which had provided the shock content of *Hamlet* twenty-one years before. Many marriages resulted from this new influx of planters, but the best known is that of Alice Southworth, who on August 14 became the second wife of William Bradford.

One public benefactor who came on the *Anne* was Francis Sprague: he established the first tavern in New England. One legend-begetter was John Faunce of Purleigh in Essex: his son John, the third and last ruling elder in Plymouth at the end of the century, started the Plymouth Rock story. One rather endearing pair who arrived on the *Little James* was the elderly Edward Burcher and his wife, who, according to Captain John Bridges, "wore as hearty as the youngest in the ship." The youngest in the ship was a new baby, born a month before arrival, Samuel, first son of John and Sarah Carey Jenney from Norwich. Despite the rough passage, both were doing well: Samuel Jenney lived to be over seventy. John Jenney, former cooper and brewer's man, built Plymouth's first mill. He was "a godly though otherwise plain man, yet singular for publicness of spirit." There were the two little Jenney daughters, Abigail and Sarah, to complete the family.

All the newcomers were appalled by what they saw in Plymouth. Some reacted with tears, others wished they had never come and were back in England, all were distressed to see the state their friends were in.

> And truly it was no marvel they should be thus affected, for they were in a very low condition; many were ragged in apparel and some little better than half naked, though some that were well stored before were well enough in this regard. But for food they were all alike, save some that had got a few peas of the ship that was last here. The best dish they could present their friends with was a lobster or a piece of fish without bread or anything else but a cup of fair spring water. And the long continuance of this diet, and their labours abroad, had something abated the freshness of their former complexion.

Most of the newcomers were "for the General" but a group of ten were "on their Particular." These nice terms meant that most intended to mix completely with the existing planters, and the ten particulars wished to be independent in all but law. These had visions of great houses in fruitful estates and a future of quick riches, "but," noted the practical Bradford, "they proved castles in the air." Conditions for the particulars included payment of a bushel of wheat, or its value, toward colonial expenses, from every male of sixteen or over, and complete prohibition of trade with the Indians.

Various fears, apprehensions, and complaints, voiced by newcomers and Adventurers alike, caused Bradford for once to go on the defensive. He made a summary of twelve specific objections and answered each separately. The twelve points were: that there was diversity of religion; that people neglected family duties on Sundays; that baptisms and communion services were not celebrated; that the children were not learning to read, nor were they taught the catechism; that the particulars would not work for the generals; that the water was unwholesome; that the land was barren; that "the fish will not take salt to keep sweet"; that the colony included a number of thieves; that the settlers were plagued by foxes and wolves; that the Dutch on the Hudson were likely to spoil Plymouth's trading prospects; and that the people were "much annoyed with mosquitoes."

Bradford flatly denied that religious wrangling existed. It was unfortunately true that lack of a minister prevented the colony from enjoying the sacraments, and of course there was no schoolmaster either, but they hoped soon to find a way of starting a school. Parents did not neglect their children's learning, however, but taught them as best they could. There were some particulars who would not cooperate, but the rest hoped they could be reformed; if not, they must go. Neglect of Sunday obligations?

> We allow no such thing, but blame it in ourselves and others, and
> they that thus report it should have showed their Christian love
> the more if they had in love told the offenders of it, rather than
> thus to reproach them behind their backs. But (to say no more)
> we wish themselves had given better example.

And as for thieving, if London had been free of that crime, the colony would have been free of it too. Stealing, when detected, was suitably punished.

Bradford dealt masterfully with the other six points. The land was much the same as anywhere else, some good, some poor. The question of the fish was ridiculous: New England drew fishermen like a magnet. Foxes and wolves harassed many communities: poison and traps would help to destroy them. If by saying the water was not wholesome the grumblers meant that it was inferior to wine or beer, that was true enough, but if they meant it was unhealthy, that was a lie: it was as sweet as any in the world "for aught we know."

The question of the Dutch trade was simple. If the English did not develop New England, the Dutch would. Regarding the mosquitoes, Bradford had the perfect and charming answer:

> They are too delicate and unfit to begin new plantations and

colonies, that cannot endure the biting of a mosquito. We would wish such to keep at home till at least they be mosquito-proof.

Yet, he added, Plymouth was no worse than anywhere else, and the settlers had learned by experience that the more land they cleared the fewer mosquitoes troubled them.

The fact that Bradford thought it proper to clear the air about these complaints indicates that they had reached a crescendo. Grumbling throughout the initial stages of settlement was constant and hearty. One pleasant example was that of Captain Bridges, who stepped ashore from the *Little James* cursing his crew: they were green, he said, and in manning the ship "cared not which end went forwards."

The Plantation was not expecting a good harvest that year. Summer had been hot and dry, no rain had fallen for ten weeks from the middle of May to the end of July, and the corn stood parched and withered. It looked so bad that the Pilgrims fixed one of their special Days of Humiliation to pray for rain. To their wonder and delight, and to the amazement of the Indians, they received a swift and gracious answer. Most of the Day of Humiliation was hot and cloudless, but toward evening the sky began to darken. Clouds appeared and piled up, and then the rain began—steady, soaking, sweet-smelling, regular, sinking into the cracked earth and freshening the dry crops. Looking across their dripping fields, the Pilgrims breathed deep happy sighs of thankfulness. From that night on they had showers interspersed with fine warm spells, and the harvest was a far better one than they had imagined possible.

The wedding of William Bradford and Alice Southworth was celebrated along with the harvest festival. Emanuel Eltham, an Adventurer who had arrived on the *Little James,* on which he had been governor for the voyage, described the harvest feast in glowing terms in a letter to his brother:

We had about twelve pasty venisons, besides others, pieces of roasted venison and other such good cheer that I could wish you some of our share. For here we have the best grapes that ever

you saw, and the biggest, and divers sorts of plums and nuts . . .
six goats, about fifty hogs and pigs, also divers hens. . . . A better
country was never seen nor heard of for here are a multitude of
God's blessings.

It is agreeable to picture the colony with its comfortable and
familiar sounds, the cluck of hens, grunt of pigs, bleat of goats,
among the hammering, sawing, chopping, and cheerful conversation.

Massasoit came, bringing the chief of his five wives, four sachems, and 120 braves, also three or four bucks and a turkey.
Eltham thoroughly enjoyed watching them dancing "with such a
noise that you would wonder." He considered that there were too
many women and children in Plymouth for the colony to be a real
success, and thought poorly of the Pilgrims as fishermen, but on the
whole he was well impressed by what he saw.

After this harvest the rations were increased. The oldcomers
arranged that as far as possible the newcomers should live on the
supplies they had brought and keep old and new stores separate, to
which both groups readily agreed.

The *Anne* was rapidly loaded up with a cargo of oak staves,
cedar, and beaver, and sailed on September 10, taking Winslow to
report in person to the Adventurers. He carried with him the
manuscript, published the following year, called hopefully *Good
News from New England.* A few days later Captain Robert Gorges,
son of Ferdinando, brought a ship into Massachusetts Bay with a
group of passengers to start a new settlement, and fixed upon
Wessagusset, funnily enough. He held a commission from the
Council for New England to be governor of the region. As assistants the Council had given him Captain ("Admiral") West and one
Christopher Levett, an Adventurer who had bought a hundred-
pound share in the Council and held a land grant of six thousand
acres. The Council had also told him to make full use of any advice
and assistance he could get from the governor of Plymouth, so this
could be said to be the moment when the colony took full status in
the eyes of the outside world.

a. 390.

GOOD
NEVVES

FROM NEW ENGLAND:

*Maxima hereticorū fautrix nova Anglia, omni doctrinarū
licentia (ut et Angl— mum) famosa.*

OR

A true Relation of things very remarkable at the Plantation of *Plimoth*
in NEVV-ENGLAND.

*Eaurge Des, dissipentur inimici tui; profligentur hereses una cum
suis autoribus et patronis.*

Shewing the wondrous providence and good-
nes of GOD, in their preservation and continuance,
*being delivered from many apparant
deaths and dangers.*

Together with a Relation of such religious and
civill Lawes and Customes, as are in practise amongst
the *Indians,* adjoyning to them at this day. As also
*what Commodities are there to be raysed for the
maintenance of that and other Plantations in the said Country.*

Written by *E. W.* who hath borne a part in the
fore-named troubles, and there liued since
their first Arrivall.

LONDON

Printed by *I. D.* for *William Bladen* and *Iohn Bellamie,* and
are to be sold at their Shops, at the *Bible* in *Pauls-*Churchyard, and at the three Golden Lyons in Corn-hill,
neere the *Royall Exchange.* 1624.

The title page from *Goode Newes from New England* by Edward Winslow.

Robert Gorges notified Bradford that he had arrived in the bay, but before the governor could visit him he turned up. He had set out to sail up to Maine, but bad weather and the lack of a knowledgeable pilot forced him back, and he came into Plymouth Harbor, where he and his men were "kindly entertained" for two weeks.

He had been going to Maine, he explained, in search of the troublesome Weston, to call him to account on the Adventurers' behalf. As luck would have it Weston came in on board the *Swan*, showing a degree of nerve remarkable even for him, and was at once confronted by Robert Gorges in a minatory frame of mind.

> He charged him first with the ill carriage of his men at the Massachusetts, by which means the peace of the country was disturbed; and himself and the people which he had brought over to plant in that bay were thereby much prejudiced. To this Mr Weston easily answered, that what was that way done was in his absence, and might have befallen any man; he left them sufficiently provided, and conceived they would have been well-governed, and for any error committed he had sufficiently smarted.

Robert Gorges let this unsatisfactory answer go for the moment, and came to his second charge, which was that Weston, having obtained a license from the Council for New England to take a large number of big guns over for defense, had sold them for his own profit. This had deeply affronted Sir Ferdinando, who was even more critical of Weston than the Pilgrims were.

Weston shifted, but could not deny the charge. Bradford and the other Plymouth leaders tried to smooth things over, and were coaxing Robert Gorges into a better temper when Weston suddenly broke out:

> He grew more presumptuous and gave such provoking and cutting speeches as made him [Gorges] rise up in great indignation and distemper, and vowed that he would either curb him, or send him home for England.

Weston, alarmed by this threat, came privately to Bradford to ask whether Robert Gorges really could send him back or put restraint on him. Bradford said the colony could do nothing to help him, and could not prevent himself from adding that if Weston had only been sensible, and kept his temper, all might have been well. Weston admitted that he had a fiery temper that was hard to control, but all the same he hoped that the governor could pacify the captain. Bradford with typical kindliness managed it, not without trouble, and Weston promised to render full accounts, but said after Bradford had gone: "They are young justices, but good beggars," meaning that the Pilgrims were not very experienced but could be persuasive. Gorges went back to the bay, thanking the colony for its hospitality, and soon sent a warrant for Weston's arrest. Bradford thought the warrant was not legal, but somebody had to clear up Weston's affairs. Accordingly Bradford wrote to Gorges, telling him that if he (Gorges) arrested Weston he would be saddled with paying all Weston's debts, which were considerable and for which Plymouth could not be responsible. For example, Weston's men were unpaid and clamoring for their wages; Weston owed money for food already bought and consumed, and was even now buying more on credit. Gorges replied loftily by sending "a very formal warrant under his hand and seal" for Weston's arrest. Matters fell out precisely as Bradford had warned. Weston had barely two weeks' supplies left for his unfortunate assistants, and Gorges was obliged to reimburse them, pay off the defrauded creditors, and restock the *Swan,* whereupon Weston, deciding that this would do for the present, sailed away to Virginia, and no more was heard of him for some time.

This business had changed Robert Gorges' mind about staying in New England. He took one more disillusioned look at Wessagusset, where the few remaining planters were drifting away, some to Virginia, some to England, and went back home himself, with the offended comment that the state of affairs in the colonial territory did not suit a man of his quality and standing.

One man who had arrived with Robert Gorges was a minister,

the Reverend William Morrell. He stayed for about a year after
Gorges left, and his standing remained forever ambiguous. No one
knew exactly what his duties were supposed to have been, nor the
extent of his pastoral charge. His quality was, on the other hand,
only too clear. He spent his time composing an ode in Latin
hexameters, which was published in 1625 in London, with an
accompanying translation also written by him. Its noble title was:
*New-England, or, A Brief Ennaration of the Air, Earth, Water, Fish,
and Fowls of that Country.*

On November 5, 1623, a fire broke out among the newcomers
in Plymouth. Several sailors, gathered together in one house, built
up a roaring fire against the freezing weather, and clustered around
it, drinking and singing to warm themselves still better. The flames
blazed up, breaking out of the chimney and setting the thatch
alight. Three or four neighboring houses caught fire and were
completely burned out, and the Plantation storehouse next door
began to burn. This was the one building it was vital to save, and
Bradford, hurriedly called to the scene, organized the firefighting
operations. He put some trustworthy helpers inside the storehouse
and others outside, armed with wet cloths, and got the fire under
control. Some people wanted to take all the stores outside, but
others knew that if they did so some of the newcomers would steal
whatever they could lay their hands on. Suspicions of arson were
heard: at the height of the tumult a voice, never identified, warned
the Pilgrims to take care, for "all were not friends that were near
them." Joined to one end of the store was a shed "wattled up with
boughs" whose leaves were dry and withered, and no sooner had the
fire died down in the storehouse than smoke was seen coming out of
this shed. At once several helpers ran to deal with this new menace,
and found to their horror a firebrand nearly four feet long tucked
inside the struts. It could not possibly have come there by accident;
someone must have deliberately placed it there. As ever, the Lord
guarded his chosen people, and the storehouse with its contents was
saved.

Robert Gorges had left his ship to go on to Virginia after a refit,

for there were several people on board to be landed there. A
number of the newcomers, whose houses, with everything in them,
had been burned to the ground, went with them, as did others who
had taken a dislike to the colony, and thought this was a good chance
to try somewhere else.

The *Little James* proved a disappointment. She had been sent
out by the Adventurers to stay in New England and make herself
useful in trading up and down the coast. A vessel of forty-four tons
could hold a lot of beaver, corn, timber, and all kinds of essential
supplies. She looked a brave sight, with her flags streaming in the
breeze, but she had brought over no trading goods, and her crew
were difficult. They had been told originally by some plausible
propagandist that they would be able to capture French or Spanish
ships and make a fortune. They were recruited on a share or bonus
basis, and only the captain, John Bridges, was to have regular
wages. Weston "and others of the same stamp" had talked to them,
so that now "neither Master nor Governor could scarce rule them."
They behaved in a most recalcitrant way, unwilling to fish or do any
trading, and, fearing that they would either run away or simply take
the ship and go, Bradford decided that they had better be paid
wages of their own. This was done, and the *Little James* was sent up
to trade with the Narragansett. The only trading goods available
were a few beads and knives, which did not impress the Indians
much, as the Dutch traders who had already visited them had much
more attractive things to barter. The *Little James* did pick up some
corn and beaver, though not much, and the crew nearly wrecked
her on the way back, saving her from driving on to Brown's Islands
only by cutting down the mainmast.

The mast was replaced, with the rigging, and at the beginning
of March the *Little James* was sent out again, this time up to
Damaris Cove. She anchored safely in the harbor, along with several English fishing vessels, and stayed there for several weeks,
presumably joining in the fishing expeditions. On April 10 a terrific
storm broke. Huge waves crashed over the ship, flinging her onto
the rocks, and holing her so badly that she sank. Bridges and one of

his crew were drowned, and the rest only just managed to survive. The cargo was completely lost.

Some of the other ships' captains sent word of this to Plymouth and said that it was a pity to lose such a fine vessel. They suggested that if the colony would meet the expenses they could raise and repair her. Plymouth paid the cost in beaver, and the ship was raised most ingeniously:

> They got coopers to trim I know not how many tun of cask, and being made tight and fastened to her at low water, they buoyed her up; and then with many hands hauled her on shore in a convenient place where she might be wrought upon. And then hired sundry carpenters to work upon her, and others to saw plank. . . . [There was] such a hole in her bilge as a horse and cart might have gone in.

The whole operation cost a great deal, and took over a year to complete.

· 7 ·

Meanwhile, back at the Plantation, Winslow returned from England in the *Charity,* arriving in March. He brought three heifers and a bull, the first cattle in the colony. He also brought the badly needed fishing equipment, and a charter, dated January 1, for a tract of ground with islands, and hunting and fishing rights, at Cape Ann. Five hundred acres were allocated for public use, and thirty in addition for each planter who went there. These were to be compact, not spread about, so the intention to set up a small town was clear from the outset.

Winslow brought some clothes with him, and three people, who were destined to have varying effects on the Plantation. One was a carpenter, an honest, hardworking man, who built two strong shallops, "a great and strong lighter," and cut the timber for two ketches. Most unfortunately the poor fellow succumbed in the hot weather, and though he received the best treatment the town afforded, he died, to the regret of everyone concerned. The second was a saltmaker, and he was just the opposite—ignorant, foolish, and obstinate. He made extravagant promises, boasted of what he could do for them, and, when he was sent to prospect for a good site for the salt pan, reported back that he had found the ideal situation. There was everything he needed, and it would show fine profits, but he must have eight or ten men to work with him all the time. They had to build a large framework for the curing shed, but as soon as this was done he said that after all the soil was wrong just there, and if he could have the lighter to carry clay for him he could find the right spot and get the whole thing working perfectly in no time.

The Pilgrims, who had already had to put up with a good deal of mutinous muttering from some of the newcomers, and to whom this was not the first problem, thought that the best way to deal with this plausible fellow was to give him plenty of rope. So they sat back quietly and let him rush upon his own destruction. He went up to try his luck at Cape Ann, telling his assistants that this was a delicate business and required expert handling such as only he could give, yet really the only task he was able to perform was that of boiling salt in pans. Eventually he managed to set fire to the Cape Ann curing shed, "and the fire was so vehement as it spoiled the pans, at least some of them, and that was the end of that chargeable business."

The third, a very troublesome newcomer, was a minister, the Reverend John Lyford, who began by embarrassing the Pilgrims at the moment of arrival.

> When this man first came ashore, he saluted them with that reverence and humility as is seldom to be seen, and indeed made them ashamed, he so bowed and cringed unto them, and would have kissed their hands if they would have suffered him; yea, he wept and shed many tears, blessing God that had brought him to see their faces, and admiring the things they had done in their

wants, as if he had been made all of love and the humblest person in the world. And all the while (if we may judge by his after carriages) he was but like him mentioned in Psalm X:10, "That croucheth and boweth, that heaps of poor may fall by his might."

This Uriah Heep claimed to be a minister, a graduate of Magdalen College, Oxford, and to have had the tenure of an Irish parish. No record exists of his name in the records of Oxford, nor of Cambridge or Dublin. He did have the Irish living, but it seems probable that he obtained it by pretending to be in holy orders. He had a wife and a large brood of children, all of whom he brought with him, and if he had been forced to leave Ireland in a hurry when they discovered he was not a properly ordained minister, he would certainly have needed to find a new post quickly. He had ingratiated himself with the Adventurers, who approved his joining the Plantation as "an honest plain man though none of the most eminent and rare," the only problem that they could see being his swarm of children. Cushman told Bradford to use his own discretion about appointing him: "He knows he is no officer amongst you, though," he added prudently, "perhaps custom and universality may make him forget himself," meaning, "He knows he has no official powers in your lawmaking, but he may forget this while living in the colony and take on authority not naturally his own."

Despite the bowing and scraping, Lyford was kindly welcomed to Plymouth, provided with the best quarters the town afforded and a bigger allowance of food than anyone else, and supplied with a servant. He was invited to sit with the Council to discuss the most important questions, and within a short time he applied formally for church membership. He made a flowery speech, saying how glad he was at the opportunity of freedom to enjoy the law of God in purity among his elect, and confessing his former disorderly walking, as he called it, which the Pilgrims took to mean being a member of the Church of England. They considered, however, that they had made a distinguished conversion, and accepted him into their meeting, inviting him to share the pulpit with Brewster.

The word "pulpit" is misleading. The meetinghouse was an affair of plain benches confronted by a low platform with a table on it, from which modest vantage point the minister and elders surveyed the congregation. Gradually over the next century the pulpit evolved in New England, rising in height and expanding in size until it resembled a castle battlement on which the soldierly black-clad minister paced back and forth, directing the fight against the Devil, hurling thunderbolts of rhetoric and arrows of argument at an assembly of eager or somnolent listeners, while the young boys and girls, gradually relegated to the gallery, fidgeted and whispered, giggled and pinched one another, pulled pigtails, moved in and out, sat down during the two-hour prayers, and even, on occasion, slipped out before the end. As the pulpit rose so did the sounding board, which became a nest of bats. These, roused at times by the minister's sound and fury, often came swooping and fluttering over the heads of the faithful, throwing the congregation into confusion.

Lyford did not produce bats, but he did something much worse. He rapidly revealed himself as a friend to all the troublemakers of Plymouth. These had received a powerful recruit in John Oldham, described by Thomas Morton as Mad Jack. Oldham's past life, like Lyford's, is veiled in mystery, but he had crossed on the *Anne*, intending to set up as one of the independent planters. He was a quarrelsome, conniving man, though at first he professed warm feelings toward the Pilgrims. This veneer soon peeled away to reveal disruption. Mutterings in corners grew in volume, crystallizing around Oldham and sympathetically heard by Lyford.

The non-Pilgrims complained that they were expected to fit in with the Pilgrims' own religious practices. This made the non-Pilgrims more likely to grumble and of course they would make the most of it to an apparently sympathetic newcomer. The first open breach of faith appeared when William Hilton's wife gave birth to a baby and the Hiltons wanted it baptized. They were Church of England members still, and did not wish to join the Pilgrim faith, so officially the baby could not be baptized in Plymouth. The Pilgrims were horrified to discover that Lyford had not only performed this office for them but had made the sign of the cross over the baby: a violation of all that the Pilgrims stood for.

The elders decided to do nothing openly about this, preferring to wait until Lyford and Oldham provided them with more ammunition to use against them. It was not long in coming. The *Charity,* after a fishing voyage up the Maine coast, put in at Plymouth preparatory to sailing home. At this time Lyford, who had been doing an unusually large quantity of writing, took a bundle of letters to William Peirce, master of the *Charity,* to deliver for him in London. Bradford now acted in a cloak-and-dagger manner uncommon in his nature. He was suspicious of Lyford and knew he had been writing a lot. So he waited until the *Charity* set off late in the afternoon, gave her a head start, and, as darkness fell, boarded the shallop and went in pursuit. Out of sight of the town he caught up with her, hailed and boarded her, and seized the letters, along with others written in Oldham's barely legible scrawl. He thanked Peirce for his help, got back on board the shallop, and was rowed back to Plymouth, where both Lyford and Oldham looked blankly at him. Nothing happened for some weeks, as far as they could tell, so pretty soon they were going about as briskly as ever, happy in the belief that their secret correspondence was a secret still.

It was not. The rest of the Council read the letters, made careful copies of them and held on to a number of the originals, for this was evidence, and prepared to summon both the offenders to trial.

Within a short time the issue was forced on them. Called to take his normal turn as watch, Oldham refused, drawing a knife on Standish, whom he called a beggarly rascal. The fiery little captain flared up in reply, Oldham's shouts redoubled, and Bradford rushed up to find out what was going on. He found Oldham bawling like a wild thing, roaring at the rebels and traitors who surrounded him. They chained him up in the fort to cool down. Lyford and his adherents, the general malcontents, promptly summoned a meeting "without ever speaking one word either to the Governor, Church, or Elder" and "set up a public meeting apart, on the Lord's Day," which went against Pilgrim custom.

This super-Separatism was more than enough. To prevent further mischief and stop the "insolent carriages" of these two hedgehogs, as Bradford pleasantly described them, the trial must take place at once. The council had read more than twenty of Lyford's letters, "large and full of slanders and false accusations, tending not only to their prejudice, but to their ruin and utter subversion," plus two that Lyford had copied:

> One of them writ by a gentleman in England to Mr Brewster
> here, the other by Mr Winslow to Mr Robinson in Holland, at
> his coming away, as the ship lay at Gravesend. They lying sealed
> in the great cabin, whilst Mr Winslow was busy about the affairs
> of the ship, this sly merchant takes and opens them, takes these
> copies and seals them up again; and not only sends the copies of
> them thus to his friend and their adversary, but adds thereto in
> the margin many scurrilous and flouting annotations.

The adversary was the Reverend John Pemberton, a well-known opponent of the Pilgrims.

The trial was organized with the most impressive show of formality that Plymouth had so far seen. Standish, carrying his sword, led his full military array, escorting the accused up the hill to the fort, where Wituwamat's skull still decorated the battlements, into the dimly lit meetinghouse, crammed with fascinated listeners, who could hear in the pauses between what people were saying the tramp of the watch overhead on the wooden planks of the roof. Bradford sat at the table with his assistants flanking him, and read out the charge.

It accused both Lyford and Oldham of plotting against the Plantation and disturbing the peace, both spiritual and temporal. The Pilgrims had come to the New World to enjoy freedom of worship and conscience, and everyone present knew what struggles and sacrifices they had made to achieve it. Lyford's passage had been paid, and his family maintained, at the town's expense, he was a member of the Pilgrim church, and had repaid all this with perfidy; Oldham was, to be sure, independent, but the colony had helped him when he could not stand alone. It was like the fable of the hedgehog:

whom the cony in a stormy day in pity received into her burrow, would not be content to take part with her, but in the end with her sharp pricks forced the poor cony to forsake her own burrow; so these men, with the like injustice, endeavoured to do the same to those that entertained them.

The accused denied this. They were "stiff and stood resolutely on the denial of most things and required proof." Bradford quietly produced the incriminating letters. Lyford was "struck mute," but Oldham shouted furiously at the court for daring to open his letters, and called on his adherents to rally round: "My masters, where is your hearts? Now show your courage, you have often complained to me—now is the time, if you will do anything, I will stand by you."

Nobody spoke. There was a pause, and then Bradford turned to Lyford and asked him if he thought it was wrong to open his letters. Lyford remained silent. Bradford had the letters read aloud.

They were full of wild accusations. Lyford had stated that the Pilgrims would only admit those of the same persuasion, that they would quickly get rid of others however honest, that they disapproved of his preaching that great men as well as meaner ones should if need be equally be criticized, that the Pilgrims were out to ruin the independent settlers, refusing to trade with them or to supply them, that food distribution was unfair, and that the Pilgrims were wasteful administrators. Bradford answered every accusation carefully, summoning witnesses:

One was called before them, and questioned, for receiving powder and biscuit from the gunner of the small ship which was the Company's, and had it put in at his window in the night; and also for buying salt of one that had no right to it, he not only stood

to back him (being one of these Particulars) by excusing and
extenuating his fault as long as he could, but upon this builds this
mischievous and most false slander, that because they would not
suffer them to buy stolen goods, *ergo* they sought their utter ruin.
Bad logic for a divine!

About the wastefulness Lyford was closely questioned, and all
he could actually say he had seen was an old hogshead or two falling
to pieces, and one or two broken hoes that somebody had carelessly
left in the fields. The matter of food shares was equally without
foundation. There was some inequality as a result of the arrangement made when the *Anne* arrived, as they all knew, but it was only
a temporary measure, and Lyford of all people, with his highest
allowance, was in no position to grumble.

But there was worse to come. As the reading went on, big black
facts emerged. Lyford had written that the ruling Pilgrims were
high-handed enough for Jesuits and must be subdued by being
outnumbered. The Adventurers must send over as many independents as they could find, and send them on the clear undertstanding
that they were to have full voting rights and eligibility to hold office.
They must on no account let John Robinson, or anyone else from
Leyden, come to Plymouth: it would spoil everything. There had
been some talk in London of sending out a new military commander, and this should be done:

> If that Captain you spoke of should come hither as a general, I am
> persuaded he would be chosen Captain, for this Captain Standish
> looks like a silly boy, and is in utter contempt.

It is easy to imagine the reaction of the "easily kindled little
chimney" to that sentence.

Lyford's letters implicated Oldham. He had written that since
he started making these reports some dispatches had come from
London indicating that Bradford (and any governor after him)
ought to have greater authority in some matters; this should be
avoided at all costs. He expected Oldham would have enlarged on

this point in his letters. He requested the recipients to keep his own share in the business quiet.

At last Lyford pulled himself together sufficiently to reply. Billington and others had complained to him. Was that enough to produce all this? wondered Bradford. Perhaps there were genuine grounds for doubt. Perhaps there had been corrupt or unfair dealing. If Lyford, or anyone else, had evidence of such, let it now be stated openly; the whole colony was present; evil must be unmasked and crushed wherever it appeared. Lyford said he could see that he had been told lies, which he in his innocence had accepted as truth. Billington and his friends, when questioned, made no attempt to come to the aid of their beleaguered pastor, but said that Lyford was making it all up, and that although they had sometimes been drawn to his meetings they had never consented to act dishonorably as he had tried to persuade them to do.

Lyford had recourse to his last weapon, and burst into tears, confessing brokenly, between sobs, that he was a miserable sinner unfit for the forgiveness of God, and that all he had said in the letters was false. He described himself as "unsavoury salt," said he had wronged them past redemption, and "all this he did with as much fullness as words and tears could express."

The two men were formally pronounced guilty, and sentenced to banishment: Oldham at once, though the Pilgrims would allow his wife and children to stay until he was in a position to provide suitable lodging for them; Lyford within six months, with a hint that the court might reconsider if he behaved well and proved sincerely repentant. At first it seemed as though he was. He spoke in church soon after, confessing all over again in a most dramatic and enjoyable fashion, at great length and with much emotion, so much so that various tender-hearted hearers, including Dr. Fuller, said afterward that they felt like going to beg his release from the court.

They did not feel like it when they found out, only a month or two later, that Lyford was writing secretly to the Adventurers again. Dating it August 22, 1624, signing it "John Lyford, Exile," he admitted that he had been indiscreet in his previous letters, but that he had said nothing that was not true. Impartial men would realize that. Some in Plymouth were "very audacious" in "whatever colours be cast to darken the truth." Out of the respect he had for the Adventurers he had stayed in New England and suffered, when he would have preferred to come back, and, unless he received better encouragement from London he would get out of Plymouth.

> I purposed before I came to undergo hardness; therefore I shall,
> I hope, cheerfully bear the conditions of the place, though very
> mean; and they have changed my wages ten times already.

He was not, he said, aiming at self-promotion. It was for the poor souls here, without a properly ordained minister, who had begged him with tears in their eyes to look after them, that he had taken on the ministry. He would wait to hear what the Adventurers had to say, "so it be within the time limited me." He remained theirs ever.

How fortunate it was, recorded Bradford, that Lyford's clandestine correspondence had been discovered. The Council faced him with it at once. Lyford had opened this letter with the peculiar statement: "Though the filth of mine own doings may justly be cast in my face, and with blushing cause my perpetual silence": first they wanted to know what filth that was:

> Some great matter sure? But if it be looked into, it amounts to no
> more than a point of indiscretion, and that's all. And yet he licks
> off that too, with this excuse, that he was stirred up thereunto by
> beholding the indirect course here.

As for criticizing the church, Elder Brewster was in no way inferior to Lyford or to some of his betters in gifts or in learning. There had been no agreement about wages, no bargain had been made, they had simply given Lyford the best they had. Even he had acknowledged in his earlier letters that they had treated him kindly and lovingly.

Mrs. Lyford now put her spoke in the wheel, complaining to one of the deacons that Lyford had "wronged her before marriage" and (presumably in a different way) since, because it had proved impossible for her to keep any maids: "he would be meddling with them." She had caught Lyford with the maids on several occasions. "A grave matron," she was taken seriously by Bradford. Before the Council, other disgraceful details came to light: in Ireland, where Lyford had "wound himself into the esteem of sundry godly and zealous professors in those parts, who having been burdened with the ceremonies in England, found there some more liberty to their consciences." There he had really behaved very badly indeed.

What had happened was this. In Lyford's congregation was a young man who had fallen in love and wished to marry, but before getting too involved with the girl he wanted to make sure that his choice was likely to meet with the favor of God. What more correct than that he should consult the minister? Lyford said he would talk to the girl, and let the young man know what he thought. After several private meetings, Lyford summoned the young man and told him that the girl would be an admirable wife: the pair were married, and all was apparently well.

> But some time after marriage the woman was much troubled in mind and afflicted in conscience, and did nothing but weep and mourn, and long it was before her husband could get of her what was the cause. But at length she discovered the thing, and prayed him to forgive her; for Lyford had overcome her and defiled her body before marriage, after he had commended him unto her for a husband, and she resolved to have him, when he came to her in that private way. The circumstances I forbear, for they would offend chaste ears to hear them related (for though he satisfied his lust on her, yet he endeavoured to hinder conception.) These things being thus discovered, the woman's husband took some godly friends with him to deal with Lyford for this evil; at length he confessed it with a great deal of seeming sorrow and repentance, but was forced to leave Ireland upon it, partly for shame and partly for fear of further punishment.

When this story came out, Winslow commented that Lyford had acted "knavishly"—a moderate comment: but Lyford's supporters picked it up and accused Winslow of calling the minister a knave. They threatened to summon Winslow before the court for slander. The colony resounded with gossip and rumor, and, to settle the matter simply, once and for all, witnesses were called and asked to testify on the question of Lyford's personal conduct, details of which, Bradford said, he was ashamed to relate. But the testimony was quite deadly enough from the witnesses,

> whose persons were so grave and evidence so plain and the facts so foul, yet delivered in such modest and chaste terms and with such circumstances as struck all his friends mute, and made them all ashamed. Insomuch as the moderators with great gravity declared that the former matters gave them cause enough to refuse him and to deal with him as they had done; but these made him unmeet for ever to bear ministry any more, what repentance soever he should pretend; with much more to the like effect, and so wished his friends to rest quiet.

This was conclusive. The Lyfords were asked to leave.

· 8 ·

They were still lingering in Plymouth when Mad Jack Oldham reappeared. He had been up to Nantasket on Boston Bay, taking with him several other malcontents as well as the capable Roger Conant, former salter of London, later founder of Salem, and the William Hiltons, who, with brother Edward Hilton, went on to the Piscataqua River, joining a Scottish trader named David Thompson. William and Edward also founded a town: Dover, New Hampshire.

Oldham was still explosively quarreling as vigorously as ever, and efforts to calm him only made him worse. Again he was locked up in the fort before being forcibly expelled. Standish lined up his troops in two long rows leading down to Oldham's shallop on the shore, and sent Mad Jack to run the gauntlet. As he went by each gave him "a bob upon the bum and a thump on the breech" with the butt of a musket, and, when he stumbled on board the shallop, told him to go and mend his manners. This hearty treatment, coming after the imposing trial, persuaded many independents to join the church, which seemed naturally to Bradford yet one more example of the providence of God.

Oldham went off to the salt-pan site at Cape Ann, where the Pilgrims had built a crude wharf in the spring. It was, they hoped, the starting place of a fishing station, but the captain of the first vessel they sent there did little but "drink and guzzle, and consume away the time and his victuals." Lyford went to Cape Ann too, and so did Conant, who acted as governor. Standish found this out when in the spring of 1625 he went up to Cape Ann to see how it might be developed further. His rage at seeing his two old adversaries there was immense: he sailed straight in and peremptorily demanded surrender. The men on the wharf piled up a barricade of barrels and laughed at him, saying that in that place the Pilgrim charter was valueless. Before Standish could blast away at them with shot as well as words, Conant and William Peirce intervened, and a compromise was with some difficulty arranged, whereby Conant's men might keep their wharf if they helped the Pilgrims to build another. Within a year Conant's men had moved fifteen miles back along the coast to Naumkeag, which in time became Salem. Oldham did well, expanding trade and growing prosperous. Later he was forgiven in Plymouth and was allowed to come and go and speak to whom he wished, as it suited him. But they never forgave Lyford, who stayed as minister in Salem until 1628, when the new wave of Puritan settlers caused him to think of trying his luck elsewhere. He selected Virginia, where he lived for the remaining year or so of his life.

His work in Plymouth had an effect, though. When the letters (though intercepted, they had been copied and sent on) of expostulation and denial, of accusation, defense, and counteraccusation reached London, many of the Adventurers declared themselves quit of the Plantation, and even the best disposed were exasperated. There was no smoke without fire. Something must be seriously wrong. Their original idea, of settling a colony that would pay its way and make a little profit for those who had invested generously in it, seemed to have disappeared under a squabble about doctrine. Some of this feeling came over in a letter signed by James Sherley, William Collier, and Thomas Brewer. The Pilgrims were contentious, cruel, hardhearted to any who disagreed with them, negligent, careless, wasteful, and thriftless, spending their time in "idleness and talking and conferring, and care not what be wasted, worn, and torn out." They had dissembled on the question of their beliefs and practices with the Adventurers and with the King. The Adventurers wondered whether they might not offend God "in building up such a people." To save "your lives and our monies" they must lay down fresh conditions, giving themselves a voice in colonial government, insisting that the Pilgrims should follow the tenets of the French Reformed Church as they had originally been willing to do, and Robinson and his other followers in Leyden could not come to Plymouth unless "he and they will reconcile themselves to our church by a recantation under their own hands."

Bradford and his assistants worriedly debated this disturbing letter. They decided to say nothing about the conditions until they could send over someone to speak in person, but they denied emphatically that there had been any dissembling. It was tyranny to force them to submit to other principles in every detail. The French, he said, could be in error, the Pilgrims could be in error for that matter, any church could be mistaken at times:

> It is too great arrogancy for any man or any church to think that he or they have sounded the word of God to the bottom as precisely to set down the church's discipline so that no other without blame may digress or differ in anything from the same.

It was all very well, Bradford thought, for the Adventurers in

London to exhort the Pilgrims: "Go on, good friends, pluck up your spirits and quit yourselves like men"—an unnecessary comment; but they added that the Pilgrims' work was to the glory of God and better worth doing than wasting the plenty of cultivated land or eating the fruit of a grown tree, if they lived as long as Methuselah in doing so, meaning that it was better working for God in the wilderness than living on the profits in London. They even preached to the Pilgrims: "Walk close with God," they told them piously. "Walk circumspectly and carry yourselves so uprightly in all your ways, as that no man may make just exceptions against you."

The *Charity* and the *Little James* were now made ready to sail to England, loaded with cargo of fish and fur. Most of the fish was on the *Charity,* most of the fur on the *Little James.* Captain Peirce disliked this arrangement, preferring to have all the cargo under his eye, but Winslow said he was under contract to fill the smaller ship, which had to be sent as there was so much cargo. Standish, who was going over as a nonmember of the church to answer the Adventurers' questions in London, changed his mind at the last minute and decided to sail on the *Charity* rather than on the *Little James.* The larger ship towed the lesser, for company and safety, and made a good crossing until they reached the English Channel, where a heavy gale forced Peirce to cut the towline. A Turkish corsair popped up out of nowhere, seized the *Little James,* and sailed away with the prize to Sallee in Morocco, a nest of pirates and slavers until at least the time of the American Revolution. Everyone on board the *Little James* was sold in the slave market, and the beaver skins, set in Winslow's contract against a bond of five hundred pounds, fetched fourpence apiece. Nothing more was ever heard of the ship or the men she had carried, and even Bradford's faith faltered slightly as he made the comment in his journal:

Some thought this a hand of God for their too great exaction of the poor Plantation, but God's judgments are unsearchable, neither dare I be bold therewith. But, however, it shows us the uncertainty of all human things and what little cause there is of joying in them or trusting to them.

Standish, who had been warned to keep his temper, placate the Adventurers, ask for help in dealing with difficult people on both sides of the Atlantic, and affirm the Plantation's need for better supplies at lower prices, carried a letter from Bradford to Cushman. It said in part:

> We will never build houses, fence grounds, or plant fruits for those who not only forsake us but use us as enemies, loading us with reproach and contumely. Nay, we will rather ruin that which is done than that they should possess it. . . . Your son and all of us are in good health (blessed be God). He received the things you sent him. I hope God will make him a good man.

Bradford added that Oldham was rumored to have gone to England: if so, Cushman should beware of him, "for he is very malicious, and much threatens you." Billington was still heard grumbling about Cushman and threatening to have him arrested, Bradford did not know why, but Billington was "a knave, and so will live and die." He had often been in trouble: in 1622 Standish had "tied him neck and heels" for refusing to do military duty.

Standish did badly in London, but it was not his fault: one of the periodic outbreaks of plague had paralyzed business in parts of the city. He heard that the self-seeking James Sherley and the other Adventurers were deep in financial difficulties because of the loss of the *Little James*. But the worst thing was that death had struck three times, each of them a blow to the Pilgrims in varying degrees. The King was dead, and his heir, now Charles I, was known to hold stiffer views on the divine right of kings and to stand closer to the perilous brink of Catholicism than his father had ever admitted. Robert Cushman, the Pilgrims' right hand in their dealings with the Adventurers, "the stay and life of the whole business," had died of the plague. And John Robinson, the pastor of Leyden, was dead too.

He had fallen ill on Saturday, February 22, 1625, but had

insisted on preaching twice on Sunday. He seemed to have a continual inward ague, possibly pneumonia, and the medicines given him, though good, did nothing: he grew weaker each day, but felt no pain and remained conscious until he died on March 1. He was not yet fifty. On March 5 he was buried in the Pieterskerk, across the street from the Green Door.

"If either prayers, tears, or means would have saved his life, he had not gone hence," the sorrowing flock reported from Leyden.* All the Pilgrims in Holland and America felt this loss as the cruelest they had to suffer. Especially did it strike in Plymouth, where the worst days had been made more endurable by the thought that their dear pastor would join them one day, bringing his calm faith, comforting assurance, and good sense. It was hard to tell whether he had been happier in his followers than they in him: each felt so much respect and affection for the other. Now that he was gone, they could truly realize what a source of strength they had lost.

Robinson's death was reported in a letter signed by Roger White of Leyden and dated April 28. In it, White commented on the death of James I, optimistically said there was "great hope" of the new king, and said that the Dutch Stadtholder had died too: "Here they have lost the old prince, Grave Maurice . . . they have made Prince Hendrick general in his brother's place." Bradford's words were simple and oddly moving:

> Thus these two great princes, and their pastor, left this world near about one time. Death makes no difference.

• 9 •

Standish brought all this news back, along with the information that he had borrowed, after a good deal of trouble, a hundred and fifty

*Appendix 3.

pounds in London, at 50 per cent interest, and had spent a lot of it in expenses. Bradford contented himself with remarking that in business matters the captain was not skillful.

The Plantation now faced the clear duty of bracing itself to the task of establishment afresh, in order to place itself financially secure and clear of debt and even beginning to show a profit. "They gathered up their spirits and the Lord so helped them, Whose work they had in hand, as now when they were lowest they began to rise again." All trade must be encouraged to show dividends. One growing venture was the fur trade.

The good ship's carpenter had built two shallops and a lighter, but working alone had not finished the two ketches when he died; Bradford called upon "an ingenious man that was a house carpenter" and asked him to do what he could. He took the biggest shallop, cut it in two, set in a new middle section five or six feet long, strengthened all the timbers, laid a deck, and created a vessel with a thirty-two-foot keel and a hold five and a half feet deep, promising sails and wooden anchors by the next year. The Plantation got seven years' good service out of it.

Tendrils of development were spreading as the Pilgrims set up the Aptucxet trading post at Manomet. It shortened the journey south, as a brief overland crossing from Buzzard's Bay to Cape Cod Bay was now easy. A few settlers built a house on the creek, planted corn, reared pigs, and were always ready to take their boat out for trading to good effect and profit.

By now, tiny scattered settlements existed in various places along the coast and on the rivers. Some of the settlers added to Plymouth's difficulties by undercutting: "they went and filled the Indians with corn and beat down the price," forcing the Pilgrims to carry bigger trading loads of corn to make any sort of profit.

Extra supplies came unexpectedly. A merchant of Plymouth in Devon had started a small plantation at Monhegan as a fishing station. His name was Abraham Jenness, and he did not prosper. Two Adventurers, Robert Aldworth and Giles Elbridge, both of Bristol, sent a planter called Abraham Shurt to take over the management from the failing Jenness and perhaps even sell out. Rumors of a bargain day at Monhegan caused Bradford and Winslow to take a boat and some men and go along to see what they could pick up. David Thompson arrived from Piscataqua for the same purpose and the proprietors, seeing competition, raised their prices and requested a package deal—all or nothing. Very sensibly Bradford, Winslow, and Thompson closed together and halved the stocks, so that what fell to the Pilgrims' share was "a parcel of goats" and corn worth in all over four hundred pounds.

In the spring of 1626 a French ship was wrecked on the lower reaches of the Kennebec River and the contents sold off. Bradford, Winslow, Thompson, and some fishermen from Damaris Cove bought up the cargo, paying for it in beaver, and the Plymouth Plantation was richer by more than five hundred pounds' worth of goods of all kinds, the largest consignment of which was Biscay rugs.

The Pilgrims now had plenty of trading goods, mainly fabrics, and were able to expand the Indian trade steadily. They were in a position to pay off Standish's debt, and they prepared a good cargo of beaver to send to London. Along with it they sent as business manager and emissary Isaac Allerton.

Allerton had recently married Fear Brewster, the Elder's younger daughter, now twenty, who had acquired three stepchildren as well as a husband. When he sailed off for London, Allerton carried with him a formally drawn-up statement, signed and sealed by the Council, giving him authority to represent the Plantation in all business dealings with the Adventurers. It was the first of many such voyages that this enterprising, self-seeking, incredibly rash man was to make on behalf of the colony, and his briefing included orders to reach some kind of understanding with the Adventurers on the claims and rights of both sides. All along he had been one of the principal organizers. He had offered to go and they had agreed. The Pilgrims did not realize (perhaps Allerton did not either) just how great a problem he was going to be to them.

He was empowered to borrow one hundred pounds, but not

more, and he was to do nothing drastic without consulting the Pilgrims.

Allerton's actions revealed the shape of things to come to anyone with the hindsight provided by three centuries. He returned to Plymouth in the spring of 1627, bringing a cargo of useful supplies and the information that he had borrowed two hundred pounds at 30 per cent. He also carried a provisional agreement from the Adventurers, which the Council seized upon and studied with the most eager attention.

· 10 ·

The draft agreement, worked out in principle on October 26, 1626, and signed on November 15, fixed the sum of £1800 to buy out the Adventurers. Payment was to be made

> at the place appointed for the receipts of money, on the west side of the Royal Exchange in London; by £200 yearly, and every year on the feast of St Michael, the first payment to be made Anno 1628.

The Adventurer signatories were John Pocock and Robert Keayne, both of whom would be members of the Bay Company two years later. Keayne, who became a prominent Boston merchant, was often in trouble with the authorities for profiteering.

The leading Pilgrims liked the scheme, although the commitment was heavy and they already had considerable financial burdens, and pledged themselves to meet the payments with a promise of thirty shillings a week each if they "missed the time." The contract was engrossed on parchment and formally signed.

In consequence of this, the Pilgrims set their own house in order. From the first they had wished for a systematic settlement and distribution of the property. What Bradford called "some untoward persons" had mixed with the original Separatists. They always had two sorts of members—general and particular. General were mostly Pilgrims plus a few loyal others like Miles Standish; particulars had come along with the rest but wanted to make their own way outside the settlement. Some had professed sympathy with the Pilgrims at first, but as time went on their true nature showed as not the kind of people the Pilgrims found easy to get on with. The best plan clearly was a fresh, specific shareholding. This was the 1627 agreement, whereby all heads of families and all single young men held shares, calculated on a strict per capita basis. A man with a wife and three children held five shares. A single man held one. Cattle, few in number, were entered as one cow to six people; goats, one to three people; pigs in similar proportion. Land was allocated at twenty acres each, not counting the single lots already in use. The allotment was entirely orderly: from one side of the town to the other, along the waterside, all tillable land was ruled off into pieces, five acres wide along the water and four deep. Those whose land came nearest the town should choose the neighbors they liked best to farm next to them, planting corn together for four years. Every season all members were told where they should mow, according to the proportion of cattle they had. No meadows were laid out, as meadowland was scarce; and the untillable parts of the area were to remain as "refuse and common." The governor and four or five other leading citizens were given the houses they lived in; the rest were

> valued and equalized at an indifferent rate, and so every man kept
> his own and he that had a better allowed something to him that
> had a worse, as the valuation went.

Bradford recorded that now "all were content and settled in mind." The objects of the shareholding were manifestly to stabilize the plantation and keep it compactly unified. In this way, the settlers would have a defensible position against possible Indian attacks; they could keep up a strong community life, attend church, and watch out for stray sinners. This was for years a deeply felt need: as late as 1656 an order was sent to one Joseph Ramsden to move to a neighborhood place within the next four months or his house would be pulled down, as he had lived "long in the woods, in an uncivil way."

An interesting shipwreck took place that year. The *Sparrowhawk,* bound for Virginia with a full complement of passengers and goods, lost her way. The master had been ill on the voyage, able only to "lie in the cabin door and give direction," and his crew were none too bright at carrying out his orders. Also the passengers grew panicky and demanded land as soon as possible, no matter where. Supplies were dangerously low after six weeks at sea: they had even burned up the empty barrels in the cooking fire, had drunk up all the beer and water aboard and were down to the last couple of hogsheads of wine. Terrified at the specter of starvation and disease now haunting them, they clamored for a quick landing and found it in Manamoyick Bay, now Pleasant Bay, by the same inlet Bradford had used on his 1622 corn voyage. The *Sparrowhawk* ran up on Nauset Beach in the night, but the sea was calm and no one was hurt. Next evening, however, the wind sprang up so fiercely that it broke the anchor cable and forced the ship over the harbor bar, drenching passengers and cargo alike. They dried out next day, when to their alarm they saw Indians approaching. Fear turned to relief when the Indians greeted them in English, asking if they were the Plymouth governor's men or friends. They feasted the Indians as best they could, gave them presents, and sent two men with a letter to the governor asking for help and supplies.

Bradford took a boat and went in person. It was not the season of the year to sail outside Cape Cod, so he went around the inner coast, hugging the shore until he reached Namskaket Creek, just over two miles overland from the *Sparrowhawk.* The Indians helped to carry the supplies over, and the governor left the passengers feeling much happier. Soon after, however, a great storm broke the ship to pieces, so the passengers asked for shelter in Plymouth, and the Pilgrims distributed them and their belongings among themselves as best they could.

For some reason imperfectly understood for generations, the

spot where the *Sparrowhawk* had settled on Nauset Beach was known as "the Old Ship." The mystery cleared in May 1863 when a storm shifted the sands to reveal the bones of a ketch-rigged vessel forty feet long. There is no doubt that this was the *Sparrowhawk*.

The majority of the *Sparrowhawk's* passengers were Irish servants, who worked energetically in the fields and raised a lot of corn. One passenger was Captain John Sibsey, who went eventually to settle in Norfolk County, Virginia, where he became a burgess and councillor. Another was a Mr. Fells, who had with him a maid-housekeeper suspected of being his mistress. Both were questioned but would say nothing; then it became obvious that she was going to have a baby. Fells, aware that this could not be concealed, took a small boat and ran away with her. They reached Cape Ann but could not get a passage to Virginia from there, so they rather ignominiously returned to Plymouth from where the elders "packed them away as soon as possible" by boat, as soon as it could be arranged for a Virginia destination. On Nauset Beach is a piece of land traditionally known as Slut's Bush, where Professor Morison suggests Fells and his girl may have camped. Along with them, the Pilgrims also packed away others "being many untoward people amongst them," though some, of course, "carried themselves very orderly." After good trading in things the Pilgrims needed, cloth, hose, and shoes, a couple of ships took the *Sparrowhawk* passengers off at the end of the summer, "and sundry of them have acknowledged their thankfulness since from Virginia."

Another complimentary letter arrived in March 1627. This was written on Manhattan Island, "in the fort Amsterdam," from Isaac de Rasières, the secretary to the governor Peter Minuit and Council, and opened (in Dutch) in a very stately fashion.

> Noble, worshipful, wise and prudent Lords, the Governor and Councillors residing in New Plymouth, our very dear friends: the Director and Council of New Netherland wish to your Lordships, worshipful, wise, and prudent, happiness in Christ Jesus our Lord, with prosperity and wealth, in soul and body.

Bradford, copying this into his journal, wrote somewhat austerely: "the rest I shall render in English, leaving out the repetition of superfluous titles."

Mynheer de Rasières congratulated the Pilgrims on having made such a good beginning, as the Dutch had had for a year now in New Amsterdam. Both mother countries were old friends and allies against the wickedness of Spain. The two colonies were not all that far apart. They could trade, if and when one had goods that the other would gladly buy. Had they at the moment any beaver or otter to sell for ready money?

Ten days later, on March 19, Bradford replied, excusing his imperfect Dutch. The Pilgrims were delighted with the friendly communication from New Amsterdam. Indeed it was good to know of the new alliance against Spanish encroachment. The people of Plymouth had every reason to feel affection for the Dutch who had sheltered many of them for so long. The trading offer was most acceptable. They did not need anything particular this year, but would be happy to deal later if the prices were reasonable. What rate would they think proper for the furs? And what of the other goods—tobacco, fish, corn—how much would they like and how much would they pay?

In due course de Rasières came to see for himself. Arriving in October at Aptucxet with a well-turned-out retinue and a flourish of trumpets, he asked for a boat to take him on to the colony. A portly man, he did not care for the idea of walking twenty miles, saying that his feet would give out if he tried it. A shallop came down from Plymouth and formally took the secretary off the *Nassau,* brought him to the Plantation and set him ashore on the quay at the mouth of the Town Brook. To him we owe that priceless thing: a firsthand description of Plymouth as it impressed a reasonably impartial outsider of intelligence.

He had a good look at everything—at the main street a cannon shot long, with the governor's house at the central crossroads where the four small *Mayflower* guns were mounted, one facing each way; at the houses and fences of hewn planks, "so that their houses and courtyards are arranged in very good order"; at the palisade with its three gates; at the fish traps and eel pots; at the method of planting corn.

> Their farms are not as good as ours, because they are more stony, and consequently not so suitable for the plough. They apportion their land according as each has means to contribute to the eighteen thousand guilders which they have promised to those who sent them out, whereby they have their freedom without rendering an account to any one.

He commented on the abundance of fish, far more prodigal than at Manhattan.

De Rasières was particularly impressed by the way the Pilgrims went to church. It was emphatically a Church Militant, and was to remain so for more than half a century. The Pilgrims walked to the meetinghouse with a gun in one hand and a Bible in the other, reminding the reader more than ever of their resemblance to the Dutch Boers who were to begin settling in South Africa twenty-five years later.

On Sundays and on lecture days, which were more often than not on a Thursday, the families assembled by beat of drum, each man with his musket, in front of Standish's house at the foot of the hill leading up to the fort. All had their neatest cloaks on. A sergeant (by which one assumes de Rasières meant the officer of one of the four companies) led the way up the slope, followed by the governor in a long robe. On Bradford's right walked Brewster, on his left Standish with his sidearms and a small cane in his hand, and behind came the rest of the men, three abreast, in good order, with the women and children bringing up the rear. In church each man carefully placed his weapon close at hand, where he could snatch it up easily.

De Rasières presented Bradford with some Dutch clothes of good quality, some linen, and a chest full of white sugar, for which Bradford gave him tobacco in return. The visitor also produced strings of wampum, but the Council raised their eyebrows when they heard that the Dutch expected to get five shillings for five yards of it. On the whole, however, the meeting was a great success and led to subsequent trade. It was also pleasant to be reminded of the years in Leyden by the Dutch gossip of their guest, and de Rasières enjoyed himself, sending Bradford a courteous thank-you letter when he departed.

Isaac Allerton, sailing for England again at the end of May in the *Marmaduke* with her master John Gibbs, carried with him a copy of what came to be known as the Undertakers' Agreement, developed from the charter of the previous year. It named as parties the colony of New Plymouth, represented by Bradford, Standish, Winslow, Brewster, John Howland, John Alden, Thomas Prence, and Allerton himself, and the London Associates, represented by Sherley, John Beauchamp, Richard Andrews, and Timothy Hatherley. Signed in July 1627, it stated that the colony undertook to pay all debts, keep the pinnace, the Aptucxet boat, the shallop or bass boat, and all implements, plus the whole stock of furs amd skins, corn, beads, and wampum. All trade from the end of September would be carried on by the colony alone, and each member would pay annually into the common stock three bushels of corn or six pounds of tobacco. Every year London would send fifty pounds' worth of shoes and stockings to be paid for in corn at six shillings a bushel. At the end of six years, all corn trade would revert to the colony as before. The aim of this undertaking was to be able to make enough money to bring over the rest of the diminished Leyden congregation.

The appointed London agents to mediate between the Adventurers and the Pilgrims were Beauchamp, salter and citizen, and Sherley, goldsmith—what today would be called a private banker. It was not the happiest of choices. Judging by his letters, Sherley was a mean-spirited crawler, seemingly humble but really feathering his own nest. He did in fact charge 30 per cent interest to the Pilgrims for money borrowed from the Adventurers. What with him and the rash Allerton, writing soothing letters and using their ostensible humility or charm to cover up the fact that they were never sending any precise accounts, the Plantation struggled for years against unnecessary financial difficulties. Sherley never sent any exact financial statements showing Plymouth the Adventurers' balance —Allerton did the same to Sherley in reverse—both told the tale to each group so that they could make personal profits. With more honest agents, New Plymouth would have shown itself one of the richest of all colonies.

Sherley suffered from indifferent health. As a safeguard, he asked John Beauchamp to assist him as well as to assist Allerton. He explained this in a particularly sycophantic letter* to Bradford, written in London on November 17, 1628:

> . . . and wherein I fail, blame yourselves that you made no better choice. Now, because I am sickly, and we are all mortal, I have advised Mr Allerton to join Mr Beauchamp and me in your deputation, which I conceive to be very necessary and good for you. Your charge shall be no more, for it is not your salary makes me undertake your business . . .

The following day the Undertakers' Agreement was drawn up afresh and sealed. Allerton returned to the Plantation bringing goods valued at £232: shoes, leather, cloth, Irish stockings, rugs (which in the invoice were spelled rudge), pitch, tar, ropes and twine, knives, scissors, lead, powder and shot, hatchets, hoes, axes, scythes, reaping hooks, shovels and spades, saws, files, nails, iron pots, and a supply of drugs and spices.

Considerable profit came to the Pilgrims from the trade in wampum. Throughout the colonial period this was written down as wampumpeag, often abbreviated to peag. Wampum was shell money. The shells of certain kinds of clam, whelk, and periwinkle were polished, cut, and holed so that they could be strung together and the strings linked into strips or belts. The different-colored shells made beautiful patterns. Throughout the seventeenth century, wampum was accepted as legal tender in New England; the

*Appendix 3.

Indians of Massachusetts Bay did not possess much of it, but the Pequot and Narragansett Indians had a great deal. At first the English did not realize its value, but in 1628 the Pilgrims bought a quantity for which they paid fifty pounds. Bradford thought it might prove a drug on the market in time, though just then it was "very vendible" especially at Fort Orange, the original settlement of the New York State capital, Albany. The real trouble was that the wampum money helped the Indians to buy guns.

The Indians were assisted in this dangerous trade in another way, too. This was by one Thomas Morton, who for a considerable time proved a great nuisance to the Plymouth settlers.

Some three or four years before, a small party had arrived in New England to start a plantation of their own near Plymouth. They included half a dozen men "of some eminency," among them one Captain Wollaston, and Morton, who had been a lawyer of Clifford's Inn with an alarming tendency to get into fights as well as lawsuits and who might be described as having left his country for his country's good. The plantation had not prospered, so Wollaston decided to dismiss some of his assistants and find them employment elsewhere. He left one Lieutenant Fitcher in charge while he and a companion named Rasdall went off to organize the transfer. Morton, who was never treated with much respect by any of the assistants, seized the opportunity to give a party for them with "strong drink and other junkets." When they were all, in his opinion, sufficiently elevated, he made a speech. "I'm going to give you some advice," he told them. "You know that the others have been sent away to Virginia. If you stay here till this Rasdall gets back, you'll be sent away too—sold into slavery like the rest of them. What I say you ought to do is get rid of this Lieutenant Fitcher. Then I, as a shareholder, will take you in as partners and associates. In that way you'll be free men, and we can all live together as equals, planting and trading and helping and protecting one another."

This egalitarian address was well received. The inflamed assistants promptly ran the unfortunate Fitcher out of the plantation and refused to have anything more to do with him. He wandered off toward the nearest settlement, where he had to ask for food and shelter, and led a most uncomfortable existence on the charity of others until he managed to get passage back to England.

Morton's newly promoted partners now turned life into one long party. Wine, women, and song, financed by Indian trading, went on for days at a stretch, with Morton as Lord of Misrule. At times, ten pounds' worth of wines and spirits was consumed in a morning. Indian women and girls were brought in, and Morton set up a maypole, around which they all danced together. He composed songs and verses, some of them simply drinking songs, such as this one:

> Make green garlands, bring bottles out,
> And fill sweet Nectar freely about.
> Uncover thy head and fear no harm,
> For here's good liquor to keep it warm.
> Give to the nymph that's free from scorn
> No Irish stuff nor Scotch over-worn.
> Lasses in beaver coats, come away,
> Ye shall be welcome to us night and day.
> Then drink and be merry, merry, merry boys,
> Let all your delight be in Hymen's joys;
> Io! to Hymen, now the day is come,
> About the merry May-pole take a room.

In this really quite innocuous doggerel, pleasantly reminiscent of the works of William McGonagall, the Irish and Scotch stuff meant merely woolen cloth.

Bradford, naturally, disapproved of these goings-on, and declared that Morton was setting up a School of Atheism, "as if they had anew revived and celebrated the feasts of the Roman goddess Flora, or the beastly practices of the mad Bacchanalians." They had even changed the name of the place: from the perfectly acceptable Mount Wollaston it was now the shocking Merrymount. They were behaving, said Bradford, as if all this jollity was going on forever.

It was not. There arrived shortly in the Bay Colony a worthy and serious gentleman, John Endecott, who had brought with him a patent "under the broad seal" for the government of the Massachusetts region. He traveled all over the territory, and when he reached Merrymount he put a stop to the high jinks at once. He ordered the maypole to be taken down, and sternly rebuked Morton and his mob of revelers, admonishing them severely and telling them to behave properly in the future. He and his companions changed the name again, from Merrymount to the classical and unexceptionable Mount Dagon.

Morton, naturally, was furious at all this, and took his revenge in a way that was deadly enough to make the Bay authorities wish they had let him alone. He introduced the Indians to the pleasures and risks of shooting. The way to load and discharge a musket, the correct proportions of powder and ball, the right shot for fowl and for deer: he gave instruction thoroughly in all these. The Indians of course went mad about guns, thinking their bows and arrows were toys in comparison. Morton therefore arranged to supply guns to them. When lead was so scarce in the colony that it fetched as much as fourpence a pound, Morton, who had been stockpiling, sold it at a shilling a pound, over three times the price, to the Indians, who were so keen to have it that they were willing to pay wild amounts like three or four shillings a pound for it. In the end they were (at least in Morton's locality) better equipped with guns than the English. In an uncharacteristic rush of passionate indignation Bradford burst out:

> O, the horribleness of this villainy! Governments should pass
> laws and take measures to stop it. Barbarous savages armed with
> our own weapons supplied by traitors could destroy the Colony.

Morton sold the Indians all the guns he could spare from his own supply, to the understandable terror of those English settlers living in the smaller and more isolated clusters. Realizing that they could expect to keep no loyal servants and that "all the scum of the country or any discontents" would flock to Morton, and hearing that he was planning to get more guns sent from England, a number of men from the scattered plantations appealed to Plymouth for help. This nest of evil, they said, must be broken up.

A kind of United Settlements command was set up under the most suitable officer, Captain Standish. Contributions flowed in from all over: Roger Conant and friends at Salem sent one pound ten shillings, Mr. Jeffrey and Mr. Burslem, having another try at Wessagusset, sent two pounds, Mr. Edward Hilton at Dover sent one pound, Mr. William Blackstone of the future Boston sent twelve shillings, and a widow, Mrs. Thompson of Thompson's Island in Boston Harbor, sent fifteen shillings. Plymouth and Piscataqua Plantations each put up two pounds ten.

While the money was coming in and the expedition getting ready, the Pilgrims decided to try persuasion. They sent a letter of friendly advice to Morton, to which he paid not the slightest attention. They wrote again, a little more severely this time, threatening Morton with the King's displeasure. Morton replied flatly that the King was dead, and his displeasure with him, and anyone coming near Merrymount should look out for trouble because he would certainly get it.

Morton never disguised his amused contempt for the earnest and church-centered Pilgrims. He had observed their methods and forms of worship, and, in spite of his claims to hold libertarian views, objected to the preaching of every Tom, Dick, and Harry who cared to take part:

The Church of the Separatists is governed by Pastors, Elders and Deacons, and there is not any of these, though he be but a cow keeper, but is allowed to exercise his gifts in the public assembly on the Lord's Day, so as he do not make use of any notes for the help of his memory, for such things, they say, smell of lamp oil, and there must be no such unsavoury perfume admitted to come into the congregation.

He had enjoyed writing about a meeting in Plymouth, reporting with malicious joy the way in which men of plain trades revealed their work in their words. One, like a grocer, weighed everything; a tailor of "more cutting disposition" begged the assembly to wear close-fitting religious garments of a suitable fashion for Christians; a tapster filled the cup of repentance; a cobbler urged his hearers to mend their ways and walk upright in the paths of righteousness; and one—"doubtless his father was some Irish footman"—took up a text and ran away with it so fast that no one present could follow him. He had fun inventing witty names, too, so that Endecott of Salem became Captain Littleworth, John Winthrop, the great governor of Massachusetts, was Joshua Temperwell, and the red-faced, red-haired little Standish was Captain Shrimp.

Suitably warned, the expedition, nine men strong, set out for Merrymount. Morton was ready for them. He had barred his doors, armed his men, set powder and bullets in dishes on the table, and primed the whole party with drink. Standish shouted a request to yield; Morton hooted defiance and insults in reply. Standish stationed his men at attack points around the house: this brought Morton and his defenders out, not to surrender but to start shooting. The drink had been too effective, however: the guns proved unaccountably heavy and Morton's men could hardly lift them. Morton himself, waving a loaded carbine, yelled threats at Standish, who, not in the least discomposed, walked up to him, pushed the carbine calmly aside, and made his arrest. No one was hurt (though Bradford admitted many might have been had Morton not over-armed his men with strong waters), except for one of the Merrymount defenders, who, as he lurched back into the house, ran his own nose upon the point of a sword held by one of Standish's troopers; "he lost but a little of his hot blood."

Morton's own account of this fracas, written later, was naturally rather different. He said that Captain Shrimp had come with his eight supporters within range like "a flock of wild geese, as if they had been tailed one to another, as colts to be sold at a fair," and threatened him with a pistol. Matters might have been really quite nasty, he said, had not "mine Host" generously yielded in order to avoid bloodshed.

Morton, taken to Plymouth, was kept there in custody of sorts until the next ship sailed for England. At first he was under a kind of house arrest, then spent some uncomfortable days on the Isle of Shoals, from which the ship sailed. He was, in fact, deported. Captain Shrimp, that quondam drummer, he wrote, had callously marooned him on the isle "without gun, powder or shot or dog or so much as a knife to get anything to feed upon or any other clothes to shelter him with, at winter, than a thin suit." Along with Morton on the ship the Pilgrims sent not only a full statement of what had happened but also a trustworthy member of the colony to give details in person in London.

This was not the only trouble the Plantation had that year. Allerton, returning from his journey to England, brought back a new minister to replace the unsatisfactory Lyford. This was one Rogers, and it was clear from the start that all was not as it should be. The poor fellow was out of his mind. The Pilgrims, Bradford wrote, "perceived upon some trial that he was crazed in his brain." He was sent back the following year, having caused them much bother and expense—he had needed provisions, clothes, and bedding as well as the cost of his passage—and they felt irritated with Allerton for adding that much more to their considerable burdens.

That was not all Allerton had done. On his previous trip he had brought over some supplies which he sold privately, a thing no other colonist had so far thought of. They had let it pass because he had (apparently) worked hard for them and they did not want to seem difficult. But this year he did it again, mixing his own stuff with theirs in the cargo so that no one knew what belonged to whom. If there had been a shipwreck the Plantation would have borne the whole cost. "Love thinks no evil nor is suspicious," said Bradford, and the elders agreed to let him go again in spite of Rogers and the cargo. They warned Allerton this time. He was to bring back fifty pounds' worth of shoes, hose, and linen, no goods for private sale, to mark the Pilgrims' stuff separately and not mix it with other cargo, to be sure to send it off promptly, not exceed instructions, and run up no further charges. Allerton agreed charmingly to these conditions.

· 11 ·

By July 1623, 233 men, women, and children had been brought to the colony of New Plymouth. By December of the same year 183 of them were still alive. Some recruits rose to eminence who came, as a trickle did come, over the rest of the decade. One such was Thomas Willet, son of an English clergyman, who crossed in 1629 aged twenty-four and eventually became one of Plymouth's leading citizens. In 1664 he went with the local expeditionary force that took New Amsterdam from the Dutch, and Governor Nicholls appointed him first English mayor of New York. He returned to Plymouth, where he died in 1674.

Willet was one of the last settlers to reach Plymouth before the mass immigration at Massachusetts Bay outnumbered the first settlement once and for all. On Easter Monday, 1629, a fleet of eight ships sailed from Cowes on the Isle of Wight opposite Southampton, carrying over nine hundred people to the new Bay Colony. They had a charter entitling them to open up and settle the valleys of the Merrimac and Charles Rivers with wide self-governing powers. The farewell sermon in the port of departure was preached by John Cotton, who himself was to emigrate to Boston two years later, and was published as *God's Promise to His Plantation*.

The principal ship was the *Arabella*, 350 tons, with a crew of fifty-two and mounting twenty-eight guns, and carrying the future leaders of Massachusetts, including Thomas Dudley, then fifty-three. Like Ferdinando Gorges, Dudley had served as a young man with the army of Henry of Navarre. Overbearing and dogmatic, he lived to be four times governor and thirteen times deputy governor of the Bay Colony, one of the first governors of Harvard, and the father of a brilliantly controversial daughter, Anne Hutchinson. He fathered his last child at the age of seventy.

The other ships were the *Charles,* the *William and Francis,* the *Hopewell,* the *Success,* the *Trial,* the *Whale,* and the *Mayflower.* Although the *Mayflower* belonged to Thomas Goffe, and Dr. Rendel Harris exerted himself to explain that it was the Pilgrim ship, there seems no doubt that it was another of the many bearing the same name. On board was young Henry Winthrop. Henry's father John, newly elected governor of Massachusetts, was sailing on the *Arabella,* and he in his turn preached a sermon. Sermons were always prominent among shipboard activities if the weather permitted: they helped to pass the time and to weld the passengers closer together, and, of course, propitiated the Almighty. Winthrop's sermon sounded the keynote of the American sense of special destiny. It included a famous sentence:

> We shall be as a City upon a hill, the eyes of all people are upon us; so that if we shall deal falsely with our God in this work we have undertaken and so cause Him to withdraw His present help from us, we shall be made a story and a byword through the world.

Cotton Mather later described this sermon as an example of

> the wonders of the Christian Religion, flying from the deprivations of Europe to the American Strand ... wherewith His Divine Providence hath irradiated an Indian wilderness.

The Winthrop family produced a number of distinguished scholars, one of them, John Winthrop IV, born in 1714 and living until 1779 so that he saw the American Revolution, the most accomplished astronomer America had so far seen.

Waiting for the newcomers on the other side of the ocean was the sternly redoubtable John Endecott, founder of Salem the year before, who was to cooperate with Winthrop and with Bradford in various colonial crises. Winthrop it was who named the first sizable ship built in New England. In 1631 the thirty-ton vessel was launched at Mystic and called *The Blessing of the Bay*. The date was neatly symbolic: it was the fourth of July.

There was a distinctly Separatist flavor about the Bay Colony, although its members were Puritans. This was made explicit in 1647 by Nathaniel Ward, writing in a work rather archly entitled *The Simple Cobbler of Aggawam*.

> I dare take upon me, to be the Herald of New England so far, as to proclaim to the world, in the name of our Colony, that all Familists, Antinomians, Anabaptists, and other Enthusiasts, shall have free liberty to keep away from us, and such as will come to be gone just as fast as they can, the sooner the better.

· 12 ·

The year 1629 saw the beginning of the great Puritan migration to Massachusetts Bay and New England generally. It is not too much to say that they could never have done it as they did without the nine years' pioneering work put in, at such cost, by the *Mayflower* passengers.

One immensely cheering thing came out of this migration for the Plymouth Plantation: some more of the Leyden congregation arrived to join them.

It was a costly enterprise. Transported from Holland to England, kept there until the sailing date, provisioned and clothed, passages paid—the total cost well exceeded £500. The Reverend Francis Higginson of Salem commented that, at a rate of five pounds for each man, ten for each horse, and usually three for every ton of goods, it was "wondrous dear." Once landed at Salem the Leyden people had to be taken down to Plymouth and there looked after at the community's expense until they could harvest a crop, which could take as long as eighteen months. But no one grumbled: everyone was far too pleased to see their friends again. Thirty-five came in early May, arriving during August; others left in March 1630 and arrived in late May in the *Lion,* William Peirce master, crossing from Bristol to Salem. Allerton returned on that voyage. In Salem he borrowed the *Lion*'s shallop to sail down to Plymouth; en route on June 12 greetings passed between him and Governor Winthrop's flagship, the *Arabella,* off Cape Ann.

Allerton had been sent to London on that occasion to complete all details of the enlarged and confirmed patent for Plymouth and the new trading post on the Kennebec River. He returned leaving many loose ends still to be tied up. Almost certainly his idea was to make sure that he was sent over again. This annoyed the colony, but they were even more exasperated to find that he had brought Thomas Morton back with him. Apparently London had not thought any prohibitive action necessary. Allerton lodged Morton in his own house and gave him various pieces of secretarial work to do. Morton, however, did not wait long before falling right back into his old ways. He returned to Merrymount, refused to recognize the Bay Company authority, and started selling guns again to the Indians. It did not take long for him to provoke the Bay Company into getting rid of him, they hoped for good this time. They dug up an incident of suspected murder of an early settler, pinned the suspicion at least to Morton, and that, with the gun trade, gave them sufficient excuse to send him under arrest to England, where he was lodged in Exeter jail. They then pulled down his house, "that it might be no longer a roost for such unclean birds to nestle in."

Morton was not finished yet. He contrived his release, and wrote a book called *The New English Canaan,* which was published in 1637 in Amsterdam. It was a lively, spiteful, funny account, sparkling with high spirits, and revealing a genuine feeling for the country and the Indians. In it, Morton tried as hard as he could to slant English opinion against the Pilgrims. Having characteristically backed the wrong horse in the English Civil War, he incredibly showed up again in Plymouth in 1643. The kindhearted Bradford allowed him to board with one of the colonists for four shillings a week, but said he was to go as soon as the spring came. Winslow wrote an account of all this to Winthrop, telling him, among other things, that Morton must be sunk pretty low, as he was "content to drink water." Morton did leave in the spring, and went up to Maine, where he took up his gun trading once more. Eventually the law caught up with him, and he spent a winter in Boston jail. This finished him. His incorrigible spirit broke at last, and he died, "old and crazy," in 1647. He had had a good run for his money.

Allerton, not content with bringing Morton back, had not kept his word. He brought back a great variety of goods and sold privately as much as possible, delivering the rest to the Plymouth stores, and blaming the high cost on anybody or anything but himself—the Leyden passage, the patent deal, Sherley (who seemed willing to play along with him on that or any other point). One reason that the Pilgrims felt reluctant to antagonize Allerton was that in 1626 he had married Fear Brewster, and they did not want to hurt the gentle old elder.

Also on board the *Lion* was Edward Ashley, described by Bradford as a profane young man (one of his harshest terms of disapproval), who had been engaged by Allerton and Sherley to manage the new trading post on the Penobscot River, close to the present site of Castine. This new commitment, determined without a word to Plymouth, no doubt horrified the colony when Sherley's letter giving details of it arrived. Ashley's profanity showed when Bradford found out that he had

> for some time lived among the Indians as a savage and went naked amongst them and used their manners, in which time he got their language. So they [the Pilgrims] feared he might still run into evil courses (though he promised better) and God would not prosper his ways.

Penobscot was estimated as 240 miles from Plymouth, and the distance prevented a close watch on Ashley. When Ashley asked for supplies, the Pilgrims agreed, thinking that if they refused it might drive Ashley and Allerton into "laying their crafty wits together" to buy them elsewhere. As a precaution, however, they sent honest young Thomas Willet to Penobscot as an assistant.

Ashley soon showed his true colors. Well supplied (so well that the Pilgrims themselves ran short and had to buy extra from Allerton, who declared that he had borrowed money at 50 per cent in Bristol, which explained the prices he was charging), he wasted no time, quickly collecting a large stock of beaver. "Like a crafty pate, he sent it all home," wrote Bradford, "and would not pay for the goods he had of the Plantation here, but let them stand still on the score and took up still more." No one could trade without a boat, and Ashley suddenly remembered he hadn't got one; so the Pilgrims found that they had to buy him a boat as well and send it with its crew to transport corn and supplies to Penobscot. One maddening extra was that all through the spring of 1631 they expected a fishing ship in Plymouth; none came, but they heard that one had gone to Ashley.

This was by no means their only problem. It seemed as though there was a hoodoo on the Pilgrims' efforts to find a suitable minister. Late in 1629 they thought they had managed it, when Ralph Smith arrived with his wife and family in Massachusetts Bay. Educated at Christ's College, Cambridge, he was a Separatist by conviction. At first he and his family stayed among the scattered folk at Nantasket, but when the Plymouth boat put in there he asked for a passage to the Plantation, explaining, as Bradford put it, that he was "weary of being in that uncouth place and in a poor house that would neither keep him nor his goods dry," and that, he having been a minister, impulse had brought him to New England. He was met with the utmost kindness in Plymouth, comfortably housed and settled, with his servants and belongings fetched across from Nantasket. They thought him a grave and sincere man and made him their minister before the year was out, "yet he proved," said Bradford ruefully, "but a poor help to them in that, being of very weak parts."

That same year the colony had parted with Dr. Fuller. John Endecott wrote from Salem asking for help. Fever and scurvy, starting at sea, had broken out among the new arrivals, though curiously enough the Leyden people escaped: further proof that they were God's elect. The governor sent Dr. Fuller to Salem, and Endecott wrote his thanks on May 11, adding that he was glad to know that the Plymouth people were not so rigidly Separatist as he had feared. "We are members one of another," he said. He hoped to see them again soon. In time they heard from Fuller himself. He wrote on July 26, 1630, that Governor John Winthrop had reported a kind of plague with some deaths at Charlestown and was appointing the Friday of that week as a day of prayer to pacify the wrath of God; would the Pilgrims kindly do the same at Plymouth? To show official approval Edward Winslow wrote his signature below Fuller's, who reported on August 2 the formation by covenant of the first church at Boston. Its four original members were Winthrop, Isaac Johnson, Thomas Dudley, and John Wilson, but five more had quickly joined and membership was "likely increasing daily."

In September 1630 came the first execution in the colony, a most tragic occasion, particularly as it involved a *Mayflower* passenger. John Billington, the most consistent troublemaker in the colony, quarreled with a young man, John Newcomen, waylaid him in a wood where Newcomen hid behind a tree "perceiving the intent of this Billington," who shot him dead. He was at once arraigned for murder. Winthrop and the other ablest members of the Bay Colony were consulted as well as the Plymouth elders; both grand and petty juries found him guilty and all agreed regretfully that he must be hanged. This took place in September. Bradford recorded: "He and some of his had been often punished for miscarriages before, being one of the profanest families amongst them; they came from London, and I know not by what friends shuffled into their company."

• 13 •

Now began the complicated and troublesome business of the two ships *White Angel* and *Friendship*. It was never sorted out, either, at least to the historian's satisfaction: exactly who ended up owning these vessels is lost in mystery.

Allerton had sailed for New England from Bristol on December 1, 1630, arriving at Nantasket Roads on February 5, a journey as long as that of the *Mayflower*. He left again from Salem on April 1 and reached London just over four weeks later after a very quick passage. Sometime that autumn he set off again for New England, entering Boston Harbor on November 2, 1631. By the standards of the time he was almost commuting between the New World and the Old, but no doubt he believed his comings and goings were necessary, either to the colony and the Adventurers or to his own reputation and profit.

Between the two crossings he made in 1631, the *White Angel* and the *Friendship* arrived, anchoring in Massachusetts Bay on June 27 and July 14 respectively. The Pilgrims expected to hear news of Allerton's progress in London by letters carried on the *White Angel*, but when they found that no word had come from him, or from Sherley either, they decided they had better send Winslow over to England to discover what was happening. Before Winslow could be ready to leave Plymouth, however, the *Friendship* came in. She had sailed earlier than the other vessel but after eleven weeks of storms had been forced to put back to England for fresh supplies of food and drink, both seriously depleted after so long. She left Barnstaple in Devon in mid-May and made the crossing in eight weeks. On board was the Adventurer Timothy Hatherley, who had originally planned to cross in the *White Angel* but thought it best to stay with the *Friendship* after her ordeal. He brought for the colony's use two parcels of Barnstaple rugs and two big barrels of metheglin, a popular English drink not unlike mead, made from herbs cooked in honey and fermented. By the time he reached New

England only six gallons of the metheglin remained: in an appealing but unoriginal excuse the rest had been "drunk up under the name leakage."

Hatherley also brought a letter from Sherley, dated March 25. It was harder than usual to follow Sherley's drift, but he seemed to be informing the Pilgrims that the Adventurers had bought the *White Angel* for the colony's use in trading and bass fishing. Hatherley, said Sherley, had come over by the Adventurers' invitation as a kind of auxiliary to Allerton: "that if it should please God the one should fail (as God forbid) yet the other would keep both reckonings and things upright"—which could be taken to mean that Hatherley was no more dependable than Allerton had been, or that the Adventurers were beginning to see through Allerton at last.

The Pilgrims read Sherley's words with mounting consternation. The *Friendship* was full of other men's goods, with hardly anything for the colony, yet they had been led to expect a big consignment. No order had gone from Plymouth to London to buy a new ship—the Pilgrims would not have risked such extravagance just then—and no hint of such a purchase had arrived from London in advance. The ships' delay had created loss of trade: those eleven weeks would be hard to make good. The Pilgrims had not planned to fish for bass specifically: it was true that the striped bass of New England was prolific, easy to catch, and could be cured like mackerel—left in brine for several days, then sun-dried—but Europeans wanted only salt cod. Of course it might be possible to persuade them to buy bass, but that would take time. Worst of all, here was the additional expense of the ship on top of Sherley's statement that the colony's debts now totaled something between £1000 and £1500.

When Allerton eventually turned up, he made matters more involved than ever. Flatly contradicting what Sherley had written, he said that the *White Angel* did not belong to the Pilgrims, and its cost was not set to their account; they need have nothing to do with it unless they liked. It was *Friendship* they were really buying. *Friendship* had cost not much above £600 and a good part of that sum could easily be paid off in freight sent to England. He had already sold £400 worth of goods to the English merchants anyway, so only £200 remained before the ship was paid for. He had as usual brought back plenty of goods for the colony—linen, bed ticking, tape, stockings, rugs, pins—which he quickly sold among the colonists; then, regardless of the Pilgrim's misgivings, he went to the ship to see about the possibilities of bass fishing as a new source of profit, while Hatherley asked for a boat to take him on a tour of inspection along both the Kennebec and the Penobscot Rivers.

The Pilgrims, sorely troubled by two contradictory plans, both of which seemed certain to commit them still more deeply into debt, asked Hatherley to clarify the question for them. His reply made them more confused than ever. He explained that the original idea had been for the *White Angel* to bring one cargo over to New England, take a shipment of fish back, and then go on to Oporto, which he called Port of Porte, to be sold. She was, he said, a well-armed ship and had won an engagement; ship, goods, and ordnance would fetch a high price. The Pilgrims refused to commit themselves to any idea of selling the *White Angel* at that point, merely observing that the vessel might be very fine but her crew were a drunken, violent lot that neither Allerton nor anyone else could manage.

Several facts were clear to the Pilgrims. London believed whatever Allerton chose to tell them rather than any written reports from Plymouth, and were quite happy as long as all was going well, but the moment complications arose they were willing to let Plymouth shoulder the burden. If there were debts, the Pilgrims must sort them out. Allerton, Bradford uncomfortably realized, was out for private gain. Gradually the damaging truths came home to them: how Allerton had sometimes made as much as fifty pounds' personal profit on a cargo of beaver, how in his first two or three years as agent he had "cleaned up £400 and put it into a brew-house of Mr Collier's in London," and how his invoices, rare and belated though they were, had a way of charging things three times over, like one item of 100 Barnstaple rugs for £75 that appeared three times. One sum of £600 never did get satisfactorily explained. His accounts were

> folded up in obscurity and kept in the clouds, to the great loss and vexation of the Plantation, who in the end were (for peace sake) forced to bear the unjust burthen of them, to their almost undoing.

Allerton's accounts were so rambling and intricate that no one could understand them or even examine them properly, let alone audit them, unless he was there, and he was very good at dodging the issue and sounding plausible when he was present. At one stage he said the colony owed him £300, but when with enormous toil part of the account was sorted out it was apparent that he owed the colony over £2000. Much was obscure past sorting. Bradford was horrified to record finding "thirty pounds given at a clap, fifty spent in a journey." He noted sorrowfully that even Allerton's relations had not escaped: "Yea, he screwed up his poor old father-in-law's account to above £200 and put it on the general account." Everyone knew that the Pilgrims would never put pressure on Brewster, and that the unworldly old man would never suspect his son-in-law of deliberately cheating.

Sherley's eventual thunderclap, the account showing a Plymouth debt of £5770. 19s. 2d. (with the aforesaid treble charges appearing in it), provoked Bradford into further reproachful comment. At the end of 1628, he said, the Plantation had owed the Adventurers barely more than £400; now "into these deep sums [over fourteen times that total] had Mr Allerton run them in two years." He discovered deeper iniquities still: an attempt by Allerton to erase the figures given in one of Sherley's letters to the Plantation, which reads unnervingly like some comments printed about the affair of the Watergate tapes:

> And whereas in the year 1629 Mr Sherley and Mr Hatherley being at Bristol, and writ a large letter from thence in which they had given an account of the debts and what sums were then

disbursed, Mr Allerton never left begging and entreating of them till they had put it out. So they blotted out two lines in that letter in which the sums were contained, and writ upon it so as not a word could be perceived, as since by them was confessed, and by the letters may be seen. And thus were they [the Pilgrims] kept hoodwinked till now they were so deeply engaged.

Sherley had apparently asked Allerton to straighten out the whole question of the debts, even requesting Fear Brewster Allerton to use her influence, but Allerton had dictated most of the letters designed to keep the colony quiet and, when any Pilgrim referred him to the terms of their patent, which stated that money matters must be scrupulously explicit, had brushed such protests aside by saying that the patent "was but a pretence and not the thing"—in other words, it was important to decide everything in the light of what was actually going on at a given moment, not of the original terms laid down for the colony. He had certainly run the colony into its difficulties and intended to leave it there: "having brought them into the briars, he leaves them to get out as they can."

The whole affair of the debts dragged on for years, revealing fresh depths before it was finally sorted out, and carrying the unresolved issue of who owned which ship, if any, along with it as an additional irritant. As early as 1631 the Pilgrim leaders told Allerton they no longer wished him to act as their agent, but it was 1639 before the full extent of his dealings was known and 1641 before the financial complex was finally disentangled and wound up. In the matter of the ships, it seemed best to sort the facts out in front of impartial hearers, so in sworn statements before Governor Winthrop and Deputy Governor Dudley on August 29 and September 7, 1639, Hatherley and Allerton admitted what had happened, more or less.

The Pilgrims had suggested that another ship would be useful, saying this in a vague way, not expecting any prompt action from London as a result. The Adventurers, without a word of advice or warning to Plymouth, hired one, loaded her with cargo, and sent her to the bay. This was the *Friendship*. During the long interval between the hiring and the *White Angel's* departure, five men—Sherley, Hatherley, Allerton, Beauchamp, and Andrews—completed the purchase of the *Friendship* and planned to buy the *White Angel* as well. Hatherley drew back at this point, possibly suspecting shady dealing or at least an overheavy commitment of the colony: he was of course the only one of the five to settle in New England later. The other four met in a London tavern with a man called William Denison and arranged the purchase of the *White Angel*. They discussed all kinds of lucrative possibilities, such as developing bass fishing in the colony and selling one of the ships quickly in Oporto or one of the other Spanish or Portuguese ports. Allerton did the actual buying in Bristol, where he beat down the price, and it is tempting to speculate how much he managed to rake off for himself in doing so. What to do with either ship was still a matter of desultory discussion in London by the time Winslow arrived there on his 1632 visit to England, during which he explained to Sherley why it was difficult to make quick profits out of bass fishing just then. Sherley exclaimed: "Feck [a seventeenth-century equivalent of "gosh," apparently], we must make one account of all!" and urged Winslow to make the *White Angel* a joint property between the colony and the Adventurers. Winslow steadfastly refused to let the colony in for this extra expense, but when he arrived back in Boston on June 5 in the *William and Francis* he reported that nothing could stop Sherley from adding the purchase price of both ships to the Pilgrims' account.

Allerton, however, came to grief at last. Bradford put it in his own way: "God crossed him mightily." He had hired a ship from Sherley at a rate of thirty pounds a month, loaded her too heavily with cargo, and set sail with "a most wicked and drunken crew" (it was curious how Allerton always managed to find wicked and drunken crews). The ship sagged, a highly dangerous sign, and could not bear sail properly, so Allerton had to agree to shelter in Milford Haven while the crew rearranged the stores. This caused a delay so long that the sales value was badly depreciated by the time the goods were landed in New England. Allerton sold to all comers as best he could, and collected a crowd of ruffianly companions "to run into every hole and into the river of Kennebec to glean away the trade of the house there." He then overreached himself, setting up a rival trading post beyond the Penobscot. It was not fully prepared when Claude de la Tour, one of the rival French proprietors at l'Acadie, sent a punitive force along to stop it. They killed two men and seized all the stocks, most of which, ordered by Allerton, were not yet paid for.

Halted by the French and cheated right and left by his own helpers, Allerton took refuge in Plymouth, where at last he could be pretty sharply questioned. He promised to disentangle himself from his debts and behave better in future. He admitted owing the Plantation £2000. The first thing he did was to break his word to Sherley. He paid nothing for the hire of his ship, nor did he return to London, which he had agreed to do. He sailed instead to Bristol, where, having held the ship for ten months, he apparently intended to load a fresh cargo and sail right back again. "It should seem he knew well enough how to deal with Mr Sherley," wrote Bradford ironically. It did, too. Incredibly, Sherley reported in a letter to Plymouth, dated December 6, 1632, that he had given Allerton a year in which to prepare a statement of account and another year in which to pay off his debts, "at six and six months." "But here's not a word," said Bradford, "of the breach of former bonds and covenants, or payment of the ship's hire. This is passed by as if no such thing had been."

Not only had Sherley allowed Allerton to wriggle free, but he told the Pilgrims that they ought not to bother Allerton on their own account during the two years. Since, to them, Sherley spoke for the Adventurers, to whom the Pilgrims were indebted, this meant that they could only look on helplessly while Allerton "made all away into other men's hands, save a few cattle and a little land and some small matters he had here at Plymouth. And so in the end removed as he had already his person so all his from hence."

If they had lost Allerton (and they had not quite yet), the

colony had gained Hatherley, who had sold out his Adventurer's partnership and planned to settle. In time he became one of the leading citizens in the township of Scituate. The one thing still troubling him was his account for the *Friendship*. He drew up a statement showing Allerton's debt of £2000 and showed it to the elders, who, understandably enough, commented that "they had been fooled long enough with such things." William Peirce and William Denison also drew up their Allerton accounts; Denison went so far as to sue Allerton for one sixth of the *White Angel* money and, amazingly, recovered it, plus damages. Peirce, meanwhile, no doubt wishing to be free of Allerton at any price, sold out to the colony his own shares in the Penobscot trading post.

Penobscot had had its share of ill luck. All the trading posts served the same double purpose: to carry the colony's trade with the Indians farther afield, and to provide overnight stops and provisioning stations for any travelers from the settlements on their expeditions all over the region. Run by good managers, the posts were a godsend; run by bad managers, they were a calamity. Ashley at Penobscot had of course done the wrong thing. Like Morton, he had traded powder and shot with the local Indians, and he had been living it up in a disreputable way with Indian girls. The colony had at the outset made Ashley sign a bond of £500 not to trade in arms with the Indians: this fortunately gave them a lawful reason to dismiss him, and send him back to England under arrest. He was lodged in the Fleet prison for some time; then, Bradford heard, "by the means of friends he was set at liberty and intended to come over again. But the Lord prevented it." He was offered the chance of a trading voyage for beaver to Russia; he accepted and went, and on the way back he was lost at sea. Penobscot now belonged absolutely to the colony.

The French then robbed it in a neat operation worthy of any Western film. The new manager and his assistants had gone down the coast to fetch supplies, leaving just a few servants in charge. A party of French with one cunning Scotsman arrived, saying that their ship was leaky: might they stay awhile to repair it? Naturally the Penobscot men agreed. The invaders made themselves at home, lavished complimentary remarks on their obliging hosts, and at last seemed to notice the guns in their rack. They began to admire these and ask questions: what type, what charge, how loaded, what range? Suddenly there stood one Frenchman with a loaded gun and one with a pistol, aimed and businesslike. The Penobscot servants had no choice but to help load up goods worth four or five hundred pounds on board the French boat. Finally the French (and the Scot) went cheerfully away, shouting: "Tell your master when he gets back that some of the Ile de Ré gentlemen have been here." This was a particularly stinging taunt, referring to a most humiliating English reverse by the French six years before, when the Duke of Buckingham had led a kind of commando raid on the Ile de Ré off the coast of France and had been forced to scuttle ignominiously back to Britain.

Sherley now wrote to say that he wanted to send over a new accountant. The Pilgrims, not surprisingly, replied: Not if it meant paying. They could manage on their own and wanted no more costs than they could help just then. Sherley, characteristically, went ahead anyway, but his choice seemed all right, at least at first. The new man was Edward Winslow's younger brother Josiah. He crossed in the still unsold *White Angel* on her next trip and set to work at once.

· 14 ·

Now came the curious episode of Sir Christopher Gardiner, which proved that the Pilgrims' struggle for survival in the New World had not softened or blunted their suspicions of Rome. Appearing abruptly in the Bay Colony, Sir Christopher announced that all he wanted was peace and quiet, and a chance to lead a godly life. He would do any humble work, and he would like to join the Pilgrim church. This sounded promising, but the first stirrings of doubt arose quickly when the elders realized that he had brought with him not only a couple of servants, which was perfectly acceptable, but also a pretty young woman he introduced as his cousin. They remembered the Fells incident only too well. Soon enough, Sir Christopher fell foul of the Bay authorities for what they considered his immoral way of life and decamped into the wilds. Whether or not he took the girl along is not clear, nor does anyone mention what happened to her. Search parties went to look for Sir Christopher without success, so a reward was offered.

Some Indians now presented themselves before Bradford and said that they knew where Sir Christopher was hiding out. Should they track him down and kill him? Certainly not, replied Bradford without hesitation. What they ought to do was to capture him, treat him with great care, and bring him safe to Plymouth. The Indians, looking dubious, murmured that this might be difficult, as Sir Christopher carried a gun and a rapier. Bradford told them that if they were careful, and used their matchless woodcraft to track him, then watched for the right moment, they could capture him without harm to anyone.

Not long afterward the Indians brought their prisoner in. His hands and arms were swollen and patched with bruises, so the governor immediately ordered these to be bathed and anointed with soothing ointment. Then he asked what had happened.

The Indians told him. They had found Sir Christopher by the side of a river, and the moment he saw them he jumped into his canoe to escape. They drew nearer. He stood up in the canoe and leveled his gun at them. At that minute, the rippling current rocked the canoe and bumped it against a boulder. He lost his balance and fell into the water, dropping the gun and his rapier too. When he scrambled out onto the bank, the Indians saw that he was gripping a little dagger. Their method of dealing with this was neat, if painful. They took long poles and struck the dagger out of his grasp.

Bathed and bandaged, Sir Christopher bitterly complained about the Indians' treatment. They protested mildly that they had only hit him a little. Bradford thanked and rewarded them, sent them away, and lodged Sir Christopher in the town.

Not long afterward a sinister discovery was made. The women of the house where the captive was living came to see Bradford in some excitement. They had been making his bed, they said, and found a small notebook. It must have accidentally fallen out of his pocket or something. Bradford examined it, and to his horror found it contained notes of the day on which Sir Christopher had been reconciled to the Pope and the Church of Rome.

This dreadful discovery was too much to worry about alone. Bradford sent it to Winthrop, then sent Sir Christopher too, and asked Winthrop's advice. The only reply he got at first was a courteous acknowledgment and the hope that all would work out well in the end. The next thing Bradford heard was that Sir Christopher was on his way back to England, where he at once presented the Privy Council with a written complaint against the Plymouth authority. It was not accepted, and that was the last they heard of him.

• 15 •

In 1632, William Peirce suffered a considerable loss. It was at the height of the Allerton problem. Peirce had brought his ship, the *Lion*, to Boston after an eight-week passage, anchoring on September 16. There were 123 passengers, 50 of them children, on board, so no doubt it was a particular relief to reach the harbor. The Pilgrims arranged to send over 800 pounds of beaver back, along with a very full set of account books and long letters explaining all about Allerton's dealings, debts, and evasiveness. The *Lion* had to go to Virginia first to pick up some other goods, and there she was wrecked on the coast in a storm. The cargo of beaver was lost, and so were the account books, though fortunately none of the letters, nor was there any loss of life. Poor Peirce reported the wreck in a letter dated Christmas Day which reached Plymouth on April 7, 1633. Though Peirce had lost his ship and the better part of his whole property, he did get back safe to England. Bradford, referring again to the Allerton affair, wrote in his journal: "I am weary of this tedious and uncomfortable subject."

That year there was a little brush with the Dutch. They had planned to build a trading post on the Connecticut River, close to the future site of Hartford, but had not done much by this stage. At one point somebody had suggested a joint post set up and run by the Dutch and the Pilgrims, but the Pilgrims had their hands full just then with the running of trading posts already set up, and let the subject drop. Then some Mohican Indians who had been driven away from their camp on the Hudson River by the local Mohawks asked permission to make a trading post with the cooperation of the Bay Colony. The Bay people hesitated; the Indians wavered; suddenly the Plymouth men said that, after all, it might be an idea to go ahead. The Dutch, belatedly realizing that they were losing a good opportunity for profitable trade, had second thoughts. Meanwhile the Pilgrims sent a party up to Matianuck (later Windsor), and got going; so the Dutch dashed along and hastily built "a slight fort" which they named Fort Good Hope. It commanded the approach to Matianuck, so they fixed up a couple of guns and threatened to stop anyone coming along. The Plymouth traders, arriving on the scene in a big new ship carrying on board the prefabricated trading house, met the Dutch challenge of "Stand or we shoot!" with the polite reply that they were the governor of Plymouth's men on a lawful and respectable commission and intended to proceed. The Dutch did not open fire. The traders went calmly on, "clapped up their house quickly," landed their provisions, stored them, sent the ship away, and at once set to work at top speed to make a palisade around the house and fortify the position properly.

The Dutch reported all this to their headquarters at Manhattan. In due course they organized a formal protest. Coming up with a warlike array of seventy men with weapons, banners, and a showy display of potential force, they nonetheless halted when they saw the fortifications at Matianuck. This might well cost blood. They contented themselves with a careful parley, and returned in peace to their base. One hundred seventy-six years later, a fictitious but delightful account of this incident appeared in print: Washington Irving put it in his book *The Knickerbocker History of New York.*

In that year, too, the future founder of Rhode Island arrived in the colony. At first the Pilgrims were pleased to meet Roger Williams, who had arrived with his family in the *Lion* at Salem in February 1631. He had preached in the Bay Colony and his teaching was admired, though some members had chafed under his sharply critical tone. Yet he was so sweet in manner that it was hard to quarrel with him. He was, however, apt to create a sensation by some of the things he said, comparing (for example) James I with some of the beasts in the Book of Revelations. Seeking fresh fields to conquer, Williams removed to Plymouth in 1632, where he was kindly received and welcomed to the church as "a man godly and zealous." Then early in 1633 he began to quarrel with everybody and "to fall into some strange opinions, and from opinion to practice." He questioned the elders' rights to govern, and even the legality of their terms of reference. Bradford, tolerant as ever, left it to God to show him the error of his ways. Williams had "many precious parts but [was] unsettled in judgment." He went again to Salem, where he made his usual excellent first impression on the newcomers he met, even captivating Endecott, but not eighteen months later he was asked to clear out of the Salem area within six weeks. After a bitterly cold journey on foot he stopped at the end of January 1635 on the Seekonk River at the edge of the Plymouth territory, then crossed the river and founded the settlement of Providence, where Rhode Island's traditional religious freedom, started by him, attracted spiritual dropouts from all parts of New England.

· 16 ·

In May 1633, Plymouth had a plague of locusts. This "great sort of flies like for bigness to wasps or bumblebees" came out of holes in the ground and swarmed through the woods, where they

> ate the green things, and made such a constant yelling noise as made all the woods ring of them, and ready to deaf the hearers.

The Indians said that sickness would follow. It did. All through June, July, and August the smallpox raged: "that great infectious fever." More than twenty died, including Thomas Blossom and Richard Masterson. Finally, to everyone's sorrow, died the good doctor and deacon, Dr. Samuel Fuller of the *Mayflower*.

It was at this time that Bradford, after a good deal of pleading, managed to avoid being made governor for a while. Edward Winslow got the job in 1633, and Thomas Prence in 1634, though they did not let Bradford off the hook completely: he was deputy governor to them both.

Bradford was less moved by personal power drive than most men who have ever held authority. He could have become the virtual dictator of the colony when the patent was made out in his name, but he never thought of such a thing. He shared his rights with the other Pilgrims, and did not hesitate to sell his own house to help pay the colony's debts when these were finally met in 1648. His quality showed from the beginning. In 1617 the Leyden elders chose him for the committee in whose hands were placed all arrangements for the emigration to America, though he was only twenty-seven years old; and the total length of time they chose him as governor, thirty-three years, shows that they saw no reason to change their minds later. From 1621 to 1657 Bradford was the true leader of the *Mayflower* company and its subsequent adherents. The weight of responsibility he carried was summed up by Winslow, who wrote that only a man of "more than ordinary piety, wisdom, and courage" could have faced up to the job, especially in the early years.

Bradford's greatest regret arose out of his deepest feeling: his wish to keep the original community compact, close, and united. Under the conditions of life in the colony this was impossible. The Plantation prospered; more cattle and oxen, more plowland and grazing, the ever-increasing market created by the rapid expansion of the Bay Colony, forced the settlers to spread out over wider and wider areas, until it was too far for many of them to center their personal and spiritual lives upon Plymouth. Even such founding stalwarts as John Alden and Miles Standish, with Jonathan Brewster and Thomas Prence, moved away to Duxbury and attended their own church there. In an effort to hold some members close to Plymouth, special land was allotted at Green's Harbor (now Marshfield) to those who promised to go on living in the town. These people, the first commuters of New England, kept it up for a while; but inevitably they found it simpler to move in the end. Seeing the original settlement thinning out in this way gave Bradford the saddest experience of the place from where, once arrived, he never departed.

· 17 ·

In 1634 occurred a tragic mishap on the Kennebec River.

The Plantation, which was now prospering so well that its large annual returns would soon clear the debts, had obtained a patent for a fifteen-mile strip along the Kennebec. One Hocking went up from Piscataqua to trade, and soon sent word back that he would like to expand farther up the river toward the falls. The man in charge of the project, John Howland, refused permission. Hocking was threatening to harm the colony and risking the liberty that had cost them so dear, by expanding trade privately in an area they hoped to trade in, and eventually keeping them out. Hocking took no notice except to say that he was going ahead: he would trade as he liked for as long as he liked. Howland's reply stated that they would have to remove him, by force and capture if necessary. Hocking's answer to this was curt: "Do your worst."

Howland now had no choice. He and John Alden took a small group of men to the Kennebec in pursuit of Hocking. Howland tried persuasion, but all Hocking would do was use bad language. Howland ordered two of his men to take a canoe and cut Hocking's anchor cable so that his boat would drift downstream with the current. The men were willing, and one of them, Moses Talbot, cut the cable; but as the canoe slid by Hocking's boat, Hocking picked up his loaded gun and shot Talbot dead. One of Talbot's friends, watching in horror from the bank, shot back and killed Hocking instantly.

A great fuss now broke out, with all sorts of wild versions of what had actually happened being spread all over New England. The story was carried to London, where sharp reactions quickly followed. The trouble was that just then the Commission of the Plantations, formed to keep an eye on religious and civic affairs as well as trade, was headed by two powerful members of the Church of England: Lord Saye and Sele, and the Archbishop of Canterbury himself, William Laud, famous for his detestation of Catholics and Separatists alike. Hocking, moreover, had been a servant of Lord Saye and Sele. Some very awkward questions were being asked in London, and Winslow was charged with the difficult task of answering these when he went over on his autumn journey.

Meanwhile the Boston authorities had acted. When Alden went there with a trading vessel they arrested him, and Standish had to go and get him out. Standish took letters to Boston from Governor Prence, and Boston governor Thomas Dudley wrote reassuringly from Newtown on May 22 to say that Standish was bound to appear on June 3 before the next court to testify. Both the Kennebec and Piscataqua (where Hocking came from) were outside the jurisdiction of the Bay Colony, and the Massachusetts authorities behaved in a thoroughly arrogant manner. Tempers flared, but the apologetic Dudley wrote to Bradford on June 4 that "time cooleth distempers."

Before the full inquiry opened at Boston, careful consultation with everybody who could possibly be concerned took place.

Winthrop counseled wisely, and in the end the hearing was very fair. The blame was placed squarely on Hocking, and reports were sent to quiet fears and criticism in England pending Winslow's arrival there.

When Winslow reached London, he presented a petition to the Commission. The Plantation had, it said, been harassed by both the French and the Dutch; so would the commissioners kindly do something about it? They should either persuade the foreigners to keep the peace, or authorize the Plantation to defend itself.

Most of the commissioners approved of the petition, but not Sir Ferdinando Gorges, who had hoped to become a kind of governor general or viceroy by Laud's appointment. Captain John Mason also disapproved, and to reinforce their argument that the Pilgrims were mismanaging affairs in the colony, they produced no less a person than Thomas Morton, formerly of Merrymount. Morton had criticized the Pilgrims in his book for the way they organized their church affairs:

> The Church of the Separatists is governed by Pastors, Elders and
> Deacons, and there is not any of these, though he be but a cow
> keeper, but is allowed to exercise his gifts in the public assembly
> on the Lord's day, so as he do not make use of any notes for the
> help of his memory. . . .

The commissioners, however, decided against Morton. They reprimanded him for his comments on Plymouth and criticized Gorges and Mason for supporting such a man.

Laud, who had hoped to swing the Commission against the Plantation authority, as he disapproved of Separatists in general, now set about questioning Winslow on church matters. He asked whether Winslow had done any preaching. Certainly, replied Winslow, when there was no minister and the brethren had stood in need of special edification; which was not often. Had he, Laud asked, performed marriages? As a magistrate he had, answered Winslow; nowhere in the Word of God was marriage tied to the ministry, when there was no minister someone had to do it, and he himself in Holland had been married by civil law, by the magistrate in the *Stadthuis,* or city hall.

Laud now threw all the weight and power of his great office into the scale. He managed to persuade the commissioners, after a good deal of vehement argument, to commit Winslow to prison for breaking English church laws. For seventeen weeks Winslow lay in the Fleet before his release could be obtained, and of course the full cost of this fell upon the Plantation.*

Winslow's plea against the Dutch had been reinforced by an incident in the early part of the year, when a Plymouth trading ship put in at New Amsterdam. There they met an Englishman, Captain John Stone, who had lived in the West Indies before moving to Virginia and was just then shipping some cattle from Virginia to Boston. He had stopped at New Amsterdam for water and had been out drinking with (among others) the Dutch governor. Bradford wrote:

> I know not in what drunken fit he got leave of the Governor to seize on their bark when they were ready to come away and had done their market, having to the value of £500 worth of goods aboard her. Having no occasion at all, or any colour of ground for such a thing, but having made the Governor drunk so as he could scarce speak a right word, and when he urged him hereabout, he answered him, "Als't u beleeft" ["as you please"].

The ship's captain and the trading party had gone ashore when Stone and his men boarded the vessel. They hijacked it, forcing the crew to set off for Virginia. The Dutch merchants were not going to stand for that dishonorable and illegal act: they rustled up a couple of ships and went in pursuit. Stone was successfully captured and brought back; the hijacked ship was handed over to the Plymouth men and Stone was sent up to the Bay, where a lawsuit against him was set in motion. Friends of both parties managed to mediate in the matter so that the lawsuit was dropped, and Stone then came to

---

* Prison was a private enterprise and paid for like a hotel. Friends in London obtained Winslow's release with representations to the government and the Adventurers.

Plymouth, where he was sympathetically received by some members of the colony, who perhaps did not know exactly what he had done. All was friendly on the surface, but "revenge boiled within his breast (though concealed)." Some of Bradford's friends kept an eye on Stone, fearing that he would do something violent; some thought he even planned to assassinate the governor with a dagger, but "by God's providence and the vigilance of some, was prevented."

Like so many people who created problems for the Plymouth community, Stone came to a sticky end. He went back to Virginia, but then for some reason came up to the Connecticut River, where somehow he fell foul of the Indians. They "knocked him on the head as he lay in his cabin" and drew the coverings over his face, possibly out of fear. Then they killed the rest of Stone's party. The only man to put up a fight was one Captain Norton, who defended himself for a long time in the galley. He might have lasted longer had not the gunpowder, "which for readiness he had set in an open thing before him," caught alight and exploded, burning and blinding the captain so that the attackers were able to finish him off. The Indians praised Norton for his courage.

They carried off all Stone's stores and sold some of them to the Dutch traders nearby. Soon, however, they and the Dutch came to blows. At the threat to cut off the Dutchmen's ship, a fracas took place in which the chief sachem was shot dead, and the surviving Indians withdrew.

As the colonies expanded in one direction they contracted in another. A Frenchman with the resounding name of Charles de Menou d'Aunay Charnisay seized the Penobscot trading post at Castine in the name of the King of France. This was a well-mannered takeover: the French turned the English out with fine phrases and complimentary speeches, making sure they had their shallop and plenty of supplies to get them home.

The English, however, were not going to take this lying down. After consultation between the Plymouth and the Bay authorities, an expedition was fitted out to go and subdue the French. They hired a ship, the *Great Hope,* commanded by Captain Girling. It was a big vessel, over three hundred tons, well armed and equipped with its own barque. Naturally Captain Standish was put in charge of the maneuver, but Girling turned out to be a feckless, trigger-happy character. Long before they came within proper range of the French he began firing madly in all directions, doing not the slightest harm but completely alerting the opposition. Standish, grieved by such an unmilitary approach, suggested going in closer and opening fire when he could see what he was doing. Girling, slightly abashed, agreed, and moved in before placing a few shots to better effect. The French, tucked away unharmed in the shelter of an earthwork and comfortably waiting for Girling to run out of ammunition, now realized that this was exactly what he was doing. Only one barrel of powder had been shipped to feed his fine guns. Standish at once set out for the nearest friendly plantation to pick up more powder. As he was doing so he heard, probably from one of his party out scouting, that Girling was likely to decamp with the barque and the Plymouth supply of beaver; this sounded so probable that Standish hurriedly arranged for the powder to be sent along and dashed back to the *Great Hope.* Girling, disappointed that events had not been livelier, simply quit, going off without a word of regret or excuse, and leaving his first mate to take charge of the ship.

Faced with this fiasco, Governor Prence sent Standish's report to Governor John Haynes of the Bay Colony. On October 9, 1635, Haynes wrote from Newtown asking for a conference to decide what to do next.

Two men, probably Hopkins and Winthrop, went up from Plymouth to discuss the matter. They had full powers to sign an agreement, provided that any such would pledge a joint venture with shared costs. Bellingham, writing politely from Boston on October 16, told Prence that the Bay men were willing to help but could not afford it. Perhaps they had second thoughts about the cost.

Not long afterward, the Pilgrims discovered that some of the

Bay merchants were busily trading with these same French. Bradford was quick to see the threat in this. The French went in for strongly built forts, while the English specialized in open farming; the French had a vigorous arms trade with the Indians (the old menace); and they had developed a highly efficient spy system through which they were kept informed of all the English did. "If these things be not looked to and remedy provided in time," wrote Bradford, "it may easily be conjectured what they may come to."

· 18 ·

Just before dawn on Saturday, August 15, 1635, the wind increased to an unusual force. It rapidly built up to hurricane pitch. It blew down some houses and tore the roofs off others, including the roof of the Aptucxet trading post. The sea boiled in fury and a twenty-foot tidal wave engulfed the coast. Many Indians climbed trees for safety, but this afforded uncertain protection, for scores of trees were uprooted: pines broken off, tall young oaks and walnuts tangled and entwined together like woven cane. The Aptucxet roof floated quite a distance before it came to a halt, leaving the bare posts sticking up forlornly on the trading house. Many ships came to grief, including a pinnace just completing the run from Ipswich to Marblehead, with the Reverend Joseph Avery and Anthony Thatcher and their families on board: many passengers were drowned. The storm, very like the great hurricane of 1938 in the same region, lasted nearly six hours before it blew itself out.

Two nights later, there was an eclipse of the moon.

· 19 ·

One of Winslow's tasks on his trip to England was to find another minister for the church at Plymouth. He discovered a certain Jose Glover and arranged for him to go to New England. Glover, a master of arts of Oxford, had been suspended from his living in Surrey for refusing to read, let alone countenance, James I's *Book of Sports*. This was a theological work, in spite of its title, published in 1604, and its content infuriated all those of Puritan or Separatist leanings. It stated that Englishmen were not to be prevented or discouraged from such amusements as dancing, leaping, vaulting, and archery, May games, Morris dances, Whitsun ales, the setting up of maypoles, "and other sports therewith used, or any other harmless recreations, on Sundays after divine service." Whitsun ales were not unlike Morris dances: the livelier young men of the parish, wearing brightly colored scarves and ribbons, with knee bells chiming as they stepped, riding hobbyhorses or dragons, would dance, piping and playing, into church and up the aisle, while the delighted worshipers would scramble up onto the pew seats to see better and greet the dancers with applause, cheers, and laughter. Increasing protests about these frivolities had prompted the King to publish his book.

Glover, with his family, sailed on the *John* in the summer of 1638, but most unfortunately fell ill and died on the voyage. Winslow, casting about desperately for a replacement, found the Reverend John Norton, a graduate of Peterhouse, Brewster's old college. He was recommended as a writer of "pure elegant Latin" and a fervent believer, spending whole days in prayer. He agreed to come to Plymouth provided that he need not be tied to one place: if he moved on, he said, he would repay to the Plantation the seventy pounds it cost to bring him over. On these terms he made the crossing and stayed a year. He was a harsh, intolerant man, who liked nothing better than to divide his time between giving highly colored accounts of his wild card-playing youth (now, of course, so happily reformed), and the careful cultivation of anyone wealthy and influential he could find. He had not been long in Plymouth when he discovered the settlement at Ipswich, where various people he knew had gone to live, some of them very comfortably off indeed. He transferred to Ipswich and paid back thirty-five pounds; the Pilgrims let him keep the rest in recognition of his work among them. He became in time one of the most powerful clerics in New England, moving in 1653 to the First Church of Boston in succession to John Cotton, and took a prominent part in the witch-hunts and Quaker persecutions that disgraced the region.

One source of spiritual controversy was a rather agreeably iconoclastic immigrant named Samuel Gorton, who signed his letters "Professor of the Mysteries, and De Primo." He held surprising views for his time, and openly expressed them, so that the Pilgrims described him as "a proud and pestilent seducer and subtle deceiver" voicing "exhorbitant Novelties." He said that faith and Christ "is all one," that sermons were tales and falsehoods, baptism a vanity and abomination, ministers magicians, communion a vanity and a spell, and churches "devised platforms." He told people to make the most of this world and get what pleasure they could out of it because there might for all they knew not be another. He lodged with the melancholy Ralph Smith, who eventually told him to get out because (so Smith said) of his "unworthy and offensive" remarks, but (according to Gorton) of Mrs. Smith's preference for his style of prayer rather than that of her husband. The Gortons' maid was caught smiling in church and rebuked; Gorton came to court to defend her, told the presiding magistrate he was Satan and said he should "come down from Jehoshua's right hand." Fined for contempt of court and ordered to leave within two weeks, Gorton departed with two converts, "very atheists looking for no more happiness than this world afforded." They went to the dropouts' haven, Narragansett Bay, where Gorton succeeded in ruffling the patience of Roger Williams, a thing no one else had ever been able to do. In a dispute over the ownership of a pig, the tolerant court at Providence criticized Gorton for calling the chief justice "a lawyer" and his assistant judges "just-asses." Years later Gorton, mellowed by time, was reconciled with Plymouth and gave valuable help at the age of eighty in acting as interpreter in efforts to prevent the conflict with the Connecticut Indians known as King Philip's War.

In addition to his difficulties in finding a minister, Winslow had problems with the beaver trade. The Adventurers had never properly accounted for all the skins they had received, and the Pilgrims, sensitive about every financial point as a result of their vicissitudes with Allerton, had announced that they would ship over no more furs until precise accounts were sent, or at least promised. Winslow persuaded them to reconsider this decision. He was confident that he could sort out the whole question in London.

Accordingly the Pilgrims shipped out three big consignments of furs; totaling 3678 pounds' weight of beaver, 409 otter skins, 55 minks, and two black foxes. They partly protected themselves by sending Sherley the bills for five hundred pounds' worth of goods bought from a Dutch trader who had been forbidden to buy and sell at New Amsterdam because the Dutch West Indies Company held a trading monopoly throughout New Netherland. The Dutchman accordingly came on to Plymouth, where the Pilgrims approved of his goods. These included kettles, and Virginia tobacco bound up tightly in what were known as "Dutch rolls" from the Dutch method of packing them.

Sherley wrote back plaintively, acknowledging receipt of eight hogsheads of beaver by Edward Wilkinson, master of the *Falcon*, and including in his letter a report of calamitous conditions just then prevailing in England. Early in the year, he wrote, there had been a great drought, with no rain for weeks at a stretch; hay cost five pounds a load; when the rain finally fell, it came in floods, spoiling the summer corn and hay harvest. A serious epidemic of plague had broken out in London, and many citizens had fled out of the capital for safety into the country districts. All this had badly affected the beaver trade, as they might well imagine: prices were low, the skins were not fetching even eight shillings a pound, but no doubt all would be well when the plague was over, which could not in the nature of things be long now. Sherley was unable to write as fully or as frequently as he would wish, because he as a prudent man was just then staying inside the boundaries of London less than one day a week, "but carry my books and all to Clapham." He had known three outbreaks of plague before, but none like this: "preaching put down in many places, not a sermon in Westminster on the Sabbath, nor in many towns about us; the Lord in mercy look upon us!"

Hardly had the Pilgrims read this when letters arrived from two other Adventurers, Beauchamp and Andrews, complaining that they had received no furs. Everything went to Sherley, nothing to them. Why was this? They even enclosed a sort of account, stating that the coat beaver had sold for twenty to twenty-four shillings a pound and the skins for about fifteen shillings a pound, certainly never less than fourteen. Black beaver fetched more still. Working from this information, the Plantation drew up its own accounts, which showed that in five years 12,530 pounds of beaver had been shipped over (Bradford added it up wrong) and 1156 pounds of otter skins. The beaver, at these rates, would have fetched just under £10,000, and the otter quite enough to pay all the freight. The full sum of the Plantation's debts, including the debatable *White Angel* and *Friendship,* came to £4770. Add to that the supplies received, which could not total more than £2000, and it was clear that the Plantation had paid its debt in full.

Why, Bradford asked the Adventurers, was it not possible for them to give exact figures instead of estimates only? He knew some of the reasons perfectly well. The new accountant, Josiah Winslow, who had after all arrived uninvited, sent by the Adventurers' decision and not by the Pilgrims' request, was not a meticulous bookkeeper: he let bills pile up, receipts get overlooked, papers drift into disorder, and relied on his memory and odd notes on loose scraps of paper so that everything was in a muddle. They had asked him to sort the whole thing out, and he had promised to do so as soon as he could find the time. He had been ill, too, which had not made matters easier. What was more, Winslow himself, ordering stocks in England, had not been given correct invoices, nor had price lists or complete bills been sent over with the goods he had ordered.

All this information went to Beauchamp and Andrews, with copies to Sherley.

In time both Beauchamp and Andrews replied, still full of indignation. Sherley had paid them nothing and had sent them no accounts. In time, Beauchamp brought a lawsuit against Sherley in the Chancery Court. The Adventurers still implied that the basic fault lay with the Plantation; and at last the Pilgrims came to the end of their patience, dismissing Sherley as their agent, and telling him to clear up the whole question once and for all, as it had dragged on for so long. There was no doubt that Beauchamp and Andrews were seriously out of pocket, however, so any available beaver should go to them personally as soon as possible.

It is difficult to avoid the suspicion that Sherley had intercepted the cargoes and had been feathering his own nest as assiduously as Allerton had for so long tried to do.

The Massachusetts planters suffered losses, too. On October 6, 1635, two shallops going to Connecticut with supplies for the new planters were wrecked on Brown's Bank in a storm. The crews were drowned and the goods scattered all along the shore, some of them washing up and lying at the high-water mark. Another supply boat was similarly wrecked soon afterward near Scusset. In both cases the Massachusetts governor sent out rescue parties to collect up the stores, salvage what they could, dry them out, and restore them to their owners. Some dubious souls suggested that the wrecks were God's rebuke for trying to colonize in Connecticut, "but," declared Bradford, "I dare not be bold with God's judgments in this kind."

• 20 •

A greater menace than storm and shipwreck now loomed up before the English planters: the Indian wars.

The Pequot Indians, who had killed Captain Stone, had also fallen out with the Dutch settlers on the one hand, and with the neighboring Narragansett Indians on the other. It seemed prudent to try to be friends with somebody; so they selected the Massachusetts English, to whom they sent presents of beaver and wampum, with polite messages. At first the English did not reply, but after some discussion they drafted out terms on which a sort of friendship might be possible. These were: that the Pequots should hand over Stone's killers; that they should allow the English whatever Connecticut planting rights they might happen to want; and that friendly trading might develop between both parties.

The Pequots promptly agreed about the planting rights and the trade, and asked the English to help them in coming to terms of peace with the Narragansetts. As for Stone's killers, only two were still alive. It had been a just fight in any case, for he had captured two Pequots, bound them, and forced them to guide him up the river. Nine other Pequots had tracked him and had killed him and his men in order to rescue their own. It was all quite simple.

A trading pinnace went up into the Pequot country from Boston, but achieved little in the way of trade or promising contact, so Governor Winthrop and his assistants concluded that they ought to let the matter drop. But then occurred an event that no one dared to overlook. Mad Jack Oldham was killed. He had taken a small boat, with very few to carry it, into Indian country to trade. A quarrel broke out, and Oldham was cornered on Block Island. Some of his killers fled for sanctuary to the Pequots, and John Endecott hastily mustered an expedition to make an inquiry. All it did was to ruffle Pequot tempers further. The situation was now serious: Stone dead, Oldham dead, loss of face among the Pequots, who had asked for friendly alliances with the English in the Bay Colony, and did not want to be accused of harboring an English enemy. Nothing useful resulted from the Endecott foray. Many English settlers scented blood and began to clamor for the hunt. They were all for rushing off at once and acting without thought, but the wiser advice of the elders held these hotheads in check for a while at least.

The Pequots did not make matters easier. A kind of guerrilla warfare began to flicker along the borders. Small hunting and fowling parties found themselves ambushed, lonely houses were attacked, until in the early part of 1637 a bigger attack took place. On the lower Connecticut River, various English men and women were working in the fields when the Pequots fell upon them, killing a number and sending the rest flying in terror for their lives. Another body of Pequots attacked a fort at the mouth of the river. They did not overcome the powerful defensive position there, but the defenders noticed their warlike, resolute bearing and determined attack, just as the farmers had observed in them "great pride and triumph, with many high threats."

The word spread like wildfire through the scattered settlements. Everywhere the English looked to their weapons and the chances of guarding their homes. In ones and twos and small apprehensive groups they began to appeal for aid in resisting the stronger attacks they felt sure must come. A local governor named Vane appealed to Plymouth, and received a willing response.

The Pequot Indians now called for reinforcement in their turn, from their old rivals the Narragansetts. They said that here were the English interlopers, taking great stretches of land, and showing every sign of ruling the whole country in time. It would not help the Narragansetts to side with the English against the Pequots: the English would simply overthrow both tribes separately. There was no idea of a full confrontation: the Pequots were simply going to kill cattle, set houses on fire, and ambush the English a few at a time. If this was systematically done, the intruders would be starved out and have to go back home. The Narragansetts wavered. These arguments were powerful, and it was true that the settlers showed every sign of staying forever. But in the end the old threat proved more powerful than the new, and the prospect of revenge against the Pequots for former injuries swayed the Narragansetts to assist the English against them.

Plymouth rapidly fitted out an armed force to meet the Indian menace. Lieutenant William Holmes with Thomas Prence and forty-two other men prepared to march, but, just as all was ready, a dispatch from the Bay told them "to stay; for the enemy was as good as vanquished and there would be no need."

Captain John Mason, commanding a Connecticut force of ninety men, and Captain John Underhill, commanding a Bay contingent of forty, with a promise of a hundred more to follow, met in Narragansett territory, where a group of Indians guided them stealthily through the night toward the chief concentration of Pequots at Mystic Fort. Mason had already had a successful brush with the enemy. For some days past little groups of settlers had been searching for stray Pequots; they had taken some prisoner, killed some, including two sachems, and gave one prisoner his life if he would guide them to the chief sachem. One such group, hearing that the chief sachem had prudently taken refuge with the Mohawks, came upon an Indian camp with eighty braves and two hundred women and children. Close by was a swamp a mile in circumference, and here most of the party got stuck. Mason, with about ten men including one Roger Ludlow, and Captain Daniel Patrick with about twenty others, started shooting, more to reveal to their comrades where they were than to attack any Indians; and Captain William Trask heard them and brought his troop of fifty to the rescue. He ordered them to surround the swamp, which was thick with shrubs; Lieutenant Richard Davenport got a nasty wound under one arm and one of his companions was shot in the head, but half a dozen others, led by Sergeants Edward Riggs and Thomas Jeffery, pulled them out to safety, slaying a number of Pequots with their swords in the process.

The Indians, speaking through the English interpreter, Thomas Stanton, now asked for a parley. This went on sporadically for a couple of hours; by then it was dark, and Stanton, approaching again as ordered, was shot at. The Indians shouted defiance, Stanton was rescued unhurt, and the men spread out around part of the swamp and hemmed in the Indians there. Showers of arrows fell about them, some sticking into their clothes and hatbrims, but miraculously no one was hurt; and in the morning the weary English found that barely twenty of the enemy had escaped. The prisoners were disposed of, some sent to the West Indies, some to Old Providence, and some to Boston, including the wife and children of Chief Mononoto. She was "a woman of a very modest countenance and behaviour," and her first request to Winthrop was not to rape her, and second, that her children would not be taken away. Mr. John Gallup arrived with a boat and supplies, and took the wounded off to the doctor and Minister Wilson, who were about twenty-five miles away. The rest of the fighting English had got their second wind, and cheerfully professed their willingness to set out again at once.

Buoyed up by this victory, Mason led his troops away to the rendezvous with Underhill. The approach to Mystic was completely successful. The English opened fire and quickly reached the fort, where they met sharp resistance. Hand-to-hand fighting broke out until some attackers managed to set the Indian huts on fire. The Pequots who dashed back to try to put the fires out found that the flames burned their bowstrings, and some were trapped by the burning houses. Altogether some four hundred were killed—some pierced or hacked to pieces with swords or stabbed with rapiers, others burned to death. The sight and the smell were both horrible, but of course it all happened through the providence of God.

The Narragansett guides had stood around critically watching the slaughter and letting the English do everything, except that they stopped any escaping Pequots they could reach. They grinned and taunted the defeated foe, but even they could not repress a murmur of admiration at the way the Pequots met their doom.

> Insulting over their enemies in this their ruin and misery, when
> they saw them dancing in the flames, calling them by a word in

their own language, signifying "O brave Pequots!" which they used familiarly among themselves in their own praise in songs of triumph after their victories.

When the killing was over, the English formed up and marched back to the waterside, where their boats were waiting, loaded with food and drink. The Pequot survivors followed, hoping to catch them on a little neck of land, but the English drew up in battle order, and the Pequots stayed clear.

The most famous Pequot who had fled to the Mohawks for sanctuary was the chief sachem, Sassacus, then seventy-seven years old. At the height of his power he had been the most influential Indian in southern New England, dominating the area from Narragansett Bay to the Hudson River, and a great part of Long Island. When the news of the fighting reached the Mohawks they killed Sassacus by cutting off his head. Some thought this was done for greed, to get hold of the considerable treasure of wampum he possessed; others, perhaps more reasonably, believed the Mohawks had read the writing on the wall and were anxious to placate the English.

The rest of the Pequots dispersed, some to make an uneasy peace with the Narragansetts, others to take refuge with the Mohican tribe ruled by Uncas. They had injuries to avenge. So had the Narragansetts, angry not to have been given full supremacy over all Pequots, which they thought they deserved to have. The climate was perfect for conspiracy.

· 21 ·

At last it looked as though the Pilgrims had managed to find a satisfactory minister. Why they had so much trouble over this is a mystery. Possibly an intensely alert, critical, scripture-minded flock daunts many shepherds. A promising one now turned up: John

Rayner, a wealthy graduate of Magdalene College, Cambridge, had emigrated the year before he came to Plymouth. He stayed, incredibly, for the best part of eighteen years. Yet in the end even he had problems with his congregation, and after a good deal of disputing he withdrew to Dover in New Hampshire, and settled there.

Trade in 1637–38 went pretty well. One shipment of beaver, sent in the *Mary and Anne,* totaled 1325 pounds in weight; half of it fetched four hundred pounds. Cattle did well in the colony: twenty or twenty-five pounds each was the average price, and twenty-eight not uncommon. Cow calves usually sold for ten pounds. Milch goats brought three or four pounds each, female kids thirty or forty shillings. Corn, at six shillings a bushel, held steady.

As June came in, New England felt an earthquake. To them it was large and terrifying, though to San Franciscans it would hardly merit attention. The rumble moved from north to south, causing plates to fall off shelves and women outdoors to hang on to posts and fences to keep upright. It lasted but a moment or two. Half an hour later came another, lesser tremor. That was all. For the next few years, however, the colonists noticed that the summers were less fine: rain fell oftener, and there were earlier frosts.

The year 1638 saw an unpleasant case of robbery and murder, ending in execution.

An ex-soldier named Arthur Peach, unwilling to work for his bread, had drifted into debt and unintentional paternity. Correctly suspecting that the area would soon become too hot to hold him, he decamped, persuading three others, Daniel Cross, Thomas Jackson, and Richard Stinnings, to go along with him. They were resting by the way, having a smoke, when an Indian came by, carrying cloth and beads from trading in the Bay. Peach invited him to join them and try the tobacco. In a low voice he told the other three that he would kill the Indian. His companions were alarmed, but Peach said: "Hang him, the rogue! I've killed many of them." This subdued the other three into uneasy silence, and Peach, drawing his rapier, ran the Indian through. He took three cloth coats and thirty feet of wampum off his victim, and the four men hurried away.

The Indian was fatally wounded, but was still alive, and managed to crawl to his camp. He died several days later, but not before he had put the finger on the guilty men. He was a Narragansett, and his fellows saw in the attack the possible truth of the Pequots' prophecies of English treachery. They sent, however, for English help, requesting Roger Williams to come and see the dying man. Williams, accompanied by Dr. Thomas James, went to the camp and quieted the Indians' fears, promised a full inquiry and a just verdict. James examined the victim and saw that his wounds were mortal.

Peach and company, believing the Indian dead where they had left him, traveled on unaware of any danger. At a river, they asked the local Indians to ferry them across in a canoe; but the Indians knew what had happened, recognized them as the wanted men, and took them prisoner. The sachem ordered them to be taken to Aquidneck Island, where the English there made a formal accusation, and prepared for the trial.

At some point, it is not clear exactly when, Daniel Cross contrived to escape. The other three, after careful questioning, pleaded guilty, and were executed on September 4, 1638, in the presence of a crowd of Narragansetts, who expressed satisfaction at the verdict. "Yet some of the rude and ignorant sort," said Bradford, "murmured that any English should be put to death for the Indians." Both the Bay and Plymouth governments agreed, sensibly enough, that justice must be seen to be done.

Cross was never brought to trial. He fled back to Piscataqua, his home, and obtained sanctuary, something that happened there on several occasions for wrongdoers escaping from the Bay territory. Perhaps in order to avoid such misdemeanors in the future, New England, over the next two or three years, looked to its internal administration. The authorities had a breathing space in which to do so, for the onset of civil war in England called a halt to the flow of emigration. Instead of the old general assembly of all freemen, representative government was set up. The borders were firmly drawn between the colonies. In Plymouth Plantation there existed now seven clusters of houses that could almost be called towns: Plymouth itself, Duxbury, Barnstable, Sandwich, Yarmouth, Taunton, and Scituate. Five of these bore familiar English names, though the letter *p* in the Devonshire Barnstaple had modified to a *b* in crossing the Atlantic. It is interesting to see that, although the majority of the *Mayflower* passengers originated from eastern England, notably from Lincolnshire, Nottinghamshire, Essex, Kent, and London, only two of the five names are eastern English (Sandwich in Kent and Yarmouth in Norfolk), while the other three belong firmly to the west country.

The civil war had a bad effect on trade. Cattle prices slumped from twenty pounds to five, goat from fifty or sixty shillings to ten or even eight. The colony, however, had established itself sufficiently solidly in twenty years to survive that difficulty. After all, a fall in prices was not much of an ordeal compared with what had passed already. And one great benefit emerged from the colony's having established itself sufficiently solidly in twenty years: the latter part of 1642 saw the final winding up of the financial payoff between the Planters and the English partners.

· 22 ·

That same year, 1642, witnessed a most curious outbreak of unnatural vice of all kinds in the Plantation. Careful and laborious letters passed between reverend gentlemen throughout the region, anxiously debating the best thing to be done. They were deeply concerned about the number of illicit unions and adulteries taking place, but even more so about the examples of not only pederasty but of vice involving animals. One lurid case was that of Thomas Granger, aged about seventeen, who was indicted on this score with a mare, a cow, two goats, five sheep, two calves, and a turkey. He was tried and condemned. Following the advice of Leviticus, the animals were killed in front of him and then he was executed, on

September 8. The slain animals were thrown into a specially dug pit and no use was made of any part of them. Poor Bradford stated: "A very sad spectacle it was. . . . I forbear particulars." His reasoned conclusion to explain these horrifying events was that the devil struck with particular spite against a community striving for purity; as the laws were stricter, so outbreaks were more violent. Plymouth was not more evil than other places; it was more publicized. It was, he thought, better to believe this than to think Satan had more power in heathen lands.

One man consulted in the elders' worried correspondence on this subject was the Reverend Charles Chauncy, a former Fellow and lecturer in Greek at Trinity College, Cambridge, who later took orders and emigrated as a minister at the same time as Rayner. He was something of an eccentric thinker for his day, especially on the subject of baptism, believing fervently in the power of total immersion. He had been brought up sharply three times in England for his opinions, either by the University or the Archbishop of Canterbury, had three times recanted, and three times gone back on his recantation. He preached the efficacy of total immersion in the colony, and the Pilgrims replied, mildly but sensibly, that it was not really convenient in that claimate. A dispute on the subject developed. All the learned and reasonable ministers were consulted in Boston, New Haven, and Duxbury, where Ralph Partridge was pastor, and all attempted to soften Chauncy's views, but he remained adamant. He moved to Scituate, where he thought he could indulge his ideas in peace, but a row soon broke out there, climaxed by an incident more spectacular than usual. Governor Winthrop's own twins were christened, and one of them fainted during the ceremony, provoking an explosion from the governor, not surprisingly. Chauncy also ran into trouble because he insisted on celebrating Communion in the evening instead of at morning worship.

This doctrinal squabble had an appealing sequel. By 1654, Chauncy was all set to give up the colonial struggle and return to England, when he was elected president of Harvard—provided that he kept his views on baptism to himself in future. He accepted.

· 23 ·

On April 18, 1643, William Brewster died at the age of seventy-seven. He had been ill for one day only, and his death was peaceful as he had always wished. He had worked in the fields as long as he was able, and right up to the end of his life he "taught twice and well" every Sunday. Bradford wrote a most handsome obituary in his journal.

Brewster was, according to Bradford, wise, discreet, and well-spoken, with a serious, deliberate style of speech, yet cheerful and pleasant among his friends. He had a modest and unassuming attitude, was humble about his own abilities, which led him sometimes to rate others too highly. His disposition was pleasant: he could tell others about their faults, both public and private, without giving offense: a rare gift. His life, like his conversation, was innocent and kind. He had compassion for those who had fallen on hard times, but his displeasure was reserved for people "risen from nothing and having little else in them to commend them but a few fine clothes or a little riches more than others."

· 24 ·

The smoldering fires of Narragansett resentment now began to flicker more brightly. The English had made friends with the Mohican sachem, Uncas, and the Narragansetts plotted murder against him, fearing he might side with the English against them. The moving spirit was Miantonomo, a Narragansett sachem who, in much the same way as the Chicago gang leaders operated in the nineteen-twenties, hired various men of his tribe to kill Uncas. Miantonomo was less well served than was Johnny Torrio or Al Capone, though, for his paid henchmen were incompetent:

Sometime they essayed to poison him; that not taking, then in the night time to knock him on the head in his house or secretly to shoot him, and suchlike attempts. But none of these taking effect, he made open war. . . .

Miantonomo, with a force numbering 900 to 1000, attacked Uncas, but failed to defeat him. Uncas won the battle and captured his adversary. Wondering what to do with his eminent prisoner, Uncas appealed to the English. They advised Uncas that he would never feel safe while his enemy was alive, and therefore dispassionate execution, with no torture, was the best answer. Uncas nodded agreement, and Miantonomo was put to death "in a very fair manner." What this meant was that the prisoner was bound, and dispatched with a hatchet wielded by Uncas's brother. This incident lay for a long time on the New England conscience. A suspicion still clings to it that the colonists welcomed the chance of making an example of Miantonomo because he had sold land to two troublemakers, Roger Williams and Samuel Gorton. True or not, the dead sachem enjoyed a picturesque revenge. In Norwich, Connecticut, the site of the execution, a statue of Miantonomo was put up in 1841, and several ships of the United States Navy have been named after him.

Occasional Indian forays on a small scale took place in the early months of 1644, put down with help from the planters of Hartford and New Haven, but on September 19 a treaty was drawn up and the Narragansetts promised to uphold it.

Edward Winslow succeeded Thomas Prence as governor that year, and further developments in settlement took place, to Bradford's distress: he was always unhappy whenever any of the colony moved away from the nucleus of Plymouth. But the arable land around Plymouth itself was narrow and restricted in formation, and the surrounding country both rugged and rocky. Extensive cultivation, therefore, could only be developed farther away. More: ships found it easier to use Boston than Plymouth. The Plymouth community and congregation did want to stick together, but land need drove them to consider moving to (for example) Nauset. On the whole, they decided, it might be best to stay where they were for the present; but a few did leave. These included John Doane, Edward Bangs, and Thomas Prence, Jr., who settled where the town and church of Eastham later sprang up.

Further troubles with the Narragansett Indians plagued the Pilgrims in 1645. They broke the peace agreement made the year before. Gathering a large army, they attacked Uncas, and because they had many guns and their force outnumbered him, they were able to slay many of his braves and wound many more. Uncas called upon the English for assistance. He received a troop of forty men from Connecticut to provide a garrison for him until the appropriate commission could meet and determine what to do, and he also had an offer of help from the Mohawk tribe.

The commissioners met, deliberated, and said that they would ask both sides to send responsible delegates to discuss the question fully together. To carry this advice to both warring parties they selected three men: Francis Smith, Sergeant John Davis, and (a name of fame in American history) Benedict Arnold. They were to tell both sides that the English were determined to prevent hostile invasions of their territory, no matter from what quarter they came.

The three messengers duly returned, bringing with them a letter received in Connecticut from Roger Williams saying that war was inevitable and that its violence would sweep the country. They had been given a contemptuous and menacing response by the Narragansetts, as well as the disquieting news, true or not, that the Narragansetts had "concluded a neutrality" with the English settlers of Providence and of Aquidneck Island. They thought it very likely this was true, as both places were havens for rebellious English dropouts. Alarmed by these reports, the commissioners thought it best to consult very carefully with the elders and magistrates of Massachusetts, which they did.

The military commanders of both areas were brought in for consultation as well, and six points were hammered into an agreement. These were: that the English had given their word to defend Uncas; this, not only against attack, but to keep him in the freedom and status he had hitherto enjoyed; that help must reach him quickly, as the threat to him was imminent; that the English were clearly in the right to assist him, so the facts should be made public; that the fifth day of the following week should be fixed as a day of humiliation (the common practice before an important event); and that certain troop dispositions should be made. Three hundred men, they thought, were required. From Plymouth and Connecticut, 40 each, from New Haven, 30, and from Massachusetts, as befitted the most populous region, 190. Forty must go from the Bay immediately, for the need was pressing, and the Connecticut forty who had gone already were supposed only to stay for a month.

What the Narragansetts had told Arnold, Davis, and Smith, speaking in the haughtiest manner, was that there could be no question of peace without Uncas's death. It did not matter to them who had started the fighting; Uncas's head in their camp would finish it. If the English would not stay clear, they would bring in the Mohawks against them, kill the English cattle until the slaughtered beasts lay in heaps as high as houses, and every Englishman who so much as stirred outside his house to relieve himself would instantly be slain too. Arnold, Davis, and Smith had, naturally, asked for guides to give them safe conduct through Narragansett territory on their way to Uncas; the Narragansetts offered them one old Pequot woman. All the time these exchanges were being made through an interpreter, three Indians with hatchets stood threateningly close, so the three Englishmen prudently withdrew. Their own Indian escort, unnerved by the hostile atmosphere, bolted away, leaving the three to get along alone as best they could.

The most sensible course seemed to be for the Plymouth forty to take up good defensive positions as fast as possible, while the rest made ready at top speed. Accordingly, Captain Standish led his party, well armed with good light flintlocks known as snaphances, up to Seekonk, on the Narragansett border. So fast did they move that they were there eight or ten days before the other forces were prepared. The Connecticut contingent under Captain Mason, and other groups under able officers, joined them, and the whole force was placed under the command of Major Edward Gibbons.

While all this was going on, the Massachusetts deputies met to debate whether what they were doing was legal. They concluded that it was. The governor sent back by two messengers and an interpreter the Narragansetts' present to him, saying that he could keep no gift from those who violated a treaty, and emphasizing that Uncas had not the slightest intention of occupying Narragansett territory. He guaranteed pardon and safety if there was no war. This worked for some reason. A meeting took place on August 27 and peace was concluded. Benedict Arnold acted as interpreter between the commissioners representing what might be described as the United Colonies and the sagamores with other influential Indians. The resulting document was signed by John Winthrop, Herbert Pelham, Thomas Prence, John Browne, George Fenwick, Edward Hopkins, Theophilus Eaton, and Stephen Goodyear. It also bore the marks of Pessacus, Mixanno, Witowash, Aumsequen, Abdas, Pummash, and Cutshamakin. This settled the matter for the time being.

· 25 ·

In the middle of May 1646 three men-of-war, looking most businesslike, entered Plymouth Harbor. They carried a number of men whose subsequent conduct was not businesslike at all. About eighty of them, strong and vigorous but thoroughly unruly, came ashore and rapidly got into a state that can only be described as mad drunk. They could scarcely be restrained, even though some of them were "punished and imprisoned." Eventually they sobered up, and stayed about five or six weeks before going off to Massachusetts, where they spent prodigally, scattering not only money but sin, despite careful surveillance from the local authorities. The captain of this force was one Thomas Cromwell (no connection with either of the other two famous Cromwells as far as one can see), who had taken prize ships from the Spanish West Indies and now carried the Earl of Warwick's commission.

Cromwell was present when a murderous quarrel broke out between two of his wild boys. He ordered them to stop, but one of the two half drew his rapier, intending to run at Cromwell. Cromwell promptly closed with him, wrested the rapier out of his grasp, and dealt him a box on the ear. This did not deter the angry attacker, so Cromwell hit him on the head with the hilt of the rapier. Unfortunately the blow was harder than anyone would have expected, for it cracked the fellow's skull, and he died a few days later.

Cromwell was called upon to testify before a council of war, where various crew members affirmed that the dead man had been a problem for a long while. Cromwell, they said, had had to lock him up under hatches on board several times because of his violent temper. The council acquitted Cromwell, who soon took his ships away to the West Indies on a three-year expedition from which he returned a very rich man. On arrival he presented Governor Winthrop in Boston with a sedan chair worth at least fifty pounds that had apparently been looted from the governor general of Mexico.

The truth was that Cromwell was a pirate. Born apparently by a kind of caesarian section like Macduff, he first came to Boston as an ordinary sailor in 1636. He joined Captain Jackson's pirate ship in the Caribbean soon after that, using the Earl of Warwick's island of Old Providence off the coast of Nicaragua as a base. (It was to Old Providence that the Plymouth authorities sent some of the Indian prisoners taken in 1637.) Cromwell's 1646 fleet entering Plymouth Harbor consisted of his own vessel and two prize ships, cedar-built frigates of sixty to eighty tons each, which he intended to take to Boston; but a gale forced him to shelter in Plymouth.

Cromwell came to a peculiar end. He fell from his horse and landed heavily upon his rapier hilt. This set up an internal bleeding, and he died of it. Bradford, seeing the coincidence of the two deaths caused by the hilt of a rapier, naturally credited such unimpeachable symmetry to the hand of God.

· 26 ·

In 1646 the colony lost Edward Winslow, who went to England to sort out fresh trouble. A remonstrance and petition had been drawn up and presented to the General Court on May 6. It was full of complaints against the Massachusetts authority. One petitioner was Samuel Gorton, a lively, amusing, but persistent troublemaker, who had been expelled from Plymouth in 1638. The reason for his expulsion, some said, was that he loudly defended a young widow whom the court wanted to deport; but Winslow said it was for abusing his landlord and trying to incite some Planters to rebel against the civil authorities. The landlord, incidentally, was the Reverend Ralph Smith—the same who had begged asylum in the colony because his Nantasket house let the rain in and he felt lonely.

The remonstrance not only made a stir in New England but caused awkward questions to be asked in London, so Winslow went over to answer them, traveling as accredited government agent and defense counsel. He exercised both functions so well that the matter was speedily cleared up, and any charges against the New England governments were quickly dropped. Various business talks and interviews delayed his return: before he could take ship again for the colony, he was persuaded by no less a person than Oliver Cromwell to join an expedition to capture Jamaica. Admiral Penn and General Venables were placed in command, and Winslow, intrigued by the offer, went along. It was a lengthy affair. The capture of Jamaica was completed in 1655. Winslow died of a fever on the voyage home and was buried at sea on May 8.

· 27 ·

The colonists framed their own laws on reasonably democratic principles, carefully not vesting too much power in any single individual, so that no truly learned lawyers on the European pattern developed throughout the whole colonial period. Laws had to conform to biblical precepts yet still be recognizably English in style. The Bible was the blueprint for the Good Society, the building of Zion on earth. Its ideas pervaded all aspects of life; small everyday details referred to it. At first church membership was the test for suffrage, and the local elders dominated public affairs, but by the end of the seventeenth century this rigorous application of scriptural rule was relaxed. It was formidable in the beginning, when intending church members had to stand up and testify that they had experienced conversion, and win the approval of the minister, the officials, and the united congregation.

Dedicated to creating a godly commonwealth, the garden of the Lord, each settlement revolved around its church with its elected minister as leader. If they moved away, they preferred to move in a group, with the minister leading them into the wilderness. Massachusetts Bay was the hive out of which new settlements swarmed away throughout the century. Every little community had its place of worship, usually termed the meetinghouse, a plain square building with no popish steeple; later, of course, bell towers were added, with steeples on top. Inside the meetinghouse the congregation sat, men on one side, women on the other, on plain wooden benches without backs. There was no light except daylight, no regular heating: occasionally members brought foot warmers, iron boxes filled with hot coals, but these made such a fire hazard that many churches prohibited their use; some members brought hot bricks or stones wrapped in blankets. But winter services were usually arctic. The wind blew through the cracks in the clapboard walls, the communion bread froze, hands and feet grew numb. Standing to pray for perhaps an hour, sitting listening to sermons for possibly two, the assembly had walked to church, sometimes for miles across a roadless landscape deep in snow or mud and bristling with the Indian menace. Yet they came—to a place where the frosty breath of whisper gave the whisperers away in winter, where in summer it was all too easy to doze off. To prevent this, a church official known as a tithingman walked around carrying his wand of office, a long rod with foxtails tied to one end. With it he tickled the faces of sleepy women and girls, tapped the heads of fidgety boys and men. It was his duty to observe, and report, any form of Sabbath-breaking, including games, frivolous behavior, loud laughter, fast walking or driving, and loitering outside the church. One young couple in Connecticut had to pay a fine of five shillings because during service in the meetinghouse "they did smile." This incident of course is parallel to that of Samuel Gorton's maid.

Attendance at church was compulsory, yet few liked to miss going, in spite of the drawbacks, because in an age without radio, television, and newspapers, in a place without theaters, the church provided company, fellowship, and drama. It was the epoch of the great sermon. Separatists and Puritans alike worked out their own plain style, with the sermons divided into three parts: doctrine (announcement and opening of the text), reasons (supports, explanation, and amplifying of the doctrine), and uses (application of the text to the needs of the listeners). Details of everyday life were drawn upon: a boy drowned while out skating, a heavy storm or earth tremor, locusts, sickness, an election, military plans, a ship arriving, anything would serve to illustrate the watchful presence of God. Shivering congregations rubbed their chill fingers as the minister preached of hellfire. A strong style was favored—in 1642 John Cotton recommended preaching after the manner of Christ, who, he said, "let fly poynt blanck"—and the hearers judged each performance like professional drama critics. Two sermons on Sunday and a lecture-sermon or weeknight meeting, usually on Thursday, were the custom, with fines of up to five shillings for absence from church. Only those who wished need go to the weeknight sermon, which was accompanied by no prayers or other teaching. Yet they were so popular in the sixteen-thirties that the General Court of Massachusetts tried to make every community hold them on the same day, to cut down all the running about from one town to the next. The preachers protested that it was in order to hear sermons that people had come to New England, so the court contented itself with the mild recommendation that listeners should at least be able to get home before dark.

Even condemned criminals joined in the vogue for sermons. On March 11, 1686, when James Morgan was executed in Boston, three sermons were preached to him by Cotton and Increase Mather and Joshua Moody (so many came to hear Moody that their combined weight cracked the church gallery), and the prisoner delivered from the scaffold a stern warning to all present to take heed from his dread example.

Sermons were so important that it is impossible to overestimate them. Hourglasses, set up by the minister, showed the sermons' length: a bare hour was not good enough. People brought paper and inkhorns to take copious notes in a specially invented shorthand; many thick notebooks filled with closely written sermon summaries have been preserved. The meetinghouse rustled with the turning of pages and the scratching of pens. Sermons were as pervasive then as political news today; they were read and discussed more eagerly than newspapers are now.

Funerals were simple affairs, but one quaint custom attached to them: the pallbearers and the pastor were given black gloves. Dr. Fuller in 1633 told his sister, Susanna Winslow, to mourn him in a pair of twelve-shilling gloves and to give Rebecca Prime a half-crown pair. Ministers received so many gloves in the course of their lives that they did a good trade in them: one Boston pastor collected 2940 pairs in thirty years, and sold them for £1442, a most useful supplement to his modest wages.

Later it became the custom to give ministers and pallbearers white linen scarves and black enameled gold rings with the name, age, and date of death of the deceased engraved inside. This in time was so ruinously costly that by 1721 the Massachusetts General Court passed a law to prohibit "scarves, wine, rum and rings" and gloves "except six pairs to the bearers and one pair to the minister." Normal expenses show in a bill for a Plymouth funeral in 1656 listing eight shillings and fivepence for five yards of lockram and thread for the winding-sheet, eight shillings for the coffin, three for digging the grave, two shillings and sixpence to the clerk of the court, and twelve shillings for "tavern charges."

It was an obsession with some settlers not to waste time. Time belonged to God, and was precious. Holidays might be sinful; in the early years, as we have seen, Christmas itself was barely celebrated, partly because it was a wicked waste of time, partly because popery and superstition clung about it. Some examples of this hatred of time-wasting are in retrospect wildly comic, or deeply pathetic, according to the reader's own nature. Major James Cudworth cast an interesting light on the subject of women smoking and his own active life when he wrote:

> My wife, as is well known to the whole town, is not only a weak woman, and has so been all along; never a day passes but she is forced to rise at break of day, or before; she cannot lay for want of breath, and when she is up, she cannot light a pipe of tobacco, but it must be lighted for her; and until she has taken two or three pipes, for want of breath she is not able to stir, and she has never a maid. And then in regard of my occasions abroad, for the tending and looking after all my creatures, the fetching home of my hay that is yet at the place where it grew, getting of wood, going to mill, and for the performing all other family occasions, I have none but a small Indian boy about thirteen years of age to help me.

Mrs. Mary Rowlandson, captured in King Philip's War, refused to accept a pipe from the Indians, although she enjoyed smoking quite as much as Mrs. Cudworth did, because it would show God that she was simply wasting time. The Reverend John Cotton, asked by one troubled father if it could be right for girls to dance and to draw valentines out of a hat, said that dancing was all right provided it was not lascivious dancing to wanton songs with amorous gestures, leading to dalliance, particularly after great feasts, and that valentines were harmless in themselves. They should not, however, be drawn out of a hat, for that was lottery, or a game of chance, and therefore sinful; one must not ask God to be frivolous or to countenance time-wasting. Children, people thought, ought not to play jokes on the first of April, traditionally the Feast of All Fools. In 1646 the Massachusetts magistrates heard a complaint against games of bowling and shuffleboard "in and about houses of common entertainment, whereby much precious time is spent unprofitably; and much waste of wine and beer occasioned." In their ambition to set up a true church state, Sunday was given an iron rigidity: all work, travel, and amusements had to stop at 6 P.M. on Saturday (an interesting echo of the Jewish sabbath), and from then on in Boston at least nobody might go into or out of the towns. Godliness was regarded as marine insurance; sabbath-breaking provoked God's wrath. With their ceaseless industry, thrift, abstinence, and sobriety, of course, the colonists made fortunes. All the more proof, they thought, of divine favor.

But the parents of young people found, as parents have found since the time of cave-dwellers with clubs, that their sons and daughters gave trouble. It is not surprising that the Pilgrims' children were as obstinate as their fathers. Constant Southworth, in his will, left his "next best bed" and furniture, and his wife's best bed, to his daughter Elizabeth, "provided she do not marry William Tokes; but if she do, then to have five shillings." Elizabeth sensibly chose William and the five shillings, in preference to two beds without him. Governor Thomas Prence similarly had a prolonged wrangle with young Arthur Howland, fining him five pounds for "inveigling" his daughter Elizabeth. He might as well have saved himself the trouble. Seven years later he fined him again and put him under bond for fifty pounds "to refrain and desist" from courting Elizabeth. It was no use. The next year the governor gave in, the couple married, and in due time the names of Thomas and Prence Howland appeared on the birth list of the Plantation. Even Isaac Robinson, son of the great pastor, strayed from the path: he became a Quaker, settled among a group of them on the site of the future town of Falmouth, and there kept a tavern for years. As for students, Harvard found it necessary in 1655 to draw up specific rules about dress. A cloak must always be worn outside a student's room; gold and silver ornaments required the president's permission; what was wanted was "a modest and sober habit without strange ruffianlike or newfangled fashions, without all lavish dress or excess apparel whatsoever" and no long hair, long curls, artificial curling, parting, or hair powder.

Some festivals were celebrated. All men must have the chance of earning a living, and intellectual life was far better than frivolity, but equally all needed opportunities for "seasonable merriment."

Disapproving of the pagan elements in them, the colonists made little of Christmas and nothing of May Day, but launched new festivals of Thanksgiving, Election Day, and Commencement. Election days started with a sermon, but went on with plenty of smoking and drinking (as they do now), and housewives baked election cakes. Muster Days began with sketchy military parades, marching on the town common or village green and going through the manual of arms, before relaxing into the party atmosphere. A few muskets, fired off, signaled the start of the celebrations: shooting contests at targets or at live ducks and turkeys, wrestling and fist fights, and flowing beer and spirits. Some places marked Shrove Tuesday with a "cock-skailing"—a man carrying a cockerel at his back, and a bell in his hand, would walk down the main street, others following blindfold, with long cartwhips, trying to strike him or the bird, and in the process hitting, by accident or design, spectators and passers-by. Judge Sewall of Boston wrote in his diary for February 15, 1687, that it had made a great disturbance. There were, naturally, harvest thanksgivings, and Guy Fawkes Day was kept.

Communities joined together for the hog-killing—every part was saved for use, providing bacon and salt pork, ham, sausages, lard, and bristles—and for corn-shucking parties on moonlit evenings in late November around a bonfire, with cakes and cookies, cider and persimmon beer. There were rat-killing contests, wrestling matches, neighborhood gatherings, picnics, church socials, visits, and family conclaves. Taverns and coffeehouses evolved as they evolved in London. People sang, read aloud, and told tales: the American love of the "tall story" came straight from this practice,

One great festival grew out of Commencement Day at Harvard, which opened with sermons and exercises (spiritual, not sporting) and went on with feasting and parties. By 1730 it was always held on a Friday so that it would not go on too long. Sunday observance started on Saturday night.

It was Cotton Mather who said that Harvard was "the best Thing that ever New England thought upon."

By 1667 Plymouth had the look of a properly established town. Two-story clapboard houses with shingled roofs, windows with glass in them, lined the main street. Each house had a big main room, usually in the southeast corner, with a massive central fireplace. Interior walls were paneled in pine, floors were laid with wide hand-cut boards, and ceiling rafters were uncovered. Simple, practical, uncomfortable furniture filled the rooms. The fireplaces had brick ovens in which cooking went on all day. Breakfast consisted of rye pudding and bread, or hasty pudding with pea or bean soup, or salt fish, or stew flavored with pork; luncheon was bean soup, or pork and beans, with vegetables such as stewed peas, onions, turnips, or squash; supper was like breakfast with the addition of gingerbread, cake, pie, or cheese. All meals were washed down with beer; milk was for the babies only. On the wealthier tables one could find butter.

Skating and sleighriding were introduced by the Dutch and adopted enthusiastically by the Pilgrims. They did not, however, generally take up or incorporate any customs or festivals that seemed to them specifically Anglican: they wished to develop their own. Although at the very start it was as much as they could do to stay alive (and many failed in that), it is surprising how soon certain modest amusements began. Among the earliest were parties, although dancing was frowned on in some quarters. So was card playing, yet it continued, and party invitations were often written on the backs of playing cards, which the preachers referred to picturesquely as the devil's picture book.

All young people were carefully watched over. Apprentices were bound by highly detailed indentures. They were to serve their masters faithfully for a full and just term of so many years, during which they would keep trade and other secrets, not play unlawful games nor stay away "unseasonably" from work, not frequent taverns, marry, be guilty of immorality, nor lend nor spend the goods and victuals of the masters without permission. Masters in their turn promised to teach the boys reading and writing in addition to the art and mystery of their craft, to provide "convenient" meat, drink, lodging, and washing, an annual sum of money for clothes (it might run to seven pounds a year), and give each boy a set of the tools of his trade at the end of his time. Standing legally *in loco parentis,* masters could beat boys for indiscipline, and did. Some apprentices did very well, marrying masters' daughters in due course.

Poor girls were similarly bound out as servants, or were apprenticed to spinning, weaving, cooking, or needlework. Many were little more than household drudges, and there were examples of really young children apprenticed—one case on record is of a child aged six. Some of the most fortunate apprentices worked for doctors, eventually winning the status that the medicine man has enjoyed in every community the world over.

Not for nothing was the codfish eventually adopted as the emblem of the Commonwealth of Massachusetts. Fishing was by far the most important commercial activity of New England for the first century of its existence. Cod, cured and dried with salt, had a bottomless market in Europe, where it was in great demand for Catholic fast days. It is nicely ironic that the great prosperity (estimated at £250,000 a year before long) of a community dedicated to the proposition that Satan was a Catholic rested upon the practices of the Catholic Church. They might comfort themselves by reflecting that they were not the only ones. Fishing vessels of many nations converged on the Grand Banks, where even in the cold misty waters of winter huge catches were easily taken. A large fat drab-colored fish of the cod type, called dunfish, came up in thousands to the bait of mackerel in brine, and was scooped up in nets, split, cleaned, and roughly salted on board. The entrails were thrown out for the multitude of screeching gulls; the heads were kept for hog food, the livers for their oil, used to treat leather. When the ships returned to port the fish were unloaded, washed in salt water, and spread out to dry on specially built platforms called flakes.

Deep-sea fishing, then as now, was work for tough men with good courage. Men and boys of less heroic mold took rowboats out along the shore and brought back mackerel, some cod, and a large herring type of fish named alewife, so plentiful that it came by the cartload and was used for fertilizer, a practice learned from the Indians.

It was on one of these local fishing trips that an excited young man called John Josselyn saw marvels. On June 26, 1639, he saw a snake, or perhaps it was a sea serpent, lying "quoiled up like a Cable upon a Rock" at Cape Ann:

> A Boat passing by with English aboard, and two Indians, they would have shot the Serpent but the Indians disswaded them, saying, that if he were not killed outright, they would all be in danger of their lives.

Josselyn listened enthralled to the story of "a young Lyon" recently killed at Piscataqua by an Indian, and then saw another surprising sight: a "Triton or Merman" in Casco Bay:

> who laying his hands upon the side of the Canow, had one of them chopt off with a Hatchet by Mr Mittin, which was in all respects like the hand of a man, the Triton presently sunk, dying the water with his purple blood, and was no more seen.

After such a day it is hardly surprising that Josselyn wrote in his journal: "There are many stranger things in the world, than are to be seen between London and Staines."

The settlers' ideas of natural history were sometimes fanciful. William Wood, writing his *New Englands Prospect* in 1634, said that among the animals found there were moose, deer, bears, lions, rabbits, hares, ferrets, foxes, the "skipping squerrell" and "quill-darting porcupines and rackoones castell'd in the hollow of an aged tree." He listed the "grim-faced ounce and ravenous howling woolfe" as well as "the civet-scented musquash," "black glistering otters and rich-coated bever." There was nothing fanciful about the whale, however: in 1654 the Plymouth Plantation passed a law that any whale cast up on private land belonged to the landowner. If not too far gone it was endlessly useful: the blubber gave lamp oil, the sperm oil was an excellent lubricant, the ambergris made a scent base, and there was all that whalebone.

Timber was a prosperous business. Specially tall trees were picked out for ships' masts and marked with broad arrows to distinguish them from the rest. Much timber was exported to Scotland, which was said to be so bare of trees in the seventeenth century that Judas could have found salvation more easily than a tree to hang himself on. Oaks built ships and barrel staves; all kinds of wood made household articles, tools (which were entirely of wood except for the iron plowshare) and the wooden spoons, plates, bowls, churns, and so on made during the long winter evenings.

Not much work could be carried on after sunset. Farming, with its heavy plowing and harvesting by hand, and the cultivation of herb gardens, had to be done in daylight; all livestock could be fed by lantern light, but that was one job among many. From the Indians the colonists learned to plant corn in the most labor-saving way: to dig holes with a sharp stick or deer antler in straight rows four feet apart, to drop into each hole four grains of corn separately, so that one did not touch another, fertilizing with fish dug in under each row, and then, when the corn stood a foot high, planting beans between the corn so that the bean vines would climb the corn stalks. It was from the Indians too that they learned to cut rings around trees, removing the bark to prevent the sap rising, so that the tree would die and thus be easier to cut down. It is noticeable that no one commented on the beauty of the forests: that came later, when life was more secure. At first the woods were simply frightening, deep, dark, unknown, full of who knew what wild creatures, thick with briars that tore cloth so that a man going into them soon realized he needed leather clothes. In an age of feeble lanterns and no pocket compass, men hesitated to enter unknown forest land.

It was really easier to explore by water. Rivers and streams were safer in a land without roads, and small sloops and rowboats, and the classic birchbark canoe, nosed up where men dared not walk. They could live in the boats, too: house-building had to be achieved on navigable water with some natural defensive protection and the promise of reasonably fertile soil. Many of the first houses were built of wattle and mud, using sticks, branches, and rough logs plastered over with clay. A crude clay-lined chimney of sticks took much of the smoke out, and roofs were thatched with pine boughs and grass. It was not until later that clapboard and shingles created the archetypal house always associated with the Pilgrim settlements. Neighbors joined in cooperative bands to build houses, each group learning by the experience of the last, and a "house-raising" was a festival occasion.

· 28 ·

On May 19, 1652, and August 7 of the same year John Eliot of Roxbury reported building progress. The town now contained more than fifty people, had elected its governing council, and with the help of Indians was building a new meetinghouse. Eliot had received books from London, the contents of two ministers' libraries. Later he bought up two more: that of Thomas Jenner, a Cambridge man who had come to New England in 1635 at the age of twenty-seven, whose 200 books Eliot bought for thirty pounds; and the volumes, 195 in number, belonging to Eliot's former colleague Thomas Weld.

The local elders had been examining the Indians on points of doctrine and had asked them to stand up and testify, an experience that puts the reader in mind of Dr. Billy Graham's meetings, and Eliot, thinking along rather more practical lines, asked for linen, cotton, and canvas for these Indians. The goods were sent in 1653, and arrived late that year; in a letter dated June 29, 1654, Eliot reported that he had received the stuff in good condition, and enclosed the invoice.* Of particular interest is the fact that the ship bringing the canvas over was the *Mayflower* of Boston, owned by a Puritan and former Adventurer named Thomas Webber.

Generally speaking, the colonists wanted to educate the Indians and convert them, though it must be admitted that education took a poor second place, and that their strongest motive for conversion was the fear that the Catholics would somehow manage to get at the Indians first. Some settlers wished to improve, as they saw it, the Indians' way of life: this same John Eliot was one such, though he did once say that the Indians were "so stupid and senseless" that they would not even ask the English to point out to them the road to salvation. When Eliot died, however, there was "sorrow in every wigwam."

Indian raids, massacres, and wars made even Eliot's faith waver at times: during the risings of 1677 he wrote dispiritedly to Robert Boyle:

> God pleased to show us the vanity of our military skill, in managing our arms, after the European mode. Now we are glad to learn the skulking way of war. And what God's end is, in teaching us such a way of discipline, I know not.

This was only a momentary quailing of the spirit: not for nothing had the Massachusetts magistrates in 1646 stoutly declared:

> Rome was not built in a day. Let them produce any colony or commonwealth in the world where more hath been done in sixteen years.

And it is important to bear in mind once again that without Plymouth there would have been no Boston: the old saying of New

*Appendix 7.

England testifies to that—"the Pilgrim saddle is always on the Bay horse."

More was learned from the tribes, on the whole, than was taught to them. Place names, of course, were frequently adopted from the Indians, as well as much everyday vocabulary. Settlers, like everybody else, borrowed words where they needed them, and coined their own for new-found objects or fresh situations, and new meanings grew upon imported English words to suit the New England scene. But a truly distinctive American vocabulary did not develop properly until half a century after the Declaration of Independence.

· 29 ·

New England as a whole was one of the most literate societies of its age, but by its very nature thoughtful, sober, and didactic. Books were practical and devout, not intended for fun and pleasure. The first books printed in the colony showed this: they were an almanac calculated for New England, and the *Freeman's Oath* recently revised, both published in 1639; and the great *Bay Psalm Book*, in 1640. By the time Boston was fifty years old, with a population of less than seven thousand, it had a well-established book trade, with half a dozen booksellers, all flourishing. The best-selling kinds were religious and school books, volumes of letters, and works of history, medicine, travel, and navigation. Citizens built up their own book collections, the best of which belonged to Cotton Mather; John Dunton in 1686 said that its seven to eight thousand volumes were equal to any library and called it the glory of New England as the Bodleian was the glory of Europe. Books could be found in every house, if only one or two: inevitably there would be a Bible. It was no accident that by 1653 Boston had a public library.

Believing books were all-important, the colonists naturally emphasized education. The plots of "that old deluder Satan" aimed to keep men from knowledge of the Scriptures. Laws passed in 1642 and 1647 ordered the officials of every township to make sure that parents and apprentice-masters had their children taught to read and understand the principles of religion and the laws of the land, and stated that every community of fifty and over must appoint one member to teach the children to read and write. No wonder the *New England Primer* was a best seller. In place after place appeared single-room schoolhouses where the master sat on a raised platform to hear the lessons. The young pupils had hornbooks, the older ones primers, readers, and copybooks, all of a tremendously elevated moral tone. Discipline was strict, reinforced with the birch rod and the hickory switch; the parents approved. Sometimes families helped to pay the school fees by providing firewood: if they failed, their child was put in the coldest part of the room, farthest from the fire, because a child who had shivered in school all day would report to its parents that they had better send wood along quickly. Most teachers were men, but some widows kept schools, especially for older girls. From the beginning girls' education was regarded as important; it is to the greatest credit of New England that its citizens realized so soon the truth of Mrs. Pandit's noble dictum that if you educate a boy you educate a man, but if you educate a girl you educate a family. Cotton Mather's daughter Katharine learned Latin and Hebrew; George Wythe's mother taught her son Greek.

Plymouth was, however, rather late setting up its first school: 1671, when John Morton, nephew of Nathaniel, the secretary, was employed to teach the children how to read, write, and cast up accounts. The Plymouth parents felt that this was not enough: it was not what they thought of as a proper education. Accordingly a year later a new schoolmaster was appointed, a Harvard graduate with the unlikely name of Anmi Ruhamah Corlet, first Harvard alumnus to have a middle name. He went to the other extreme, basing his instruction on the classics, and before this torrent of Latin and Greek the parents protested again, returning to their former position that it was quite good enough if their children knew how to write, cipher, and read the Bible. Corlet would not compromise on any account, so he resigned, and Plymouth remained without a schoolmaster for nearly twenty years. When at last a new and unexceptionable man was found, it was high time, for the Town Farmers' decree fixing costs was poorly spelled to say the least:

> Every scollar that Coms to wrigh or syfer or to lern latten, shall paye three pence per weke; if to Read onlie, then to pay three half pence per weke.   ·

Even an Indian could write better than the Town Farmers. A delightful letter came from the Indian chief known as King Philip to Governor Prence in 1672, and apart from the King's preference for lower-case letters the style is excellent.

> to the honoured governir, mr thomas prince, dwelling at plimouth.
>
> honoured sir.
>
> king philip desires to let you understand that he could not come to the court, for tom, his interpreter, has a pain in his back, that he could not travel so far and philips sister is very sick. philip would entreat that favour of you, and any of the magistrates, if any english or enjians speak aboute the land, he pray you to give them no answere at all. the last summer he made that promise with you, that he would not sell no land in seven yeares time. he has not forgot that you promoted him. he will come as sune as possible he can to speak with you, and so i rest your very loving friend, philip, dwelling at mount hope nek.

With their zeal for both religion and education, the colonists soon felt a need for a college to ensure an adequate supply of ministers. The first step was taken when a group of Cambridge scholars, most of them from Emmanuel College, got together to plan it. "It pleased God to stir up the heart" of the Reverend John Harvard to take the lead and contribute half his estate, in all about £1700, and his entire library; the rest followed suit and put in what they could afford. So in 1636 in the place appropriately named

Cambridge in Massachusetts, described as "pleasant and accommodate" for such a project, they set up a college that supplied instruction in grammar and rhetoric, Latin, Greek, and Hebrew, logic, mathematics, astronomy, physics, metaphysics, philosophy, and divinity. Living conditions were Spartan: cold water, outdoor privies, hard beds, a chest to keep belongings in, and no sports fields. Two main meals a day, lunch at eleven and dinner at seven-thirty, consisted of boiled beef or mutton with bread and beer; the wife of the first president, Nathaniel Eaton, provided badly cooked meat, the bread went moldy, and the beer was sour. Two light meals known as "bevers"—one in the early morning and one in the middle of the afternoon—eked out this plain or unsatisfying fare. So many hungry students visited Mrs. Vashti Bradish's tavern and bakery that the college authorities decreed not more than two visits a week should be permitted, and then only one pennyworth of food at a time could be bought.

College fees were paid, as often as not, in goods rather than in cash. A quarter's tuition could be more than paid for with one and a half bushels of wheat; Joe Farnsworth's father paid for six months' study and rent for his son with four bushels of barley malt and "a little brown cow." Gershom Bulkeley was kept for a year on a side of beef and a small side of bacon, five bushels of wheat and fourteen of corn, fifteen and a half bushels of apples, and a cask of butter. Zachariah Brigden was kept a term for the fee of a fat hog, six bushels of malt and one of parsnips; he also knocked off a portion of his bills by ringing the bell and waiting at table, an early example of an intensely American tradition.

The wretched Eaton did not last long as president. He was addicted to the rod, which he used with gusto on students and staff alike; and when he thrashed his chief assistant with what Governor Winthrop called a cudgel big enough to have killed a horse, there was an investigation; Eaton was fired and left New England, taking with him a substantial packet of John Harvard's legacy.

In the next president the college was more fortunate. A Cambridge graduate named Henry Dunster, he made a fresh start, setting his sights high so that by 1652 he had established full four-year courses leading to B.A. and B.S. degrees. He also had a good deal to do with one of New England's glories, the early setting up of the printing press.

The Reverend Jose Glover, who had died on board the *John* in 1638, had not sailed unaccompanied. With him went his wife, five children, several servants, a printing press costing twenty pounds, a quantity of printing paper worth forty pounds, and a type-setting given to him by some of the English people living in the Netherlands. Moreover, there was the Day family: Stephen Day, a Cambridge locksmith under indenture to work for Glover in operating the press, his wife and son Matthew, and Mrs. Day's children by her first marriage, called Bordman. The *John* has been described with justification as the publishers' *Mayflower.*

Grieved but undaunted by her widowhood, Mrs. Glover bought one of the biggest houses in Cambridge, and a small one close by for the Days, and set up the press. It was Stephen Day who produced the original *Bay Psalm Book.* Twenty-three publications in ten years does not sound much, but it was miles ahead of any other small scattered colony. Apart from two editions of the *Psalm Book,* there were ten almanacs, a speller and catechism, five college commencement reports, a piece of propaganda for an Indian war that did not take place, and the *Book of General Laws and Liberties.* Stephen Day, finding himself with plenty of leisure time, left some of the work to Matthew and went off to promote ironworks and prospect for minerals. Mrs. Glover meanwhile married Henry Dunster, president of Harvard.

The marriage did not last long, for the new Mrs. Dunster died before the family could move into the newly built president's lodge in 1645, but Dunster moved in, taking on all the Glover and Bordman children and the press too. He also gave house room to a student, Richard Lyon, who helped him to revise the *Psalm Book* for its second, and far better, edition. This was the great best seller that sold on both sides of the Atlantic for over a century. Another best seller was Michael Wigglesworth's 224-verse thunderbolt, *Day of*

Doom, published in 1662. Its first edition of 1800 copies sold out in a year, so that Wigglesworth was able to take a trip to Bermuda, and within ten years two more editions appeared. It too sold on both sides of the Atlantic for over a century. The first New England biography came out: Increase Mather's *Life and Death of that Reverend Man of God, Mr Richard Mather,* in 1670. And in 1669 appeared the first colonial history, *New Englands Memoriall.*

Its full title was elaborate, to say the least: *New Englands Memoriall: or, A Brief Relation of the Most Memorable and Remarkable Passages of the Providence of God, Manifested to the Planters of New-England in America; with Special Reference to the First Colony thereof, Called New-Plymouth.* It was an official publication, paid for by Plymouth Plantation, who gave the printer twenty pounds' worth of corn and a barrel of "merchantable beef" when he grumbled about a hard bargain. Nathaniel Morton, nephew of Bradford, had crossed the Atlantic at the age of ten, lived in Bradford's house, and in time became secretary of the colony, an office he held for forty years. He dedicated the *Memoriall* to Thomas Prence, stating that the bulk of his information for the book had come from his "very much honoured Uncle" and from "certain Diurnals" by Edward Winslow. Certainly the *Memoriall* is largely composed of extracts from both; Morton added little that was new. But he did name the *Mayflower.*

Neither Bradford nor Winslow had done that; it is Morton who sent the little ship sailing into legend and immortality. He also said that the Dutch *had* bribed Jones to steer clear of the Hudson River; but subsequent researchers have thought this unlikely. Morton's great achievement, however, was that, two hundred years before Bradford's journal with its matchless quality was published, he revealed the heroic story of the *Mayflower,* set the tradition of the Pilgrim Fathers firmly on its feet, and made them folklore, so that in spite of the facts that Jamestown was earlier and Boston superior it is Plymouth that has the place of honor in American history.

· 30 ·

Other colonies cultivated money, property, and material prestige: New England, led by Plymouth, put its trust in education and ethics.

These were deeply and inevitably rooted in Puritan ideals. Humanism produces sweeter circumstances, but cannot flourish in a daily grind of sheer survival. The choice was between the Puritan and the material. Right from the start education had to be set up and paid for by the community as a whole; there were no great endowments, it was a system financed by small contributions from everybody, astonishingly progressive for its time. It was designed to be universal, and for all age groups, from the very start. To create citizens rather than Puritans as such, both Massachusetts and Connecticut passed laws, the one in 1647, the other in 1650, for the compulsory provision of schools, incorporating the nicely ingenious clause that any fine levied on one community for failing to do this must be handed to the nearest place that had not so failed. Rivalry was a powerful spur, and the authorities, who were forcing through a high standard of education over the heads of a poor population aiming to keep their children working all hours at fishing or farming, criticized those who did not realize the value of the "Angels bread" of learning. The commencement sermon of 1655 spelled this out, the speaker, President Chauncy, referring to such ignorant parents as "covetous earthworms." At that time it was estimated that 89 per cent of the men in New England, and 42 per cent of the women, could sign their names; thirty years later the men's score was the same, but the women's had risen to 62 per cent, a far higher total than Europe could boast.

Grammar schools, closely modeled on those of England, were set up; Plymouth, always small, had its grammar school in 1673, specifying the teaching of literature "for the good and benefit of posterity"—a significant point. The most famous schoolmaster in New England was the delightful Ezekiel Cheever: educated at the

London Bluecoat School (where the medieval uniform of long blue coat, yellow stockings, and hatless head is still worn) and at Emmanuel College, Cambridge, he emigrated to New Haven. He taught there, then at Ipswich and Charlestown, finally in Boston, this last for thirty-eight years, and died in harness at the age of ninety-two, after seventy years' teaching without one day's absence. School Street, Boston, was named because of him.

In 1644 the New England Confederation took over the full responsibility for Harvard, and levied a tax on every family in New England for its support. They could pay a shilling a year, or a shilling's worth of wampum, or a quarter of a bushel of wheat. Ten years later the Bay Colony paid the president a salary of £100 to £150 a year, and gave the college the toll money from the Boston–Charlestown ferry. Harvard set up a department for Indian studies, but found that the Indians preferred the bread and beer to the Latin and Greek. One Indian took to drink and was jailed for debt, eventually breaking loose and running away to sea to escape the trials of culture. But at least the college press printed the Bible in Algonquin, and employed an Indian known as James the Printer to act as devil. Matthew Day had died in 1649, and the next head of the printing press was one Samuel Green, who combined this function with those of Harvard's man-of-all-work. He was sergeant of the college militia, college barber and stationer and head mechanic, and he worked for Harvard for forty-three years.

To assist Green came one Marmaduke Johnson, a lively young man who in spite of having a wife in England courted Green's daughter (one of his nineteen children). Green took him to court, where he was fined five pounds' damages and ordered to return to England, but, putting first things first, not before he had finished work on the Algonquin Bible. By the time it was done, however, Mrs. Johnson had run away with another man, so Marmaduke stayed on and presumably managed more discreetly.

Harvard based itself solidly on the classics. Those who disapproved of this pagan foundation showed themselves madly anti-collegiate, vociferously protesting until it was put to them that they would be far better off in Rhode Island; to which revolutionary but comparatively unlettered haven they soon went. By 1645 New England averaged one graduate to every forty or fifty families, a high proportion, and their influence was much greater than their numbers. It was the men of learning who were selected as leaders.

One strong interest throughout New England was poetry. All schoolboys were taught to write verse as a matter of course: it was, after all, the age of Milton, Donne, Herbert. From Greek and Latin verse they turned automatically to verse in English. Funeral poems abounded. The Puritans held no funeral services as such, because they could find no scriptural warrant for them; the minister would go to the house, speak an extempore prayer to the family and friends grouped around the coffin, then lead the party in silence to the burial ground, where no further word was spoken. But funeral poems were printed, copies given to all who might be interested, and, as often as not, a copy attached to the coffin itself. These poems were modeled closely on the classic elegy, and usually incorporated an anagram on the dead person's name. Sometimes the printed sheets were decorated with woodcuts crammed with symbols of skeletons, skulls and crossbones, hourglasses run out, and the Grim Reaper himself.

Students enjoyed poetry of all kinds, often loving or lively verse filled with jokes and puns, and copied pieces they liked into thick commonplace books. The love of poetry pervaded all age groups. One pleasant amateur was John Saffin, ward of Edward Winslow. He came to New England when he was twelve, and ten years later fell in love with Martha, daughter of former fur trader Thomas Willet, who was now assistant to the colony. Willet agreed to the marriage provided Saffin made some money, and sent him to trade for four years in Virginia. Before leaving, Saffin went to say goodbye to Martha. She was asleep, so he kissed her without waking her up (it is fascinating to speculate who let him into her bedroom) and went off, writing a poem on the journey: "Sweetly, my Dearest, I left thee asleep," which includes the following lines:

> Thus in sad silence, I alone and mute,
> My lips bade thee farewell with a salute,
> And so went from thee. Turning back again,
> I thought one kiss too little; then stole twain,
> And then another.

It ended happily. Saffin made a modest fortune in the four years, sailed home, writing poetry on the way, married his Martha, lived with her for twenty years during which he went on writing poems to her, and never stopped thinking how pretty she was: "in Splendid Beauty," he wrote tenderly, "she did much Excell." This idyll does not fit the conception of a loveless community. Actually the Puritans and Separatists believed in love and marriage. It was in no way a monastic or celibate faith: clergy and laity alike were expected to marry young and often, and it is clear that they all enjoyed obeying the commandment to be fruitful and multiply. Abstinence was the opposite of creation; men who came over without their wives were told to send for them or else go back. Divorce, that European bugbear, was easier in the New World; the Planters wanted every marriage to be a success, for they believed in love. The Pilgrims never tried to force unhappy couples to stay together as they did (and sometimes still do) in many parts of Europe. Better to split and remarry, thus making two good marriages instead of one bad one —or so they hoped. It is often tragically overlooked even yet that divorce creates marriage, not destroys it.

As well as liking poetry, the students had an interest in science, as did others. Zachariah Brigden, that same who worked his way through Harvard by ringing the bell and waiting at table, wrote an essay on astronomy which was put into the 1659 almanac. In it he cheerfully quoted Galileo and Copernicus, whose theories were still too heretical to be acknowledged by the ministers. But the official reaction was admirably tolerant: the Reverend John Davenport of New Haven said that the young man was misguided, but no matter—"let him enjoy his opinion."

The greatest scientist was the younger John Winthrop, later governor of Connecticut. Aged twenty-five when he arrived there, he followed the sciences with engaging enthusiasm: practiced physics, assayed minerals, prospected for them, experimented in alchemy and chemistry, still regarded as a branch of physics, set up the first successful salt pans and ironworks in New England, and studied astronomy, importing the first telescope, three and a half feet, after a trip to London in 1663. He was elected a Fellow of the new Royal Society, and resisted all beguiling invitations to return to his native land. He presented the telescope to Harvard. His library had over a thousand volumes by 1640. The best in Plymouth, of course, was that of Brewster, which was principally theological as it needed to be since he preached three times a week, but whose more than four hundred books included works on medicine and herbal remedies, the cultivation of silkworms and the surveying of timber, and, oddly enough, a life of Messalina, of all people. More than a hundred of these books had been imported from England.

· 31 ·

It is an immensely difficult, if not impossible, task to judge precisely where Separatism ends and Puritanism begins. The word "Puritan" is emotive: pictures come to mind of killjoys in black, with set jaws and cold eyes, thundering denunciations in church, prohibiting this, damning that, practicing a totally unnatural degree of self-control, and from time to time darting into the woods and reappearing clutching a turkey. Of course a grain of truth exists inside this metaphorical sand pile: but only a grain.

True, it required a Puritan ethic to survive in New England. The English government left the colonists severely alone; they were free to formulate and enforce their own laws and way of life. Those who disagreed were expelled. In the tough conditions of pioneer life, small groups struggling to make over a portion of the earth in the spirit of Christian philosophy as they saw it, building a new City of God in the wilderness and making a fresh experiment in Christian living, it must be so. They worked on the basis of linking family with education, church with state, ethic with behavior, all intertwined.

Actually two close but different types of church government impelled the Puritan-Separatists. Those of Presbyterian cast supported the idea of the representative assembly or synod; those of the Congregational persuasion believed that each separate congregation was a gathering of God's elect, or visible Saints. The more democratic Congregationalists were the true founders of New England. Both groups, however, encouraged the laity to play an influential part in church and state affairs, and the elders were expected to guide and comment on all aspects of life. John Cotton, for example, called upon Robert Keayne to stand up in church and submit to a scathing criticism of his business ethics: as a profiteering merchant he was going against the Right Way.

What has given Puritanism its dark image is the core of the Puritans' belief that man is corrupt, vile, and far too readily won over by evil without the help of God. Man deserves to fry in hell forever without the divine grace. This is the clear opposite of a viewpoint like that of Rousseau, who said that man was born good and corrupted by civilization. Yet the diehard Calvinist theory of predestination was not that of the Puritans. Salvation was within the grasp of all, they said; God helps those who help themselves, as he is concerned with his created people, and they were not fatalists. If God was kind, it was because they had in some way deserved it. The world was a divine enterprise in which every man had a place, but it was not a fixed place beyond change. John Harvard had some of Calvin's books in his library, but he had more volumes of Thomas Aquinas than of Calvin. John Cotton's habit was to read Calvin before going to bed (sweetening his mouth with a bit of Calvin, he called it), yet he was exceptional; the Puritans did not usually quote from, or refer to, Calvin's works. Coming as their graduate members did mostly from Cambridge, it was the great theologians of that university they quoted: Ames, Chaderton, Perkins, Preston. Influenced by the England from which they sprang, they created communities based on the concepts of Church and Commonwealth, Town and Gown. Unlike the royalists in the South, they were by nature republican: God was the only king.

One criticism leveled at New England was its lack, or comparative lack, of good native-born writers for so long. It is true that those born in England produced the best colonial writing: John Cotton, John Wilson, Thomas Hooker, Thomas Shepard, the rebellious and fluent Roger Williams, naughty Thomas Morton, above all the superb Bradford himself. But they were so busy trying to stay alive and establish their Zion that it is amazing that there was any writing done at all. Also they were few: by the law of averages one cannot expect a Milton or Bunyan in a colony that by 1640 numbered some eighteen thousand and had only a little passed the hundred-thousand mark by 1700.

They banned three art forms. There must be no drama. (Yet they were pleased, critical, and attentive audiences for a dramatic sermon.) Erotic poetry was out. This is easier to understand: plain living and high thinking do not readily go with hedonistic or sensual imagery. They prohibited religious music. Secular music was all right: they liked that; but there was no scriptural warrant for music in church, and besides, with their never-failing grasp of the practical, they feared it made people dreamy. No anesthetics must intervene between sinful man and his attentive awareness of the Word of God.

Every boy in the colonial territories was taught to bear arms, to shoot accurately, and to drill with the militia. The colonial troops were in truth a civilian army, loosely organized and quickly called to mobilization. During King Philip's War, for example, on the night of September 23, 1675, the alarm sounded at a town thirty miles out of Boston brought 1200 militiamen mustered and ready for action within an hour. The New England military picture puts one forcibly in mind of the South African Boers of the late nineteenth century: they were a civilian army, called upon when and where

Of plimoth plantation

And first of y occasion, and yndusments ther vnto; the which
that y may truly vnfould, y must begine at y very roote & rise
of y same The which y shall endeuor to manefest in a plaine
stile; with singuler regard vnto y simple trueth in all things,
at least as near as my slender judgmente can attaine
the same.

1 Chapter

It is well knowne vnto y godly, and judicious, how euer since y
first breaking out of y lighte of y gospell, in our Honourable Nation of England (which was y first of nations, whom y Lord adorn-
ed ther with, affter y grosse darknes of popery which had couer-
ed, & ouerspred y Christian world) what warrs, & oppositions euer
since, satan hath raised, maintained, and continued against the
saincts, from time, to time, in one sorte, or other. Some times by
bloody death & cruell torments, other whiles ymprisonments, banish-
ments, & other hard vsages As being loath his kingdom should goe
downe, the trueth preuaile; and y Churches of god reuerte to their
anciente puritie, and recouer, their primatiue order, libertie, &
bewtie. But when he could not preuaile by these means, against
the maine trueths of y gospell, but that they began to take rooting
in many places; being watered with y blood of y martires,
and blesed from heauen with a gracious encrease He then begane to take him to his anciente strategemes, vsed of old against
the first Christians. That when by y bloody, & barbarous persecutions of y Heathen Emperours, he could not stoppe, & subuerte
the course of y gospell; but that it speedily ouerspred, with
a wounderfull celeritie, the then best known parts of y world
He then begane to sow errours, heresies, and wounderfull
disentions amongst y proffessours them selues (working vpon their
pride, & ambition, with other corrupte pasions, yncidente to
all mortall men; yea to y saints them selues in some measure)
By which wofull effects followed; as not only bitter contentions, &
hartburnings, schismes, with other horrible confusions. But
satan tooke occasion & aduantage therby to foyst in a number
of vile ceremoneys, with many vnprofitable cannons, & decrees
which haue since been as snares, to many poore, & peacable
souls, euen to this day So as in y anciente times, the persecuti-

Facsimile of first page of Governor Bradford's *History of the
Plimoth Plantation*. (THE BETTMAN ARCHIVE)

required, seeing their army duty as a disagreeable necessity; their way of life had made them fine shots, and a local defense force was gathered together in a way that suggests picking up a team. This kind of fighting could, and did, in both South Africa and New England, defeat and bewilder the British professional army. But the Boers were Separatists even from one another: they shunned the close community, moved away alike from their neighbors and the law, and wanted none of the pattern of settlement shown from the first in the New World.

The Pilgrims, of course, were basically pacific in outlook and intent. Their fight was the spiritual one. But they could go to war when they had to, and observed with the keenest interest the course of the great struggle out of which England wrested her liberty. Bradford's reaction to the English Civil War was partly typically unwarlike:

> Full little did I think that the downfall of the Bishops and their courts, canons and ceremonies had been so near when I began these scribbled writings.

But its result made him quite untypically jubilant too. Nowhere else in his journal does he break out into such a tone of barely contained gleeful exultation:

> Rejoice, yea, and again rejoice, and say Hallelujah, salvation, and glory, and honour, and power to the Lord our God, for true and righteous are His judgments. Hallelujah!

It was enough, he thought, to have lived to see "that joyful harvest."

· 32 ·

It is essential to remember that although in numbers and way of life the Massachusetts Bay colonists rapidly overshadowed those of

Plymouth, yet none might have gone there had it not been for the *Mayflower*. The Puritans who began to pepper the shores of the Bay with settlements from 1630 were unlike the original Separatists in that they intended to stay more or less inside the church framework and "purify" it from within. To simplify the ritual, eliminate the bishops (dislike of bishops equally pervaded both groups), and set up their own dominant theocracy was the Puritan aim. Stricter and sterner than the Separatists, they began by establishing the "Bible commonwealth" under such demanding spiritual leaders as John Cotton and Increase and Cotton Mather. It was under the Bay influence, not that of Plymouth, that the extremes of intolerance like the Salem witch-hunting took place.

In some ways, however, both groups had ideas in common. Both found comfort in the democracy of town meetings; both were English in origin, similar in language, manners, piety, and ways of thought; both sprang from like stock, minor squires, yeomen, farmers, shopkeepers, mechanics, with a stern pride in their origin, a full concept of opportunity and a sense of special destiny. The Royalist conformists went to Virginia; the New England settlers, who imported no slaves, had to become jacks-of-all-trades. Every man must be prepared to act if necessary as doctor, lawyer, architect, planner, diplomat. New England had from the first a zeal for education that dwarfed that of Virginia. Within five years of its foundation, Boston had its public Latin School; Harvard started the following year. So did industry: the fast-running rivers and streams of the North encouraged the development of water mills, there were sawmills and gristmills in plenty, leather tanning, rum distilling, wool spinning; soon the foreign commerce of Boston alone showed a staggering total of six hundred vessels. Most households were self-supporting, making their own furniture and shoes. On the small farms in the stimulating climate the owners worked with their own hands, unlike those of Virginia, who saw their overseers in the fields supervising slaves under a hot sun.

In the South were great plantations, but in the North were the compact towns, each with its local government chosen by its people. In both areas, land was the key to social success, but the two interpretations were utterly different. It is not too much to say that from the beginning, planted in the New World, lay the seeds of dissent that were to bloom two centuries later into the American Civil War.

It seems as though the North scored over the South in general contentment. No complaints appear in contemporary accounts that can compare with Governor William Berkeley of Virginia's lament in 1676 about the burden of power:

> How miserable that man is that Governes a People when six parts
> of seaven at least are Poore, Endebted, Discontented, and
> Armed.

Possibly the reason may lie in the basic concept common to Puritans and Separatists alike that work is valuable in itself. Hard-headed, if narrow, enterprise, piety, industry, thrift, coupled with the belief that idleness is sin and that the New England colonists were the chosen people, elect of God, forged their character, which set its stamp forever on the best, and some of the worst, of American attitudes. The worst was the killjoy intolerance that has made life a misery for many lively souls; the best, far outweighing this, was the heroic strain that gave America its finest quality: the New England conscience. Oliver Wendell Holmes touched upon it in a comment he made soon after 1865. He was writing of medical treatment, and it is plain that New England was very sensible in such matters. In Plymouth and the Bay, people used simple naturalistic remedies. Smallpox, that great scourge, was treated by a regimen of no meat, no wine, fresh air, small beer warmed, water gruel, something called water pottage, and other easily digestible food including stewed apples and warm milk. For all illness, simple herb medicines were employed, though Governor Winthrop did prescribe a paste made from woodlice (it is not clear what to cure). Holmes wrote:

I suspect that the conditions of rude, stern life, in which the colonists found themselves in the wilderness, took the nonsense out of them, as the exigencies of a campaign did out of our physicians and surgeons in the late War. Good food and enough of it, pure air and water, cleanliness, good attendance, an anaesthetic, an opiate, a stimulant, quinine, and two or three common drugs, proved to be the marrow of medical treatment.

Certainly it is true that after the first terrible winter the Pilgrims lived long and healthily.

In 1650, thirty years after the great voyage, Bradford wrote a summary in his journal of what had become of the survivors. What strikes the reader most forcibly is how very well established those survivors were. John and Elizabeth Tilley Howland had ten children and five grandchildren. Love Brewster, who had died that year aged thirty-seven, had four children living; Jonathan Brewster and his nine or ten children and one or two grandchildren were still alive, and so were other Brewster grandchildren.

Then there were Richard More and his wife and their four or five children; Edward and Susanna White Winslow and their two children of marriageable age; George and Mary Becket Soule and their eight children; Miles and Barbara Standish and their four sons; John and Priscilla Mullins Alden, their eleven children and five grandchildren; Resolved and Judith Vassall White with five children; Peregrine White with two children.

Alive too were Giles and Catherine Wheldon Hopkins, with four children; Constanta Hopkins Snow and twelve children; Francis Billington with eight; Henry and Ann Plummer Sampson with seven; Joseph Rogers with six; Samuel and Jane Lothrop Fuller with at least four; Samuel and Martha Billington Eaton with one; Francis Cooke; John and Sarah Warren Cooke with four.

Bradford's second wife, Alice Carpenter Southworth, was still alive, and so were their four children, three of them married.

"Of those few remaining," wrote Bradford, "are sprung up above 160 persons in this thirty years. . . . And of the old stock, of

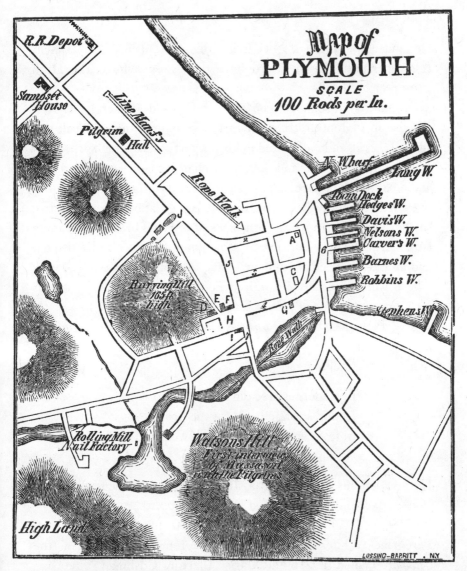

A. Joanna Davis House—Cole's Hill.
B. Plymouth Rock and Wells's Store.
C. Universalist Church.
D. First Church.
E. Church of the Pilgrimage.
F. Post-Office—Site of Gov. Bradford's House.
G. Saml. D. Holmes's House—Site of Common House.
H. Town Square
I. Town House.
J. Court-House Square.

1. Court-street.
2. North-street.
3. Middle-street.
4. Leyden-street.
5. Main-street.
6. Water-street.
7. Market-street.

A map of Plymouth, Massachusetts, in the 1880s. (BROWN BROTHERS) one and other, there are yet living this present year, 1650, near thirty persons. Let the Lord have the praise, who is the High Preserver of men."

Bradford himself died on May 9, 1657, aged sixty-eight. He left a house in Plymouth valued at forty-five pounds, an orchard, and several parcels of land. Listed in his property were ten chairs (six of leather, three carved, and one great chair), a court cupboard, ten and a half pairs of sheets and a large quantity of table linen, about five dozen pewter dishes, cups, and bowls, a great beer bowl and two smaller ones. There were clothes: a suit of red Turkey grogram, a stuff suit with silver buttons, a "sad-coloured" suit, a red waistcoat and an old violet cloak, and two hats, one black and one colored. There were about four hundred books, many in Dutch, others including John Speed's *Prospect of the Most Famous Part of the World*, Peter Martyr's *De Orbe Novo*, Jean Bodin's *De Republica*, and Pierre de la Primaudaye's *The French Academy*. He left some hymn verses, including:

> In wilderness He did me guide,
> And in strange lands for me provide.
> In fears and wants, through weal and woe,
> A Pilgrim passed I to and fro.

He also left his journal. After 1691 his dream ended, when the Plymouth colony was absorbed by Massachusetts.

Resolved White was still alive in 1690, John Cooke in 1694, Peregrine White in 1700. The last female survivor of the *Mayflower* died in 1699: Mary Allerton Cushman. She was eighty-three.

PART FOUR

The Freshest

Advices

It took time, of course, for the Pilgrims to become folklore. When they did, as is usual with folklore, the original concepts were wildly inaccurate. Subsequent generations grew up with hazy mental pictures of a group of stiff, solemn-faced persons in unrelieved black, stepping ashore precisely onto the Rock, kneeling down to give thanks, watched at close quarters by impassive braves. By the opening years of the nineteenth century something more obviously romantic was called for: the simple facts, few of them known still, required dressing in more colorful garb. Accordingly the Pilgrims were displayed on the stage. In 1808 "A New Melo Drama" was performed in Boston,* and highly spectacular it turned out to be, incorporating a snowstorm, an Indian march, wedding and marriage dance, a demonstration of "the Indian method of lying in ambush," and some singing. The scenario is full of the wildest inaccuracies. The moment the Pilgrims land, Governor Carver orders one of them to set to work with a chisel to engrave the date, December 22, 1620, on the Rock. Apart from anything else he would have been ten days out in his reckoning. One scene shows "a dreadful combat with clubs and shields" between Samoset and Squanto. This is the more remarkable because in the previous act Samoset has been thrown down a cliff by somebody called Juliana, apparently Winslow's girl friend, whose function throughout seems to be similar to that of Fanny in *Joseph Andrews,* forever threatened with seduction and rape. Not only does Samoset spring up briskly from the foot of the precipice to fight Squanto, but the Indians as a whole appear to bear no malice, for the act ends with "a Procession of Indians,

*Appendix 8.

311

carrying Winslow and Juliana on their boughs." The whole production concludes superbly, as "the Genius of Columbia descends in a Magnificent Temple, surrounded with Clouds."

The Melo Drama included a comic scene between an Irish boatswain named Blunder and an Indian squaw somewhat oddly called Yankee, and its cast list included four specific Pilgrims—Carver, Winslow, Standish, and Cushman (who as we know was not there at all)—and what is spaciously termed "other Pilgrims." It was presented three times in 1808 and 1809, and one actress who played the part of an "other Pilgrim" was pregnant at the time. Her baby was Edgar Allan Poe.

The man responsible for making the Pilgrims into a legend was Henry Wadsworth Longfellow. He was also responsible for much of the confusion on the subject that still exists in the minds of many, for he drew no distinction at all between the Plymouth settlers and the Bay settlers, lumping them all together as Puritans. He claimed *Mayflower* ancestry: John Alden, William Brewster, and Robert Bartlett of the *Anne* were among his forebears. Soon enough all manner of people were saying that they were descended from the original stock, many on the flimsiest grounds. It was not to be expected that the most prominent citizens could fail to show a connection, and four presidents of the United States are credited with *Mayflower* ancestry: Zachary Taylor descended from William Brewster and Isaac Allerton; Ulysses S. Grant from Richard Warren; William Howard Taft from Francis Cooke; and Franklin Delano Roosevelt shows the most glittering pedigree of all, from Cooke and Allerton, Warren, John Howland and John Tilley, and the De la Noye family.

In the latter part of the nineteenth century Americans began to travel to Europe for pleasure, partly to enlarge their cultural background, increasingly to hunt out the homes of their ancestors. As time went on, certain fixed spots were more and more regarded as essentials in a reversed pilgrimage. Societies dedicated to the discovery and preservation of family records and positive links with places of origin sprang up all over the United States, but New

A modern day recreation of early Plymouth. (PHOTO PLIMOTH PLANTATION)

England took and held the lead in that, as in so many other enterprises.* A perfect rash of commemorative plaques appeared to mark every discoverable spot the Pilgrims had stepped upon. Some of these are now gently decaying, seldom visited by any but the most thorough.

One such is at Immingham, on the muddy shore of the Humber, marking the place where the Dutch captain took the men on board for that terrifying crossing to Holland. The monument, a tapered column of stone mounted on rough granite blocks, is twenty feet high, topped with a piece cut from the Rock itself, set up in 1925 by the Anglo-American Society. It stands north of the dock at the edge of a small creek by the remains of a tiny pier, and is left for the most part proclaiming its message to the air and the wheeling gulls.

Scrooby fares little better. Few stop there to note the place that Wolsey stayed at, or Margaret Tudor on her way to marry James

*Appendix 9.

IV of Scotland, or Henry VIII himself, who held a meeting of the Privy Council. Archbishop Sandys, who supported the claim of Lady Jane Grey to the English crown, often visited the manor held by his kinsmen. As for William Brewster, not much is left in Scrooby to remind the passer-by of his presence. Because some people believed he had lived at the old inn, now reduced to a few cottages near the church, a plaque on the wall inaccurately informs the reader:

> Here lived William Brewster from 1588 to 1608, and where he organised the Pilgrim Church, of which he became the ruling. elder, and with which, in 1608, he removed to Amsterdam, in 1609 to Leyden, and in 1620 to Plymouth, where he died April the sixteenth, 1644.

He did in fact live in Scrooby from 1575, and died in 1643, and he lived in the manor house: but at least there is the plaque, and the inn is called the Pilgrim Fathers. The sign is painted with a picture of two rather grim-looking Pilgrims.

Scrooby church dates from 1390, was modernized in the last century, and the carved screen Brewster knew has been cut up to furnish the back of the so-called Brewster pew and two small seats in the chancel. The vine-and-grape pattern can still be recognized, but the font has gone to America, along with the village stocks. A stone in the floor bears the name of Penelope Sandys. Some of the windows are Tudor, the nave arcade and the porch are four-teenth-century, and the massive carved end of the Brewster pew is fifteenth-century. The roof has battlements, and the fine square tower is chamfered at the top to make an octagon ornamented with battlements and four pinnacles. Above these rises the spire, twice struck by lightning, and around the building flows the grass of the churchyard.

The manor house, a truncated portion of what it was, has a few bits dating from Brewster's time: a few stone window frames, roof beams in an outbuilding, an arch showing in one of the outer walls, and the old dovecote. Not far from the back of the house runs the main line of the Eastern Region of British Rail, where every day the express trains whiz by on the long route between London and Edinburgh. The bulk of today's road traffic uses the motorway and leaves Scrooby quiet. One recent reminder is the Mayflower housing estate, but this is small by metropolitan standards. Not many Americans find their way to the place now.

Even fewer go to Sturton-le-Steeple, "the town on the street." Most of the church was destroyed by fire in the early years of the present century, and although it has been rebuilt in the original style using much of the original material, all that remains of the building John Robinson knew is the fine tower. The lower half is six hundred years old, the upper four. It has a tall arch and nine windows, a crown of battlements and twelve pinnacles. Barely half a dozen signatures in the visitors' book over half a dozen years reveal how seldom any Americans come to see it.

Gainsborough hardly beats that. Tourists who go there seem more interested in George Eliot. The John Robinson Memorial Chapel, a Congregational church, stands beside the Church of All Saints, and dates from 1896. Apparently many people were under the impression that Robinson was born in Gainsborough. Certainly only a handful of visitors go there looking for references to him. Most tourists are on the track of Tom and Maggie Tulliver.

The name of Austerfield is at least twelve centuries old. Overlooking the wide spread of the Carr lowlands, it is a nondescript cluster of red-roofed houses among which is the birthplace of William Bradford. An unpretentious building, it still has its original attic, and a twisting steep staircase in what was really a chimney. Legend says that Bradford once had to hide in a copper in the cellar while the local magistrates searched the house in vain for him, but this is doubtful. His baptism in 1589 is listed in the church register, and the font is the same one. The church aisle was rebuilt by the Society of *Mayflower* Descendants in 1897: a plaque records its debt to them and "other citizens of the United States" in memory of Bradford as "the first American citizen of the English race who bore rule by the free choice of his brethren."

The plain little church has a Norman doorway with zigzag and beakhead carving on the arch, and a dragon on the tympanum. A Norman buttress still exists at the west end, where there is a thirteenth-century lancet window. One or two other windows are fourteenth-century. Like the other neighboring Pilgrim places, Austerfield attracts only a very occasional tourist.

Boston, of course, is different. But here the problem is to separate Plymouth from the Bay Colony, an impossible task. Those Americans who come to see the namesake of the leading city in Massachusetts and those who come to trace the Pilgrims' steps usually have a quick look at both aspects of the agreeable old town. In South Street stands the Guildhall, the fifteenth-century hall of the Guild of St. Mary, containing a small art gallery and museum. The gabled west front has a stone mullioned window set with the original glass, and the minstrels' gallery and the old stairs leading up to it are the ones the Pilgrims saw. Next door to the Guildhall is the courtroom where the magistrates questioned the Pilgrims. The remains of the steps down to the kitchen were there then, also the old fireplace, and, focal point of interest, the little iron-barred cells in which the Pilgrims were confined.

In the early years of the seventeenth century the population of London was about 150,000, not quite double that of Leyden. It has already been noted that Christopher Jones's home village of Rotherhithe was a scene of rural peace when he lived there. Today it is still curiously tranquil, though not countrified. The Thames at Rotherhithe makes a wide shallow curve, lined with warehouses, some of them still hollow shells unaltered since 1945. Directly behind Rotherhithe station, in the street running parallel with the river, stands the Mayflower inn, a diminutive building with whitewashed walls and blackened beams, lit by lanterns and carrying a gilt model ship on its sign. The brewery company of Messrs. Charrington supplies its beer, and it is split up into three sections: the Mariners' Bar, the New Settlers' Bar, and the Pilgrims' Restaurant. The ceilings are low and the walls decorated with ship drawings and charts. At the back a little oblong balcony overhangs the water, and out there with the evocative river smell and the anchored barges and the wash of a passing launch making ripples on the greenish stone of the wall, one can see, away to the left, the tips of the Tower Bridge turrets, and on the right, along the north bank, the small white shape of another famous waterside inn, the Prospect of Whitby. It is the easiest thing in the world, even today, staring across at the faded yellowish front of the Gun Wharves, to picture the *Mayflower* anchored below.

Behind the inn, a few paces to the west, past a narrow house decorated with the painted statues of two Victorian children, stands St. Mary's Church, where Christopher Jones is buried. A leaflet inside tells the visitors that there has been a church on this site for over a thousand years. The present building is later than Jones, completed in 1715. Its roof frame shows that shipwrights built it. Four tall pillars are actually full tree trunks encased in plaster shells. There is a communion table made from the oak of the *Temeraire*, which fought at Trafalgar and was broken up at Rotherhithe. On the wall above this are two plaques, one bearing a bas-relief carving of a *Mayflower*-style ship and dedicated to Captain Anthony Wood, who died in 1628, and the other, set up in 1965, in memory of Christopher Jones. Three other part owners of the *Mayflower* are buried at St. Mary's. Most of the original churchyard has been turned into a children's playground, and the old indecipherable tombstones have been neatly aligned, shoulder to shoulder, along the north wall.

· 2 ·

The spot where *Mayflower* and *Speedwell* lay in Southampton is now covered by streets and buildings. The old West Gate, through which would come anyone having business with the two ships, bears a commemorative plaque to the Pilgrims mounted below one for Agincourt. Midway between the West Gate and the Royal Pier stands the tall *Mayflower* monument, crowned by a bronze model of the vessel poised on the narrow canopied top. It was unveiled on August 15, 1913, and has since acquired other tablets, including those set there by the descendants of Alden, Brewster, and Winslow, and (perhaps not entirely inappropriately) a plaque commemorating the American forces that sailed from Southampton with the liberating armies to invade the Normandy coast on June 6, 1944.

In the days when American travelers came by sea and the great port of entry was Southampton, more of them paused between passing customs and setting out for London to look at the memorial and the West Gate. Now, with the vast majority arriving by air, this no longer happens.

Dartmouth is so exquisitely beautiful that the first thought in the visitor's mind is amazement that anyone could bear to leave

Dartsmouth, Bayard's Cove today. (PHOTO NICHOLAS SERVIAN FIIP,

WOODMANSTERNE LIMITED)

such a scene forever. From the center of the present-day town the sea is invisible: the Dart curves in a big bend, cutting off the seaward view. On a fine summer day it is splendidly photogenic: blue sparkling water, dotted all over with boats, patches of shade under the trees lining the quay, handsome buildings painted in white and pastel colors, river steamers cruising by, the ferry chugging stolidly across to Kingswear, the huge pink bulk of the Royal Naval College high on its hilltop to the north, and the whole framed in a delectable sweep of patchwork fields and waving woods under a cloudless blue sky. The thing to do is to walk south along the riverbank. In a few moments it is obvious that here is the older part of the town. An opening in the wall, forbidden to motorists, leads to Bayard's Cove, which is not a cove at all but a short quay lined with charming old houses including the pale pink Customs House. Now the end of the estuary is visible, a gap of open sea beyond the rocky silhouette of the old castle. At the end of Bayard's Cove is a little round tower with deep-set embrasures in the thick rough walls: through these one can see fragments of the view in each direction. At the north end of Bayard's Cove is a stone plaque set on the wall in 1955 and unveiled in 1957: no other memorial exists to mark the two ships' repair stop in 1620.

Not far from the plaque, in a street lined with shops, stands Speedwell House, but the name seems quite fortuitous: it carries a small inscription stating that the house dates from 1365 and was restored six hundred years later. It looks undistinguished. Only the name catches the eye. A bit farther along is the Mayflower Gift Shop, so called, incongruously enough, by an Italian who came over after World War II to work on mosaics at the Naval College. He took a liking to Dartmouth, decided to stay, set up shop, and gave it its present name.

In the center of Dartmouth stands the town's showpiece, the Butterwalk, a well-preserved wooden arcade of shops, among which is the town museum. This is crammed with ship models, among them a model of the *Mayflower*. Regrettably there appears to be none of the *Speedwell*. Suspended from a large carved chimneypiece

hangs a framed and illuminated poem of rather deplorably senti-
mental quality on the subject of the *Mayflower* and the Pilgrims.
Dartmouth is packed with holidaymakers in summer, but they seem
to be almost entirely from Scotland and the north of England:
voices heard in the street are more likely to reveal the flat vowels
and ironic intonation of the north of England than the creamy
warmth of the west country.

The traveler hopefully looking for Americans approaches Plymouth with greater optimism. Surely, one thinks, they must at least
come here. The place to make for is of course the Barbican. There
are two ways of walking to it, both interesting. Either one can come
from the Hoe, past the citadel gate dated 1670, over Lambhay Hill
by a neat little complex of modern houses called Paton Watson
Quadrate to a flight of stone steps overlooking Sutton Pool, or one
can come up Southside Street. This narrow thoroughfare, with little
side paths quaintly named Parade Ope, Southside Ope opposite Pin
Lane, and Citadel Ope, is obviously in the oldest part of Plymouth.
Past the Pilgrims' Rest eating house and the Mayflower Antiques,
the road opens out a little to reveal, on the opposite side of the
street, the Dolphin Hotel, an enchanting shop called Charles R.
Cload Limited, Ship and Yacht Chandler, the Mayflower cake shop,
and an inn named Sir Francis Chichester. Then, facing the harbor,
is the Pilgrim gift shop, whose proprietress says that quite a lot of
Americans call in "but all·they buy is a postcard."

New Street, a tiny narrow cobbled way that was new in 1584,
runs uphill on the right. Two ancient little buildings stand on its
southern side: the Elizabethan House, now a museum, with a
hand-written label pinned to one of the corner beams announcing
forbiddingly "Danger—falling slates," and the Green Lanterns
restaurant, displaying two green lanterns on the fascia board and an
elaborately archaic menu card, clearly worked out for 1970, in the
window. It looks appealing, all the same, but again the Americans
who come to Plymouth tend to whiz through on coach trips and
make it plain that as far as England is concerned the great attraction
is Shakespeare.

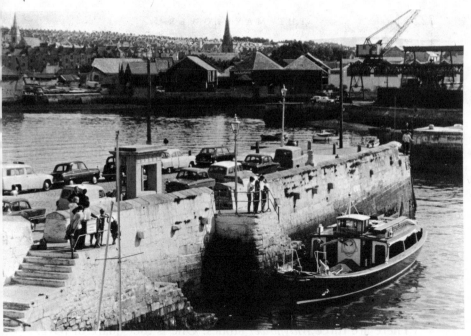

Plymouth, the *Mayflower* steps today. (PHOTO NICHOLAS SERVIAN FIIP, WOODMANSTERNE LIMITED)

Past New Street is the small irregularly shaped island site of Island House, facing the side of the gift shop where a brown wooden board lists "the Pilgrim Fathers who sailed from here The Barbican Plymouth in the Mayflower 1620." It would seem from that as though fifty-two adult males went to the New World: not one woman is listed, and the boys such as Richard More, aged seven, and Jasper More, aged six, are named in precisely the same way as the rest.

Jutting out at right angles to the Barbican is the stone jetty on which the *Mayflower* monument stands. Here is another surprise for the visitor. The Barbican pier is positively cluttered with plaques. There are eight of them—nine, if the Royal Australian Air Force tablet a few yards away at the foot of Lambhay steps is included. There are three pavement stones as well.* The *Mayflower* was not the first memorable colonist ship: the *Sea Ven-*

* Appendix 10.

ture set out for Virginia in 1609, and was wrecked on a reef in Bermuda, unwittingly starting the existence of Britain's oldest colony. The *Tory,* sailing in 1839 to begin the settlement of New Zealand, is remembered with a plaque and a stone. The arrival in 1919 of the United States Navy seaplane NC 4, having completed the first transatlantic flight, has a tablet in its memory. So have the Tolpuddle Martyrs. So has the Queen, who left Plymouth from that spot in 1962 after an official visit. Perhaps the nicest, and certainly the handsomest, of the plaques is the one dated 1826 that simply informs the reader that

> IRON PIPES for the better supply of water to the inhabitants and shipping were commenced being laid at the expence of the Corporation in the Mayoralty of W. H. Hawker, Esq.

There are three *Mayflower* stones. One is the square of pavement the passerby can step on, saying merely "MAYFLOWER 1620." One explains that the American Ambassador, the Honorable Walter Annenberg, unveiled it to mark the 350th anniversary of the *Mayflower* voyage. The third, mounted upright on the wall next but one to Mr. Annenberg's, is protected by a narrow stone canopy on pillars in the classic style, and was placed there in 1891, to commemorate not only the sailing, but also "the visit to Plymouth in July of that Year of a number of their Descendants and Representatives."

Its opening quotes Winslow:

> On the 6th of September, 1620, in the Mayoralty of Thomas Fownes, after being 'kindly entertained and courteously used by divers friends there dwelling,' the Pilgrim Fathers sailed from Plymouth in the MAYFLOWER, in the Providence of God to settle in NEW PLYMOUTH. . . .

It mentions that the ancient cawsey, or causeway, from which the Pilgrims embarked was destroyed "not many Years afterwards," but that the exact spot is marked by the pavement stone.

Coach parties of Americans stop at the Barbican, walk up to the arch, take a picture, look across the opaque water of Sutton Pool, resist for the most part the blandishments of men in dark-blue jerseys who want to take them for a nice sail around the Sound, look in a few shop windows, and go on their way in about twenty minutes or half an hour. Not often do they stay long enough to have a look around the city. Of course a great deal of it has been rebuilt during the last thirty years, since Plymouth took a battering in the bombing raids of World War II, when wide stretches of the city were flattened out. Here and there a new building has struck a *Mayflower* note. The Plymouth branch of W. H. Smith, the big chain of booksellers, has a large mural in bas-relief, colored in brilliant enamels, of the *Mayflower* and the Pilgrim Fathers, mounted on its staircase. In the Plymouth telephone directory there are twenty-one Mayflowers, fourteen of them in Plymouth itself, including an aquarium, a cinema, a dress shop, a hairdresser's, an insurance broker's, a sailing club, and a car-servicing shop. (The Southampton directory has four, Exeter three, and Boston three. None of the Exeter Mayflowers is in the city itself: there is one at Cullompton, one at Okehampton, and a hotel at Torquay.)

Up on Plymouth Hoe stands the Mayflower Post House, built for the 350th anniversary in 1970. It is uncompromisingly modern, luxurious, and designed for businessmen as well as for tourists. Conferences are referred to the Standish Suite. By an odd quirk of blurred historical sense, or it may be for general appeal, the hotel contains a drinking room called the Boston Bar. An enormous carved black mural in the lounge hall shows a somewhat grim-faced, mournful procession of Pilgrims trailing toward their ship. The restaurant menu is massive, but at the time of writing contains only two items that might be connected with the *Mayflower:* Chicken Barbican, and a dish described as "scampi and veal Massasoit."

Certainly the hotel occupies a magnificent site, at the western end of the Hoe, its ten stories commanding a splendid view of the sound with Drake's Island and the twin mounts. But it is Drake whose personality pervades the Hoe still. Among the monuments, the old lighthouse, the aligned flagpoles flying the flags of many nations, the bright flowerbeds and the clipped lawns bordering the broad walk, it is Drake's statue that catches the eye, forcing itself on the spectator's attention, although it is one of the smallest objects in sight. Members of the hotel staff inform the visitor that quite a lot of Americans stay in the Post House, but not nearly so many of their ancestors crossed on the *Mayflower* as they apparently did in the past.

· 3 ·

It is not certain what happened to the *Mayflower*. Apparently by 1624 she had three joint owners, Robert Child, John Moore, and Mrs. Josian Jones, widow of the captain. These three applied in that year to the Admiralty for an appraisal. It was carried out by four mariners and shipwrights of Rotherhithe, who valued the vessel at the unpretentious total of one hundred and twenty-eight pounds, eight shillings, and fourpence. Dr. Rendel Harris was so dissatisfied with that figure in 1920 that he declared it must have been Mrs. Jones's share only. By the will of one Robert Sheffield of Stepney, dated September 10, 1625, his share of the *Mayflower* was bequeathed to his wife Joan or Josian. Was this the former Mrs. Jones? If it was, she had married three times and went on to make it four, for Robert Sheffield's widow married Simon Jefferson of Blackfriars in 1630, whereupon Sheffield's heirs brought out a lawsuit against Jefferson in 1636 concerning "the *Mayflower* and other property." Who in fact inherited? Was this the same *Mayflower,* or was she, as some suggest, broken up after the 1624 appraisal?

The kind of confusion awaiting the historian is well shown by the following example. In 1621 Captain Richard Swan sailed in the *Hart* to the Arabian coast, a voyage listed in the marine records of the East India Company. Swan joined a fleet which set out from the port of Surat in the Punjab on April 6. The fleet, heading for the Persian Gulf, captured on May 1 a two-hundred-ton Portuguese vessel, the *San Antonio,* bound for Goa with a cargo of rice. This prize was renamed *Mayflower.* She sailed so badly (Swan called her "that leeward cart") that she delayed the fleet, but on June 7 four ships, *London, Andrews, Primrose,* and *Mayflower,* anchored beyond Ras-al-Hadd, referred to by the English as Cape Rosalgate. Here they enjoyed "all sorts of refreshments" until a guerrilla force of "certain Portingals" arrived to defend the port and drive the English out. The English riposted briskly, defeated the Portuguese, and "for their dishonesty burned the town and spoiled many of their date trees." Then the fleet went on to the Persian Gulf where the soi-disant *Mayflower,* which had been leaking badly, was broken up for firewood. The account of the whole affair was written by Richard Jefferies on October 5, 1621.

Now it is clear that the ci-devant *San Antonio* had not the remotest connection with the great *Mayflower.* What has muddled historians is the *Mayflower* of 1629 and 1630. Thomas Prence wrote in his journal in August 1629:

> Thirty-five of our friends with their families arrived at Plymouth. They shipped at London in May, with the ships that came to Salem, which brings over many pious persons to begin the churches there. So that their being long kept back is now accomplished by Heaven with a double blessing. . . . The charge is reckoned on the several families, some fifty pounds, some forty, some thirty, as their numbers and expenses were, which our undertakers pay for gratis, besides giving them houses, preparing them grounds to plant on, and maintain them with corn, etc., above thirteen or fourteen months, before they have a harvest of their own production.

James Sherley sent a letter with the new arrivals, dated March 25, 1629, which said in part:

> Here are now many of yours and our friends from Leyden, coming over who though for the most part be but a weak company, yet herein is a good part of that end ordained, which

was aimed at, and which hath been so strongly opposed, by some of our former Adventurers. But God hath His working in these things, which man cannot frustrate. With them we have also sent some servants in the ship called the *Talbot* that went hence lately; but these come in the *Mayflower*.

And Captain John Smith wrote under the date 1629:

In this year a great company of people of good rank, zeal, means, and quality, have made a great stock, and with six good ships in the months of April and May they set sail from Thames for the Bay of Massachusetts, otherwise called Charles River; viz. the *George Bonaventure* of twenty pieces of ordnance, the *Talbot* nineteen, the *Lions Whelp* eight, the *Mayflower* fourteen, the *Four Sisters* fourteen, the *Pilgrim* four, with three hundred and fifty men, women and children.

The master of the *Mayflower* was William Peirce. Roger Harman commanded the *Four Sisters* and William Wobridge the *Pilgrim*. (It is interesting to find *Pilgrim* as a ship's name so early.) The *Mayflower* reached Salem on June 30 in one account, on May 15 in another. Although she carried many Puritans for the Bay Colony, there were a few passengers for Plymouth, including Dr. Thomas Blossom, his wife Anne Heilsdon Blossom, their son and daughter Thomas and Elizabeth; Richard and Mary Goodall Masterson and their son and daughter Nathaniel and Sarah; Thomas Willet; and Kenelm Winslow, one more of the eminent Winslows who played so large a part in New England history.

In 1630 the *Mayflower* sailed from Southampton with the *Whale*. She was listed as "*Mayflower* of Yarmouth." Peirce was by then master of the *Lion*.

A *Mayflower* of Yarmouth, tonnage between 240 and 250, owner Thomas Howarth, is registered as sailing under letters of marque to the fishing grounds off Greenland on July 23, 1626, October 3, 1627, and June 29, 1631.

Then there is the *Mayflower* commanded by Thomas Webber

of Boston, the ship that brought John Eliot's order of canvas to America from England in 1654. She was about two hundred tons burden, and when she was riding at anchor in Boston Harbor on October 6, 1652, Webber sold one sixteenth of her "for good and valuable considerations" to one John Pinchon of Springfield, Massachusetts. Next day he sold another sixteenth to Theodore Atkinson, a Boston feltmaker, "as well as of said ship as of all and singular her masts, sails, sailyards, etc."

A visiting British scholar, Sir Edwin Arnold, speaking in 1889 at Harvard on the subject of Sanskrit studies, told his audience about a *Mayflower* that had been sunk off the coast of Coromandel in 1659. He mentioned Masulipatam and Malabar. This *Mayflower*, he said, was 240 tons burden, carried twenty-four guns and a crew of fifty-five, and had sailed to Coromandel with the *Eagle* and the *Endymion* in 1655. The three ships had arranged to rendezvous at St. Helena on the way home if they happened to get separated at sea. This *Mayflower* had arrived at Plymouth, Devon, on August 26, 1657, and had set out for Coromandel again on February 22, 1658, with a cargo of bullion worth £7500. She had sunk the following year, apparently in shallow water, for the wreck passed into the hands of an Indian broker in Surat on February 16, 1660, and he managed to repair the vessel sufficiently to use her afterward for local trading, though she was never again capable of making a full voyage in the open sea.

All this goes to show how complex a matter it is to find out what precisely happened to the Pilgrims' *Mayflower*. Dr. Rendel Harris, who performed twists of reasoning worthy of an expert contortionist to prove that there were fewer *Mayflower*s than his researches suggest, patiently worked out the comings and goings of every *Mayflower* recorded in the English port books for the first two thirds of the seventeenth century. What he found out includes specific information about Christopher Jones's *Mayflower*.

On January 28, 1620, Jones brought the *Mayflower* in to London and landed a cargo of 113¼ tons of French wine in eight lots, the biggest 30¼, the smallest 8 tons. During the next three days

Jones unloaded a further 37¾ tons in four consignments. On May 15, 1620, the *Mayflower* brought in another wine cargo, 50¼ tons of ordinary wine and 19 of "conyacks wine" (cognac). No other cargoes appear for 1620, naturally, but in 1621 there are several. On March 20 Jones unloaded 197 hundredweight of tallow and 17½ tons of beef, and a further 64½ hundredweight of tallow on March 23. On April 9 and 10 four tons of English beef. On July 17 "two maunds and half unbound books" and 200 bolts of "Lyons thread." In August the *Mayflower* came from Madeira with an intriguing cargo unshipped on the twenty-first as follows:

> 99 hundredweight whites
> 74 hundredweight musk con rosel
> 2¾ hundredweight panner sugar
> 635 hundredweight woad [or wood?]
> 32 hundredweight 90 pounds green ginger

On September 21 she arrived back from Ireland with a mixed shipment:

> 3½ packs Irish yarn
> 100 ells Irish linen
> 1700 pounds candles
> 40 raw Irish hides
> 39 raw Irish calfskins
> 1 barrel and 1 hogshead Irish salmon
> 11 hundredweight Irish tallow
> 75 hundredweight pipestands
> 20 hundredweight headings for pipes
> 20 hundredweight stands
> 23 hundredweight 80 pounds Scottish yarn
> 7 hundredweight feathers
> 13 dozen goatskins
> 1400 "permyscitty in the oyle" [parmaceti]
> 1¾ pecks Irish yarn
> 2 hundredweight Irish wool

2¾ hundredweight tallow

44¾ hundredweight Scottish proynes [prunes?]

100 tons oaken timber

These were unloaded between September 21 and 28. On October 19 she brought in "60 way bay salt" and on October 31 sailed for La Rochelle with "42 way and ½ bay salt." On November 21 she was back with 21½ hundredweight of currants, 7½ of it "in 31 butts and 4 cartells"; and on November 29 Jones unshipped a mixed load of cotton wool, goats' hair, cotton yarn, gum arabic, and more currants. Unloading over the first half of December read:

December 1: 14½ hundredweight currants

December 5: 4 packages "in all Reisons"

December 13: 30 hundredweight hops

December 16: 58½ hundredweight currants

December 18: 1930 pounds cotton yarn

                  "yards of Turkey grograine"

                  12 hundredweight currants

This is the last mention of Captain Jones's *Mayflower*. On September 13, 1626, the *Mayflower* of Yarmouth, Robert Jary, master, carried coals from Newcastle. Records exist of a *Mayflower* built at Aldeburgh by two of the former *Mayflower* owners, Child and Moore: Aldeburgh is close to Yarmouth as ships go and it is at least logical to suppose that this was the one commanded by Jary. On January 22, 1631, the *Mayflower* of Yarmouth, William Tracey, master, discharged 206 tons of Bordeaux wine at Hull.

An obviously different *Mayflower* appears in 1637 in the Thames: 346 or 350 tons, 24 guns, 140 or 145 men, 28 barrels of gunpowder, master William Baddilow on His Majesty's Service, first noted on March 18 but by May 3 in company with four other ships: *Unicorn, Pleiades, Industry, Richard and Mary.* On September 22 Sir John Pennington wrote from the Downs that he had discharged *Mayflower* and *Pleiades.*

Now comes Thomas Webber's *Mayflower*. On May 28, 1651,

the Council of State gave Webber permission to trade with Virginia; on June 20 *Mayflower* arrived at the Downs en route to New England; in October she anchored in Boston. On August 27, 1653, Webber petitioned the Council of State for protection for twenty seamen against impress, and for the grant of letters of marque; on September 12 the order went out to send to Virginia the *Mayflower* (160 tons, 18 guns), the *Bonaventure* (100 tons, 14 guns), and the *Hope* (120 tons, 8 guns).

One other *Mayflower* can be traced. Samuel Vassall of London gave the name to his ship *Christopher and Mary* in 1634. Her master was Peter Andrews. The ship was supposed to carry emigrants to the Carolinas but went instead to the James River. She took supplies to Virginia in 1641, anchoring on October 20; in 1642 she was put at the disposal of the parliamentary forces and spent three years patrolling home waters, and in 1645 she headed the list of merchant ships taken into the Navy. Vassall claimed unpaid compensation as late as 1654. The ship was 400 tons.

All these tempting but unprofitable trails have been carefully paced out by researchers whose optimism has had to compensate for their lamentable lack of hard facts. Dr. Harris, for example, tried hard to make all these *Mayflowers* total two, or at most three, while he and other historians have struggled to place the timbers of the Pilgrim ship. Dr. Anderson investigated a claim that the pillars in the old schoolroom at Abingdon in Berkshire were either the masts of the *Mayflower* or those of William III's ship of 1688, the *Brielle*, and, after much painstaking measuring, concluded that whatever they were they could not be from the *Mayflower*. He added the salutary remark that it was unlikely that the *Mayflower* as such would create much interest in seventeenth-century England. Many people sincerely believe that *Mayflower* timbers were used to build the celebrated barn in the Buckinghamshire village of Jordans. (Dr. Harris commented disarmingly that after all the Greeks have preserved pieces of wood supposed to be part of the *Argo.*) Ship's timbers were certainly incorporated into the barn: if the visitor stands on his head he can see the roof beams have the shape of a ship's keel; and one of the beams bears a faint adumbration of the letter M. That, it seems, is good enough for most visitors. The barn is worth a look anyway, and so is the associated meetinghouse of the Religious Society of Friends a little farther along the lane. Jordans is a pretty, tranquil village, scattered among trees a mile or two on the London side of Beaconsfield; visitors who go into the barn and sit quietly for a few minutes, thinking their own thoughts, feel an atmosphere that can perhaps be said to breathe the air of Leyden and New Plymouth. But it is all highly conjectural.

All that one can truly say is that the little *Mayflower* did on one occasion fight her way across the Atlantic and back. In the course of doing so, somehow or other against all the odds, in spite of all the speculation, ignorance, snobbery, and legend, she came back immortal.

· 4 ·

The New England settlers consciously intended to transport European civilization as they understood it across the sea with the rest of their baggage. They seemed intuitively to know that a struggle for sheer existence erodes all culture, and were prepared to make sacrifices in order to preserve the learning they possessed. They were people of strong mental alertness and a surprisingly open attitude toward the new scientific discoveries. Their leaders remained poised receptively toward liberty of thought and enlightened attitudes. The framework of values they cherished was one that generations to come could use and respect. In their love of learning for its own sake, as well as for the inner security it could bring, their feeling for the humanities, and, above all, their good sense in emphasizing values other than the purely material, they established a moral order that has produced all that is best (as well as a good deal that is harshest) in American life; that redoubtable thing the New England conscience has time and again redeemed America when nothing else could.

The *Mayflower*'s achievements started with the Compact. The system of laws and management set up by the Pilgrims may not seem startlingly democratic today, but it was a great advance on anything seen before then. They made a plantation, and kept it going in spite of death, disease, terror, storm, and tempest on the spot, exploitation and swindling from within and without. They dealt fairly with one another and with all they met. Steadfast endurance in trials, inspiring leadership, dauntless faith sustained them. They created one of the best-ordered and most successful colonies ever known.

They came to America looking for peace, not fame. They did not think of themselves as heroic, only "not as other men." Moral courage was part of their daily existence. Without looking back, with no return ticket, without any idea that they could always come home if the great design did not work, an utterly dedicated group intent on spiritual survival, they went with no intention to move on westward, or to make quick profits. The central hope was to create a new life in a new land for themselves and their children's children. The most impressive fact is that when the *Mayflower* sailed back, after those first dreadful weeks, not one member of the community asked to return with Captain Jones. And because they set up their dwelling in Massachusetts, the other Protestant English came that way. By any standards the Pilgrims accomplished a heroic achievement.

· 5 ·

Perhaps, after all, the most satisfying summing up is the simplest. The Reverend Jared Eliot of Connecticut, grandson of John Eliot, who ordered canvas for the Indians, wrote in 1748:

When we consider the small Number of the first Settlers, and coming from an old Cultivated Country, to thick Woods, rough unimproved Lands; where all their former Experience and Knowledge was now of very little service to them: they were destitute of Beasts of Burden or Carriage; Unskilled in every Part of Service to be done: it may be said, That in a Sort, they began the World a New.

Appendices

The Passenger List

Ages, where known, are given in brackets after each name. An asterisk (*) denotes that the person died during the first winter. Names in *italics* are of passengers who set out from Leyden in the first place.

1   Alden, Mr. John (21)
2   Alderton, Mr. John (21 +) *
3   *Allerton, Master Bartholomew* (8)
4   *Allerton, Mr. Isaac* (34)
5   *Allerton, Miss Mary* (4)
6   *Allerton, Mrs. Mary Norris* (32) *
7   *Allerton, Miss Remember* (6)
8   Billington, Mrs. Ellen/Eleanor/Helen (32)
9   Billington, Master Francis (14)
10 Billington, Mr. John (36)
11 Billington, Master John (8)
12 *Bradford, Mrs. Dorothy May* (23) *
13 *Bradford, Elder William* (31)
14 *Brewster, Master Love* (9)
15 *Brewster, Mrs. Mary* (52)
16 *Brewster, Elder William* (54)
17 *Brewster, Master Wrestling* (6)
18 *Britteridge, Mr. Richard* (21 +) *
19 *Browne, Mr. Peter* (20)
20 *Butten, Mr. William* (died at sea) (22)
21 Carter, Mr. Robert *
22 *Carver, Deacon John* (54) *
23 *Carver, Mrs. Catherine White Leggatt* (40) *

24   Chilton, Mr. James (57) *
25   Chilton, Miss Mary (15)
26   Chilton, Mrs. Susanna *
27   *Clarke, Mr. Richard* *
28   *Cooke, Mr. Francis* (43)
29   *Cooke, Master John* (8)
30   Cooper, Miss Humility (8)
31   *Crackston, Mr. John* (35) *
32   *Crackston, Master John*
33   Dotey, Mr. Edward (27)
34   *Eaton, Mr. Francis* (25)
35   *Eaton, Mrs. Sarah* (30) *
36   *Eaton, Master Samuel* (infant)
37   Ely, Mr. (seaman)
38   English, Mr. Thomas (30 at least) *
39   *Fletcher, Mr. Moses* (38 at least)*
40   *Fuller, Mrs. Ann* *
41   *Fuller, Mr. Edward* (25? 45?) *
42   *Fuller, Master Samuel* (5)
43   *Fuller, Dr. Samuel* (35)
44   Gardiner, Mr. Richard (20)
45   *Goodman, Mr. John* (25) *
46   *Holbeck, Mr. William* *
47   *Hooke, Master John* (13–14) *
48   Hopkins, Miss Constanta (15)
49   Hopkins, Miss Damaris (3)
50   Hopkins, Mrs. Elizabeth (at least 20)
51   Hopkins, Master Giles (13)
52   Hopkins, Master Oceanus (born on voyage) *
53   Hopkins, Mr. Stephen (35)
54   *Howland, Mr. John* (28)
55   Langemore, Mr. John *
56   Latham, Mr. William
57   Leister, Mr. Edward
58   *Margerson, Mr. Edward* *

59   Martin, Mr. Christopher (45)*
60   Martin, Mrs. Marie Prower (at least 40)*
61   *Minter, Miss Desire* (20)
62   More, Miss Ellen (8) *
63   More, Master Jasper (6) *
64   More, Master Richard (7)
65   More, Master (brother to Richard) *
66   Mullins, Mrs. Alice *
67   Mullins, Master Joseph (6)*
68   Mullins, Miss Priscilla (18)
69   Mullins, Mr. William (40) *
70   *Priest, Mr. Digerie* (40) *
71   Prower, Mr. Solomon *
72   *Rigdale, Mrs. Alice* *
73   *Rigdale, Mr. John* *
74   *Rogers, Master Joseph* (12)
75   *Rogers, Mr. Thomas* (30 +) *
76   Sampson, Master Henry (6)
77   *Sowle, Mr. George* (21)
78   *Standish, Captain Miles* (36)
79   *Standish, Mrs. Rose* *
80   *Story, Mr. Elias* (42) *
81   *Thomson, Mr. Edward* *
82   *Tilley, Mrs. Ann* *
83   *Tilley, Mrs. Bridget van der Velde* *
84   *Tilley, Mr. Edward* (46) *
85   *Tilley, Mr. John* (49) *
86   *Tilley, Miss Elizabeth* (14)
87   *Tinker, Mr. Thomas* (39)*
88   *Tinker, Mrs. Thomas* *
89   *Tinker, Master* (son of above)*
90   Trevor, Mr. William (21 approx.)
91   *Turner, Mrs. John* (35) *
92   *Turner, Master* (elder son of above)*
93   *Turner, Master* (younger son of above) *

94   Warren, Mr. Richard (40)
95   *White, Master Peregrine* (born on arrival)
96   *White, Master Resolved* (5)
97   *White, Mrs. Susanna Fuller* (26)
98   *White, Mr. William* (28) *
99   *Wilder, Mr. Roger* *
100   *Williams, Mr. Thomas* *
101   *Winslow, Mr. Edward* (25)
102   *Winslow, Mrs. Elizabeth Barker* (23) *
103   Winslow, Mr. Gilbert (20)

APPENDIX 2
The MAYFLOWER Compact

In the name of God, Amen.

We whose names are underwritten, the loyal subjects of our dread Sovereign Lord King James, by the Grace of God of Great Britain, France, and Ireland King, Defender of the Faith.

Having undertaken, for the glory of God and advancement of the Christian faith and honour of our King and Country, a voyage to plant the first colony in the northern parts of Virginia, do by these presents solemnly and mutually in the presence of God and one of another, covenant and combine ourselves together into a civil body politic, for our better ordering and preservation and furtherance of the ends aforesaid; and by virtue hereof to enact, constitute, and frame such just and equal laws, ordinances, acts, constitutions, and offices, from time to time, as shall be thought most meet and convenient for the general good of the colony, unto which we promise all due submission and obedience.

In witness whereof we have hereunder subscribed our names at Cape Cod, the eleventh of November, in the year of the reign of our Sovereign Lord King James, of England, France, and Ireland the eighteenth, and of Scotland the fifty-fourth. Anno Domini 1620.

John Carver
Isaac Allerton
William Bradford
William Brewster
Edward Winslow
Miles Standish
Francis Cooke
Francis Eaton
Edward Fuller
Samuel Fuller
Stephen Hopkins
John Howland
Christopher Martin
William Mullins
Digerie Priest
Edward Tilley
John Tilley
Richard Warren
William White

John Alden	John Billington
Peter Browne	Richard Britteridge
James Chilton	Richard Clarke
John Crackston	Edward Doty
Moses Fletcher	John Goodman
William Holbeck *	William Latham *
Edward Margerson	Solomon Prower *
John Rigdale	Thomas Rogers
George Sowle	Edward Thompson *
Thomas Tinker	John Turner
Roger Wilder *	Thomas Williams

* Names marked thus are conjectural. Some accounts state that Compact signatories included people like Gilbert Winslow, John Allerton, Constant and Thomas Southworth, none of whom sailed on the *Mayflower*. This is as close a list as the author, unable to see the original document, has succeeded in compiling.

Typical Letters to and from the Pilgrims

"It is not with us as with other men"

Right Worshipful:

Our humble duties remembered, in our own, our messengers, and our church's name, with all thankful acknowledgment of your singular love, expressing itself, as otherwise, so more specially in your great care and earnest endeavour of our good in this weighty business about Virginia, which the less able we are to requite, we shall think ourselves the more bound to commend in our prayers unto God for recompense; Whom, as for the present you rightly behold in our endeavours, so shall we not be wanting in our parts (the same God assisting us) to return all answerable fruit and respect unto the labour of your love bestowed upon us. We have with the best speed and consideration withal that we could, set down our requests in writing, subscribed as you willed, with the hands of the greatest part of our congregation, and have sent the same unto the Council by our agent and a deacon of our church, John Carver, unto whom we have also requested a gentleman of our company to adjoin himself. To the care and discretion of which two we do refer the prosecuting of our business. Now we persuade ourselves, Right Worshipful, that we need not provoke your godly and loving mind to any further or more tender care of us, since you have pleased so far to interest us in yourself that, under God, above all persons and things in the world, we rely upon you, expecting the care of your love, counsel of your wisdom and the help and countenance of your authority. Notwithstanding, for your encouragement in the work, so far as probabilities may lead, we will not forbear to mention these instances of inducement.

1. We verily believe and trust the Lord is with us, unto whom and whose service we have given ourselves in many trials; and that

He will graciously prosper our endeavours according to the simplicity of our hearts therein.

2. We are well weaned from the delicate milk of our mother country, and inured to the difficulties of a strange and hard land, which yet in a great part we have by patience overcome.

3. The people are, for the body of them, industrious and frugal, we think we may safely say, as any company of people in the world.

4. We are knit together as a body in a most strict and sacred bond and covenant of the Lord, of the violation whereof we make great conscience, and by virtue whereof we do hold ourselves straitly tied to all care of each other's good and of the whole, by every one and so mutually.

5. Lastly, it is not with us as with other men, whom small things can discourage, or small discontentments cause to wish themselves at home again. We know our entertainment in England and in Holland. We shall much prejudice both our arts and means by removal; who, if we should be driven to return, we should not hope to recover our present helps and comforts, neither indeed look ever, for ourselves, to attain unto the like in any other place during our lives, which are now drawing towards their periods.

These motives we have been bold to tender unto you, which you in your wisdom may also impart to any other our worshipful friends of the Council with you; of all whose godly disposition and loving towards our despised persons we are most glad, and shall not fail by all good means to continue and increase the same. We will not be further troublesome, but do, with the renewed remembrance of our humble duties to your worship and (so far as in modesty we may be bold) to any other of our wellwillers of the Council with you, we take our leaves, committing your persons and counsels to the guidance and direction of the Almighty.

Yours much bounden in all duty,

JOHN ROBINSON

WILLIAM BREWSTER

Leyden, December 15
Anno: 1617
to: Sir Edwin Sandys

"Your perplexed, yet hopeful brethren"

To their Loving Friends John Carver and Robert Cushman, these,
etc.:

Good brethren, after salutations. We received divers letters at
the coming of Mr Nash and our pilot, which is a great encouragement unto us, and for whom we hope after times will minister
occasion of praising God. And indeed, had you not sent him, many
would have been ready to faint and go back, partly in respect of the
new conditions which have been taken up by you (which all men are
against), and partly in regard of our own inability to do any one of
those many weighty businesses you refer to us here. For the former
whereof, whereas Robert Cushman desires reasons for our dislike,
promising thereupon to alter the same, or else saying we should
think he hath no brains, we desire him to exercise them therein,
referring him to our pastor's former reasons, and them to the
censure of the godly wise. But our desires are that you will not
entangle yourselves and us in any such unreasonable courses as
those are; viz. that the merchants should have the half of men's
houses and lands at the dividend, and that persons should be de-
prived of the two days in a week agreed upon, yea every moment of
time for their own Particular; by reason whereof we cannot conceive why any should carry servants for their own help and comfort,
for that we can require no more of them than all men one of
another. This we have only by relation from Mr Nash, and not from
any writing of your own, and therefore hope you have not proceeded far in so great a thing without us. But requiring you not to
exceed the bounds of your commission, which was to proceed upon
the things or conditions agreed upon and expressed in writing (at
your going over about it) we leave it; not without marvelling that
yourself, as you write, knowing how small a thing troubleth our
consultations, and how few, as you fear, understands the business
aright, should trouble us with such matters as these are.

Salute Mr Weston from us, in whom we hope we are not

deceived. We pray you make known our estate unto him, and if you think good, show him our letters; at least tell him that, under God, we much rely upon him and put our confidence in him. And, as yourselves well know, that if he had not been an adventurer with us, we had not taken it in hand; presuming that if he had not seen means to accomplish it he would not have begun it. So we hope in our extremity he will so far help us as our expectation be no way made frustrate concerning him. Since therefore, good brethren, we have plainly opened the state of things with us in this matter, you will, etc.

Thus beseeching the Almighty, who is all sufficient to raise us out of this depth of difficulties, to assist us herein; raising such means by His providence and fatherly care for us, His poor children and servants, as we may with comfort behold the hand of our God for good towards us in this our business which we undertake in His name and fear, we take leave and remain

Your perplexed, yet hopeful brethren,

SAMUEL FULLER

EDWARD WINSLOW

WILLIAM BRADFORD

ISAAC ALLERTON

Leyden, June 10
Anno: 1620

"Mr Weston makes himself merry with our endeavours"

My dear Friend and Brother, whom with yours I always remember in my best affection, and whose welfare I shall never cease to commend to God by my best and most earnest prayers:

You do thoroughly understand by our general letters the estate of things here, which indeed is very pitiful, especially by want of shipping and not seeing means likely, much less certain, of having it provided; though withal there be great want of money and means to do needful things. Mr Pickering, you know before this, will not defray a penny here, though Robert Cushman presumed of I know not how many hundred pounds from him and I know not whom. Yet it seems strange that we should be put to him to receive both his and his partner's adventure; and yet Mr Weston writ unto him that in regard of it he hath drawn upon him £100 more. But there is in this some mystery, as indeed it seems there is in the whole course. Besides, whereas divers are to pay in some parts of their moneys yet behind, they refuse to do it till they see shipping provided, or a course taken for it. Neither do I think is there a man here would pay anything, if he had again his money in his purse.

You know right well we depended on Mr Weston alone, and upon such means as he would procure for this common business; and when we had in hand another course with the Dutchmen, broke it off at his motion and upon the conditions by him shortly after propounded. He did this in his Love I know, but things appear not answerable from him hitherto. That he should have first have put in his moneys is thought by many to have been but fit. But that I can well excuse, he being a merchant and having use of it to his benefit; whereas others, if it had been in their hands, would have consumed it. But that he should not but have had either shipping ready before this time, or at least certain means and course and the same known to us for it; or have taken other order otherwise, cannot in my conscience be excused. I have heard that when he hath been moved in the business he hath put it off from himself and referred it to the others; and would come to George Morton and enquire news of him about things, as if he had scarce been some accessory unto it. Whether he failed of some helps from others which he expected, and so be not well able to go through with things, or whether he hath feared lest you should be ready too soon and so increase the charge of shipping above that is meet, or whether he have thought by withholding to put us upon straits, thinking that thereby Mr Brewer and Mr Pickering would be drawn by importunity to do more, or what other mystery is in it we know not; but sure we are that things are not answerable to such an occasion.

Mr Weston makes himself merry with our endeavours about buying a ship, but we have done nothing in this but with good reason, as I am persuaded, nor yet that I know in anything else, save in those two: the one, that we employed Robert Cushman who is known (though a good man and of special abilities in his kind) yet most unfit to deal for other men by reason of his singularity and too great indifferency for any conditions; and for (to speak truly) that we have had nothing from him but terms and presumptions. The other, that we have so much relied (by implicit faith, as it were) upon generalities without seeing the particular course and means for so weighty an affair set down unto us. For shipping, Mr Weston, it should seem, is set upon hiring, which yet I wish he may presently effect; but I see little hope of help from hence if so it be. Of Mr Brewer you know what to expect; I do not think Mr Pickering will engage except in the course of buying, in former letters specified.

About the conditions, you have our reasons for our judgments of what is agreed. And let this specially be borne in minds, that the greatest part of the colony is like to be employed constantly, not upon dressing their particular land and building houses, but upon fishing, trading, etc. So as the land and house will be but a trifle for advantage to the Adventurers, and yet the division of it a great discouragement to the Planters, who would with singular care make it comfortable with borrowed hours from their sleep. The same consideration of common employment constantly by the most is a good reason not to have the two days in a week denied the few planters for private use, which yet is subordinate to common good. Consider also how much unfit that you and your likes must serve a new apprenticeship of seven years, and not a day's freedom from task.

Send me word what persons are to go, who of useful faculties and how many, and particularly of everything; I know you want not a mind. I am sorry you have not been at London all this while, but the provisions could not want you. Time will suffer me to write no more; fare you and yours well always in the Lord, in Whom I rest.

Yours to use,

JOHN ROBINSON

Leyden, June 14, 1620
to: Mr John Carver

"We may go scratch for it"

Loving Friend:

I have received from you some letters, full of affection and complaints, and what it is you would have of me I know not; for your crying out, "Negligence, negligence, negligence," I marvel why so negligent a man was used in the business. Yet know you that all I have power to do here shall not be one hour behind, I warrant you. You have reference to Mr Weston to help us with money, more than his adventure, when he protesteth but for his promise he would not have done anything. He saith we take a heady course, and is offended that our provisions are made so far off, as also that he was not made acquainted with our quantity of things; and saith that in now being in three places so far remote, we will, with going up and down and wrangling and expostulating, pass over the summer before we will go. And to speak the truth, there is fallen already amongst us a flat schism, and we are readier to go to dispute than to set forward a voyage.

I have received from Leyden since we went, three or four letters directed to you; though they only concern me, I will not trouble you with them. I always feared the event of the Amsterdamers striking in with us. I trow you must excommunicate me or else you must go without their company, or we shall want no quarrelling; but let them pass. We have reckoned, it should seem, without our host, and counting upon a 150 persons, there cannot be found above £1200 and odd moneys of all the ventures you can reckon, besides some cloth, stockings and shoes which are not counted, so we shall come short at least £300 or £400. I would have had something shortened at first of beer and other provisions, in hope of other adventures; and now we could, both in Amsterdam and Kent, have beer enough to serve our turn, but now we cannot accept it without prejudice. You fear we have begun to build and shall not be able to make an end. Indeed, our courses were never established by counsel; we may therefore justly fear their standing.

Yea, there was a schism amongst us three at the first. You wrote to Mr Martin to prevent the making of the provisions in Kent, which he did, and set down his resolution, how much he would have of everything, without respect to any counsel or exception. Surely he that is in a society and yet regards not counsel may better be a king than a consort. To be short, if there be not some other disposition settled unto, than yet is, we that should be partners of humility and peace shall be examples of jangling and insulting. Yet your money which you there must have, we will get provided for you instantly. £500 you say will serve; for the rest which here and in Holland is to be used, we may go scratch for it. For Mr Crabb, of whom you write, he hath promised to go with us; yet I tell you I shall not be without fear till I see him shipped, for he is much opposed, yet I hope he will not fail. Think the best of all and bear with patience what is wanting, and the Lord guide us all.

Your loving friend,
ROBERT CUSHMAN

London, June 10
Anno: 1620
to: Mr. John Carver

"He having faithfully finished his course"

Loving and Kind Friends:

I know not whether this will ever come to your hands or miscarry, as other my letters have done. Yet in regard of the Lord's dealing with us here, I have had a great desire to write unto you. Knowing your desire to bear a part with us, both in our joys and sorrows, as we do with you. These are therefore to give you to understand that it hath pleased the Lord to take out of this vale of tears, your and our loving and faithful pastor and my dear and Reverend brother, Mr John Robinson, who was sick some eight days. He began to be sick on Saturday in the morning, yet the next day, being the Lord's Day, he taught us twice. And so the week after grew weaker, every day more than other; yet he felt no pain, but weakness all the time of his sickness. The physic he took wrought kindly in man's judgment, but he grew weaker every day, feeling little or no pain, and sensible to the very last. He fell sick the 22 of February and departed this life the 1 of March. He had a continual inward ague, but free from infection, so that all his friends came freely to him. And if either prayers, tears or means would have saved his life, he had not gone hence. But he having faithfully finished his course and performed his work which the Lord had appointed him here to do, he now resteth with the Lord in eternal happiness.

We wanting him and all church governors, yet we still by the mercy of God continue and hold close together in peace and quietness; and so hope we shall do, though we be very weak. Wishing (if such were the will of God) that you and we were again united together in one, either there or here. But seeing it is the will of the Lord thus to dispose of things, we must labour with patience to rest contented till it please the Lord otherwise to dispose.

For news here is not much, only as in England we have lost our old King James, who departed this life about a month ago; so here they have lost the old prince, Grave Maurice. Who both departed this life since my brother Robinson, and as in England we have a new King, Charles, of whom there is great hope; so here they have made Prince Hendrick general in his brother's place. Thus with my love remembered, I take leave and rest

Your assured loving friend,
ROGER WHITE

Leyden, April 28
Anno: 1625
to: William Bradford and William Brewster

"Blame yourselves that you made no better choice"

Sir:

I have received yours of the 26th of May by Mr Gibbs, and Mr Goffe, with the barrel of otter skins according to the contents, for which I got a bill of store, and so took them up and sold them together at £78 12s sterling; and since, Mr. Allerton hath received the money, as will appear by the account.

It is true (as you writ) that your engagements are great, not only the purchase, but you are yet necessitated to take up the stock you work upon, and that not at 6 or 8 per cent as it is here let out, but at 30, 40, yea and some at 50 per cent. Which, were not your gains great, and God's blessing on your honest endeavours more than ordinary, it could not be that you should long subsist in the maintaining of and upholding of your worldly affairs. And this your honest and discreet agent Mr Allerton hath seriously considered and deeply laid to mind, how to ease you of it. He told me you were contented to accept of me and some few others, to join with you in the purchase as partners, for which I kindly thank you and all the rest, and do willingly accept of it. And though absent, shall willingly be at such charge as you and the rest shall think meet, and this year am contented to forbear my former £50 and two years' increase for the venture, both which now makes it £80, without any bargain or condition for the profit you, I mean the generality, stand to the adventure, outward and homeward. I have persuaded Mr Andrews and Mr Beauchamp to do the like, so as you are eased of the high rate you were at the other two years. I say we leave it freely to yourselves to allow us what you please, and as God shall bless. What course I run Mr Beauchamp desireth to do the same, and though he have been or seemed somewhat harsh heretofore, yet now you shall find he is new moulded.

I also see by your letter, you desire I should be your agent or factor here. I have ever found you so faithful, honest and upright men, as I have even resolved with myself (God assisting me) to do you all the good lieth in my power. And therefore if you please to make choice of so weak a man, both for abilities and body, to perform your business, I promise (the Lord enabling me) to do the best I can according to those abilities he hath given me; and wherein I fail, blame yourselves that you made no better choice. Now, because I am sickly, and we are all mortal, I have advised Mr Allerton to join Mr Beauchamp with me in your deputation, which

I conceive to be very necessary and good for you. Your charge shall be no more, for it is not your salary makes me undertake your business. Thus commending you and yours, and all God's people, unto the guidance and protection of the Almighty, I ever rest,

Your faithful loving friend,
JAMES SHERLEY

London, November 17
Anno: 1628
to: Governor William Bradford.

"We were here first"

Sir:

The Massachusetts men are coming almost daily, some by water and some by land, who are not yet determined where to settle, though some have a great mind to the place we are upon, and which was last bought. Many of them look at that which this river will not afford, except it be at this place which we have; namely, to be a great town and have commodious dwellings for many together. So as what they will do I cannot yet resolve you. For this place there is none of them say anything to me, but what I hear from their servants, by whom I perceive their minds. I shall do what I can to withstand them. I hope they will hear reason, as that we were here first and entered with much difficulty and danger both in regard of the Dutch and Indians, and bought the land, to your great charge already disbursed, and have since held here a chargeable possession and kept the Dutch from further encroaching, which would else long before this day have possessed all, and kept out all others. I hope these and such-like arguments will stop them.

It was your will we should use their persons and messengers kindly, and so we have done and do daily, to your great charge; for the first company had well nigh starved, had it not been for this house, for want of victuals; I being forced to supply twelve men for nine days together. And those which came last, I entertained the best we could, helping both them and the other with canoes and guides. They got me to go with them to the Dutch, to see if I could procure some of them to have quiet settling near them, but they did peremptorily withstand them. But this later company did not once speak thereof; also I gave their goods house room according to their earnest request, and Mr Pynchon's letter in their behalf, which I thought good to send you, here enclosed. And what trouble and charge I shall be further at I know not, for they are coming daily, and I expect these back again from below, whither they are gone to view the country. All which trouble and charge we undergo for their occasion, may give us just cause in the judgment of all wise and understanding men, to hold and keep that we are settled upon.

Thus with my duty remembered, I rest

Yours to be commanded,

JONATHAN BREWSTER

Matianuck, July 6, 1635

APPENDIX 4

Passengers from Delftshaven to Southampton (on SPEEDWELL)

1 Allerton, Master Bartholomew
2 Allerton, Mr. Isaac
3 Allerton, Miss Mary
4 Allerton, Mrs. Mary Norris
5 Allerton, Miss Remember
6 Blossom, Dr. Thomas
7 Blossom, Master (son of above)
8 Bradford, Mrs. Dorothy May
9 Bradford, Mr. William
10 Brewster, Master Love
11 Brewster, Mrs. Mary

12 Brewster, Mr. William
13 Brewster, Master Wrestling
14 Britteridge, Mr. Richard
15 Browne, Mr. Peter
16 Butten, Mr. William
17 Carver, Mrs. Catherine White Leggatt
18 Clarke, Mr. Richard
19 Cooke, Mr. Francis
20 Cooke, Master John
21 Crackston, Mr. John
22 Crackston, Master John
23 Cushman, Mrs. Mary Singleton
24 Eaton, Mr. Francis
25 Eaton, Mrs. Sarah
26 Eaton, Master Samuel
27 Fletcher, Mr. Moses
28 Fuller, Mrs. Ann
29 Fuller, Mr. Edward
30 Fuller, Master Samuel
31 Fuller, Dr. Samuel
32 Goodman, Mr. John
33 Holbeck, Mr. William
34 Hooke, Master John
35 Howland, Mr. John
36 King, Mr. William
37 Margerson, Mr. Edward
38 Minter, Miss Desire
39 Priest, Mr. Digerie
40 Rigdale, Mrs. Alice
41 Rigdale, Mr. John
42 Rogers, Master Joseph
43 Rogers, Mr. Thomas
44 Sowle, Mr. George
45 Standish, Captain Miles
46 Standish, Mrs. Rose
47 Story, Mr. Elias

48   Thomson, Mr. Edward
49   Tilley, Mrs. Ann
50   Tilley, Mrs. Bridget van der Velde
51   Tilley, Mr. Edward
52   Tilley, Miss Elizabeth
53   Tilley, Mr. John
54   Tinker, Mr. Thomas
55   Tinker, Mrs. Thomas
56   Tinker, Master (son of above)
57   Turner, Mr. John
58   Turner, Master (elder son of above)
59   Turner, Master (younger son of above)
60   White, Master Resolved
61   White, Mrs. Susanna Fuller
62   White, Mr. William
63   Wilder, Mr. Roger
64   Williams, Mr. Thomas
65   Winslow, Mr. Edward
66   Winslow, Mrs. Elizabeth Barker

Note: John Carver and Robert Cushman joined the ship in Southampton. Since, however, they were originally members of the Leyden congregation, they can be listed as *Speedwell* passengers. Carver's name is italicized in the *Mayflower* passenger list as a Leyden member for that reason.

APPENDIX 5

Passengers on the FORTUNE, 1621
Thomas Barton, Master

1   Adams, Mr. John (26 or 31)
2   Adams, Mrs. Ellen
3   Bassett, Mr. William (21)

4   Beale, Mr. William
5   Brewster, Mr. Jonathan (28)
6   Briggs, Mr. Clement (27 at least)
7   Bumpus, Mr. Edward
8   Cannon, Mr. John
9   Corner, Mr. William
10 Cushman, Mr. Robert (43 or 44)
11 Cushman, Master Thomas (14)
12 Deane, Mr. Stephen
13 De la Noye, Master Philip (16)
14 Flavel, Mr. Thomas (31 at least)
15 Ford, Mr. William
16 Ford, Master William (6)
17 Ford, Mrs. Martha
18 Hicks, Mr. Robert
19 Hilton, Mr. William (25 at least)
20 Hilton, Mr. Edward (25 at least)
21 Morgan, Mr. Benedict (24)
22 Morton, Mr. Thomas (32)
23 Nicolas, Mr. Augustine
24 Palmer, Mr. William (51)
25 Palmer, Mrs. Frances
26 Palmer, Miss Anne
27 Palmer, Master William
28 Pitt, Mr. William
29 Prence, Mr. Thomas (just 21)
30 Simonson, Mr. Moses (20)
31 Stacey, Mr. Hugh
32 Steward, Mr. James
33 Tench, Mr. William
34 Wright, Mr. William (33)

Passengers on the ANNE and LITTLE JAMES, 1623

Since it is not known exactly who traveled on which ship, all the passengers are listed alphabetically together.

1 Altham, Mr. Emanuel
2 Annable, Mr. Anthony
3 Annable, Miss Hannah
4 Annable, Mrs. Jane Momford
5 Annable, Miss Sarah
6 Bangs, Mr. Edward
7 Bartlett, Mr. Robert
8 Becket, Mrs. Mary
9 Brewster, Miss Fear
10 Brewster, Miss Patience
11 Bridges, Mrs. Mary Oldham
12 Bridges, Mr. William
13 Burcher, Mr. Edward
14 Burcher, Mrs. Edward
15 Clarke, Mr. Thomas
16 Conant, Master Caleb
17 Conant, Mr. Christopher
18 Conant, Mrs. Sarah
19 Conant, Mr. Roger
20 Cooke, Mrs. Esther Mayhew
21 Cooke, Miss Esther
22 Cooke, Master Jacob
23 Cooke, Miss Jane
24 Dix, Mr. Anthony
25 Dix, Mrs. Tabitha
26 Faunce, Mr. John
27 Flood, Mr. Edmund
28 Fuller, Mrs. Bridget Lee

29 Godbertson, Mr. Cuthbert
30 Godbertson, Mrs. Sarah Priest
31 Hatherley, Mrs. Alice Collard
32 Hatherley, Master Nathaniel
33 Hatherley, Mr. Timothy
34 Heard, Mr. William
35 Hicks, Miss Lydia (Mrs. Edward Bangs)
36 Hicks, Mrs. Margaret
37 Hicks, Miss Phoebe
38 Hicks, Mr. Samuel
39 Hilton, Mrs. Mary
40 Hilton, Mr. William
41 Hilton, Master William
42 Hilton, Miss Mary
43 Holman, Mr. Edward
44 Jenney, Mr. John
45 Jenney, Mrs. Sarah Carey
46 Jenney, Miss Abigail
47 Jenney, Miss Sarah
48 Jenney, Master Samuel (born on voyage)
49 Kempton, Mr. Menassah
50 Long, Mr. Robert
51 Mitchell, Mr. Experience
52 Morton, Mr. George
53 Morton, Mrs. Juliana Carpenter
54 Morton, Mr. Thomas
55 Morton, Master Ephraim
56 Morton, Master John
57 Morton, Master Nathaniel
58 Morton, Miss Patience
59 Morton, Miss Sarah
60 Newton, Mrs. Ellen Adams
61 Oldham, Mr. John
62 Oldham, Miss Lucretia
63 Palmer, Mrs. Frances
64 Penn, Miss Christian

65   Pratt, Mr. Joshua
66   Priest, Miss Mary
67   Priest, Miss Sarah
68   Rand, Mr. James
69   Ratcliffe, Mr. Robert
70   Snow, Mr. Nicholas
71   Southworth, Mrs. Alice Carpenter
72   Southworth, Mr. Constant
73   Southworth, Mr. Thomas
74   Sprague, Mrs. Anne
75   Sprague; Mr. Francis
76   Sprague, Miss Mercy
77   Standish, Mrs. Barbara (maiden
       name unknown)
78   Tracy, Mr. Stephen
79   Tracy, Mrs. Tryphosa Lee
80   Tilden, Mr. Thomas
81   Waller, Mrs. Joyce
82   Waller, Mr. Ralph
83   Warren, Mrs. Elizabeth
84   Warren, Miss Abigail
85   Warren, Miss Anne
86   Warren, Miss Elizabeth
87   Warren, Miss Mary
88   Warren, Miss Sarah

APPENDIX 6

Officers of the Plymouth Plantation

Until 1636 the governor was also secretary-treasurer. In 1624
Bradford tried to get out of office: the Plantation replied by increasing the number of assistants from one to five. In 1633 this
number was enlarged to seven. From then on there were always

either six of seven assistants. The assistant governors are listed, for the sake of clarity, on a separate chart.

GOVERNORS

1620	John Carver
1621–1632	William Bradford
1633	Edward Winslow
1634	Thomas Prence
1635	William Bradford
1636	Edward Winslow
1637	William Bradford
1638	Thomas Prence
1639–1643	William Bradford
1644	Edward Winslow
1645–1657	William Bradford
1658–1672	Thomas Prence
1673–1680	Josiah Winslow
1681–1686	Thomas Hinckley

SECRETARIES

1636–1644	Nathaniel Souther
1645–1684	Nathaniel Morton
1685–1686	Nathaniel Clarke
1687–1692	Samuel Sprague

TREASURERS

1636–1651	William Paddy
1652–1655	Miles Standish
1656–1658	John Alden
1659–1679	Constant Southworth
1680–1686	William Bradford the younger

PASTORS

At Gainsborough	1606–1607	John Smyth
At Scrooby	1607–1608	Richard Clifton

At Amsterdam	1608–1609	Francis Johnson
At Leyden	1609–1625	John Robinson
At Plymouth	1624	John Lyford
	1628	Rogers
	1629–1636	Ralph Smith
	1636–1654	John Reyner
	1659	James Williams
	1665	William Binstead
	1669–1697	John Cotton the younger

TEACHERS

At Scrooby	1607–1608	John Robinson
At Amsterdam	1608–1609	Henry Ainsworth
At Plymouth	1631–1643	Roger Williams
	1636	John Norton
	1638–1641	Charles Chauncy

RULING ELDERS

At Amsterdam	1608–1609	William Brewster
At Leyden	1609–1620	William Brewster
At Plymouth	1620–1643	William Brewster
	1649–1691	Thomas Cushman

DEACONS

At Amsterdam	1608–1609	Christopher Bowman
At Leyden	1609–1625	Robert Cushman
At Plymouth	1620–1633	Samuel Fuller
	1617–1621	John Carver
	1629–1633	Richard Masterson and Thomas Blossom
	1634–1644	John Doane
	1634–1651	John Cooke and William Paddy
	1652–1687	Robert Finney
	1669–1693	Ephraim Morton

ASSISTANT GOVERNORS, 1621–1686

1621–1632	I. Allerton
1624–1635	M. Standish
1624–1632	E. Winslow
1624–1636	S. Hopkins
1624–1628	R. Warren
1629–1635	J. Howland
1631–1639	J. Alden
1633–1634	W. Bradford
1633	W. Gilson
1633	J. Doane
1634–1635	E. Winslow
1634–1637	Collier
1635–1637	T. Prence
1636	W. Bradford
1636	Hatherley
1636	P. Browne
1637–1641	M. Standish
1637–1638	E. Winslow
1637–1640	Jenney
1637	Hatherley
1638	W. Bradrord
1638–1645	P. Browne
1638	Atwood
1639	T. Prence
1639–1640	Hatherley
1638	W. Bradford
1638–1645	P. Browne
1638	Atwood
1639	T. Prence
1639–1640	Hatherley
1639–1651	Collier
1640–1646	E. Freeman
1640–1657	T. Prence
1641–1643	E. Winslow
1641–1657	Hatherley

1642–1644	W. Thomas
1645–1656	M. Standish
1645–1647	E. Winslow
1647–1650	W. Thomas
1647–1655	P. Browne
1650	E. Winslow
1651–1672	J. Alden
1651–1665	T. Willet
1652–1653	T. Southworth
1654–1665	Collier
1656–1657	J. Cudworth
1657–1672	J. Winslow
1658–1681	W. Bradford, Jr.
1658–1659	T. Southworth
1658–1680	Hinckley
1665–1666	J. Brown
1666–1673	N. Bacon
1666–1686	J. Freeman
1670–1678	C. Southworth
1673–1680	J. Cudworth
1673–1683	J. Brown
1679–1686	D. Smith
1681–1686	B. Lothrop
1682–1686	J. Thatcher
1684–1686	J. Walley

APPENDIX 7

The *MAYFLOWER Bill of Lading, June 29, 1654*

Invoyce of Goods Sente on yᵉ May-Flower of Boston (Master Thomas Webber) for Boston in New England consigned onto Mr John Eliott Pastor of yᵉ Church of Roxbury fr̃ Mr Jonathan Hamner, yᵉ Cost and Chardges, viz.

	£	s	d
1 Ballott of Canvas N^r 3 q^r 180 Awnds Cost	010	14	09
1 Ballott of Canvas n^r 6 q^r: 210 Awnds Cost	016	04	04
100 yards of Course Dowlis at 10½ d p y^d is	004	07	06
Chardges paide on those Goods at Bristoll is	000	05	08
	031	12	03
2 qts of Tourkinge Cloth of 45 yds: ys. white cost	16	00	00
p^d for canvas & packinge ye Tourkinge cloth	000	05	06
p^d for Cartidge to ye Water Side	000	00	08
p^d for Carryadge of ye Canvas from Bristoll	000	14	00
p^d for makeinge bills of entry and clearinge ye Canvas at ye Custome House	000	03	06
p^d for Custome of 50 ells of Canvas, entered short	000	02	08
p^d for portidge, cartidge, craneidge, boatidge and warfidge, & warehouse roome for ye Canvas	000	04	08
p^d for Warehouse rooms, Warfidge, portidge Craneidge & boatidge for ye 2 q^{rs} Tourk-Cloth	000	04	08
p^d for fraight & primadge	002	11	00
p^d Severall petty chardges on those goods	000	00	08
Sum is	051	19	07
p^d out of mony Nuttall forming a Certificate f^r ye Shippinge out of ye 2 ballotts of Canvas at shippinge office in London	00	00	06
	52	00	1

The Melo Drama, 1808

The first known dramatization of the Pilgrim Fathers took place in 1808 at Boston, Massachusetts, and the playbill reads as follows:

THE PILGRIMS
Or, THE LANDING OF OUR FOREFATHERS AT
    PLYMOUTH ROCK
A New Melo Drama in Three Acts

In the course of the Melo Drama, the following Scenery, Incidents, &c.

A View of the Rock and Plymouth Bay, and the landing of the Pilgrims. The whole scene represents Winter, with a snow storm. After returning thanks to Heaven for their safe arrival, Carver orders one of the Pilgrims to cut on the Rock, DECEMBER 22nd, 1620, the day of their landing.

An alarm of Indians.

A comic scene between an Irish Boatswain and an Indian Woman.

The perilous situation of Juliana through the treachery of one of the Pilgrims.

The Act concludes with a GLEE and CHORUS.

In Act II: Scene First Represents several half finished Houses. A shell sounds to announce the arrival of Massasoit.

A grand INDIAN MARCH.

A Treaty of Peace and Amity.

The treachery of Samoset, who attempts to carry off the person of Juliana. She struggles and seizes his Tomahawk and pursues him—he implores her pardon—which she grants—he wrests the Tomahawk from her and aims a dreadful blow, when Winslow rushes in to her rescue—his gun misses fire—he draws his sword and a combat ensues—in the meantime Juliana takes the gun and fires at Samoset, without effect—Winslow is wounded, and Samoset pursues Juliana—who is seen ascending a rock—she reaches the summit, and as Samoset is following, she strikes him with a fuzee, and he falls headlong down the precipice.

THE INDIAN METHOD OF LYING IN AMBUSH.

And the Act concludes with a Procession of Indians, carrying Winslow and Juliana on their boughs.

In Act III: The Indians preparing to sacrifice one of the Pilgrims.

A DREADFUL COMBAT WITH CLUBS AND SHIELDS, BETWEEN SAMOSET AND SQUANTO.

Scene Last: A View of an Indian Encampment, A Marriage and A Nuptial Dance.

AFTER WHICH

The Genius of Columbia descends in a Magnificent Temple, surrounded with Clouds

The list of characters included:
Standish
Carver
Winslow
Cushman
Other Pilgrims
Blunder, the Boatswain
Yankee, an Indian Woman

The *MAYFLOWER* Menu, May 26, 1897

On May 26, 1897, the Bardford manuscript, which had been discovered in London, was formally handed into the custody of the State of Massachusetts. By decree of the Consistory Court Meeting on March 25, 1897, in St. Paul's Cathedral in London under the chairmanship of an eminent lawyer, Thomas Hutchinson Tristram, QC, the manuscript was handed to the American ambassador to deliver "with all due care and diligence to the Governor of Massachusetts at his official office in the State House in the City of Boston." The manuscript was described as: "A certain book known as and entitled 'The Log of the *Mayflower*,' containing an account as narrated by Captain William Bradford, who was one of the Company of Englishmen who left England in April 1620 in the ship known as the *Mayflower*." It might be difficult to fit a greater number of inaccuracies into a description of Bradford's journal than this, but never mind. It is where Governor Roger Wolcott put it, in the Boston State Library, in excellent condition, as legible as when Bradford wrote it. To celebrate the handing over, the American Antiquarian Society gave a banquet for forty-four people at ten dollars a cover at the Parker House in Boston on the evening of May 26. The forty-four guests included representatives of both the Bradford and Winslow families. The menu was as follows, in nine courses.

Hors d'Oeuvre	Little Neck Clams and Oysters
Soup	Clear Green Turtle or Cream of Lobster
Fish	Boiled Salmon, Hollandaise Sauce
	Fried Soft Shell Crabs, Tartare Sauce
Removes	Roast Spring Lamb, Mint Sauce

Fillet of Beef, Sauce Béarnaise
Boiled Philadelphia Capon

Entrées   Sweetbreads Larded, Sauté Fresh Mushrooms
Patties of Lobster Newburg
Fried Bananas Glacé, Benedictine

Relève   Frozen Tom and Jerry

Game   English Snipe or Plover

Sweets   Frozen Pudding
Sultana Roll
Strawberry Shortcake
Maraschino Jelly

Dessert   Strawberries
Pineapples
Ice Cream
Olives
Sherbet
Cake
Coffee

(The relève was normally a kind of sorbet to afford eaters a breathing space before setting to again. The name, of course, enchants the modern reader in this particular example.)

APPENDIX 10

The Inscriptions at the Barbican, Plymouth, Devon

I. On the wall below Lambhay Hill, by the bottom of the steps:

TO THE PEOPLE OF PLYMOUTH

WITH AFFECTION AND ADMIRATION

FROM THE MEMBERS OF 10 SQUADRON

ROYAL AUSTRALIAN AIR FORCE
WHO OPERATED FROM MOUNT BATTEN
1939–1945

II. On the quayside wall, in order, from right to left:

[pavement stone] TORY 1839

CITY OF PLYMOUTH

THIS TABLET COMMEMORATES THE

DEPARTURE FROM PLYMOUTH IN MAY 1839

OF THE TORY, THE PIONEER SHIP

IN THE COLONISATION OF NEW ZEALAND

October 1939   George S. Scoble
                Lord Mayor

III. [pavement stone] MAYFLOWER 1620

On the 6th of September, 1620, in the Mayoralty of Thomas Fownes, after being 'kindly entertained and courteously used by divers friends there dwelling,' the Pilgrim Fathers sailed from Plymouth in the MAYFLOWER, in the Providence of God to settle in NEW PLYMOUTH, and to lay the Foundations of the NEW ENGLAND STATES—The ancient Cawsey whence they embarked was destroyed not many Years afterwards, but the Site of their Embarkation is marked by the Stone bearing the name of the MAYFLOWER in the pavement of the adjacent Pier. This Tablet was erected in the Mayoralty of J. T. Bond, 1891, to commemorate their Departure, and the visit to Plymouth in July of that Year of a number of their Descendants and Representatives.

This Memorial presented by Alderman Mr Frederick Winnicott J.P. was unveiled by the Right Worshipful the Mayor of Plymouth (Mr Councillor E. Stanley Leatherby) on the 5th September 1934.

IV.   Borough of Plymouth

THIS TABLET WAS ERECTED BY THE PLYMOUTH BOROUGH

COUNCIL TO COMMEMORATE THE ARRIVAL ON THE 31st DAY
OF MAY 1919, OF THE AMERICAN SEAPLANE N.C.4, IN
PLYMOUTH SOUND, ON THE COMPLETION OF THE FIRST
TRANSATLANTIC FLIGHT, AND THE RECEPTION BY THE
MAYOR OF PLYMOUTH OF THE COMMANDER, PILOTS AND
CREW, ON THEIR LANDING AT THE BARBICAN.

J. P. Brown, Mayor.	R. J. Fittall, Town Clerk.
Lt. Com. A. C. Read	Lt. E. F. Stone
U.S.N. Commander	(Pilot)
Lt. (Junior Grade) W. Hinton	Lt. J. S. Breeze
U.S.N. (Pilot)	U.S.N. (DesForce)
Ensign H. C. Rodd	Or. Machinist E. C. Rhodes
(Radio Operator)	U.S.N.

V.   THE HONORABLE WALTER ANNENBERG
UNITED STATES AMBASSADOR
TO THE COURT OF ST JAMES'S
UNVEILED THIS TABLET ON THE
6th SEPTEMBER 1970. THIS DAY BEING
THE 350th ANNIVERSARY OF
THE SAILING OF THE 'MAYFLOWER'

         Councillor Eric D. Nuttall J.P.
         Lord Mayor

VI. *The Tolpuddle Martyrs*

     THIS PLAQUE PLACED HERE BY MEMBERS
OF THE VARIOUS TRADES UNIONS AFFILIATED
TO THE PLYMOUTH AND DISTRICT TRADES
COUNCIL COMMEMORATES THE LANDING
NEAR THIS SPOT ON 18th MARCH 1838
OF
JAMES LOVELESS, JAMES BRINE,
THOMAS AND JOHN STANFIELD
(FOUR OF THE SIX DORSET FARM WORKERS

AFTER EXILE IN AUSTRALIA)

FREEDOM AND JUSTICE WAS THEIR CAUSE

5th May 1956

VII.   18—26

IRON PIPES

FOR THE BETTER SUPPLY OF

WATER TO THE INHABITANTS

AND SHIPPING WERE COM-

MENCED BEING LAID AT THE

EXPENCE OF THE CORPORA-

TION IN THE MAYORALTY OF

W. H. HAWKER, ESQ.

VIII. [pavement stone] SEA VENTURE 1609

This tablet was erected in 1959 by the people of Bermuda to commemorate the 350th anniversary of the wreck on a Bermuda reef of 'Sea Venture,' Captain Christopher Newport, flagship of Admiral Sir George Somers, whose fleet sailed from Plymouth Sound on 2nd June, 1609, to carry settlers and supplies to the infant colony at Jamestown in Virginia. On board 'Sea Venture' were 150 persons including Sir Thomas Gates, Governor Designate of Virginia, and all these were landed on the uninhabited island of Bermuda. In ten months they built two vessels and sailed on to Jamestown.—Sir George Somers having returned to Bermuda for more supplies died there on 9th November. His heart is buried at St George's Bermuda and his body at Whitchurch Dorset. His name was given to the Bermuda or Somers Islands, now Britain's oldest colony.

Inserti quo fata ferunt ubi sistere detur contrahimusque viros. Virgilis Aeneid Book 3 line 7.

IX.   H.M. Queen Elizabeth
        and H.R.H. The Duke of Edinburgh
        embarked from this quay on the occasion
        of Their visit to the City of Plymouth
        26th July 1962

APPENDIX 11

The Founding Fathers

These people were the surviving settlers of New Plymouth. Some arrived on the *Mayflower,* some followed later. Dates are given where known. Each alphabetical section starts with *Mayflower* passengers, if any.

1   Alden, John
2   Alden, Priscilla Mullins (married 1623)
3   Allerton, Isaac (1586–1659)
4   Allerton, Fear Brewster (1606–1634)
5   Annable, Anthony
6   Annable, Jane Momford (married 1619; died 1643)
7   Annable, Hannah (born 1622; married 1645)
8   Annable, Sarah (born 1620; married 1638)
9   Armstrong, Gregory
10 Armstrong, Ellen Billington (married 1638)
11 Atwood, Henry
12 Atwood, Sarah Masterson (born 1622; married 1640)

13 Brewster, William (1566–1643)
14 Brewster, Mary Wentworth (1568–1627)
15 Brewster, Jonathan
16 Brewster, Lucretia Oldham (born 1606; married 1624)
17 Brewster, Love (1611–1650)

18 Brewster, Sarah Collier (married 1634) (see also Sarah Parks)
19 Brewster, Wrestling (1614–1635)
20 Bradford, William (1589–1657)
21 Bradford, Alice Carpenter Southworth (1590–1670)
22 Bradford, Jonathan (1615–1678)
23 Bradford, Martha Bourne (married 1640)
24 Bangs, Edward (1592–1678)
25 Bangs, Lydia Hicks (born 1608; married 1627)
26 Bartlett, Robert (1603–1676)
27 Bartlett, Mary Warren (1608–1680)
28 Bassett, William
29 Billington, Francis (born 1606)
30 Billington, Christian Penn Eaton (born 1608; married 1626 and 1634)
31 Blossom, Dr. Thomas
32 Blossom, Anne Heilsdon (later Anne Blossom Rowley)
33 Blossom, Thomas (married 1645)
34 Blossom, Elizabeth (married 1637)
35 Bridges, William
36 Bridges, Mary Oldham
37 Briggs, Clement
38 Browne, Peter
39 Browne, Martha Ford
40 Browne, John (arrived 1632; died 1662)
41 Browne, Dorothy (died 1674)
42 Bumpus, Edward

43 Cooke, Francis (1577–1633)
44 Cooke, Esther Mayhew (1592–1675)
45 Cooke, John (1612–1695)
46 Cooke, Sarah Warren (1614–1676; married 1634)
47 Cooke, Jane (1615–1666)
48 Cooke, Esther (1616–1666)
49 Cooke, Jacob (1618–1675)
50 Crackston, John the younger

51   Carpenter, Mary (1577–1667; arrived 1647)
52   Church, Richard
53   Church, Elizabeth Warren (1616–1670; married 1636)
54   Clarke, Thomas (1599–1697)
55   Collier, William (1585–1670; arrived 1633)
56   Collier, Jane (born 1590)
57   Cole, Job
58   Cole, Rebecca Collier (1610–1698)
59   Churchill, John (married Hannah Pontus [q.v.] 1644)
60   Conant, Christopher (born 1596)
61   Conant, Caleb (1620–1644)
62   Conant, Roger (1592–1642)
63   Conant, Sarah (1600–1642)
64   Combe, John
65   Combe, Sarah Priest
66   Cushman, Thomas (born 1607)
67   Cushman, Mary Allerton (1616–1699; married 1635)

68   Doty, Edward (died 1655)
69   Doty, Faith Clark
70   Deane, Stephen
71   Deane, Elizabeth Ring
72   De la Noye, Philip (married Mary Pontus Glass 1657)
73   De la Noye, Hester Dewsbury (died 1657)
74   Dix, Anthony (died 1638)
75   Dix, Tabitha

76   Eaton, Francis (1595–1633)
77   Eaton, Samuel (born 1620)
78   Eaton, Martha Billington

79   Fuller, Dr. Samuel (1585–1633)
80   Fuller, Bridget Lee (married 1617; died 1664)
81   Fuller, Samuel (1616–1683)
82   Fuller, Jane Lothrop
83   Faunce, John (1610–1687)

84 Faunce, Patience Morton (1616–1691; married 1634)
85 Flavel, Thomas
86 Flavel, Elizabeth Hayward
87 Flood, Edmund

88 Godbertson, Godbert (1590–1633)
89 Godbertson, Sarah Allerton Vincent Priest (1590–1633)
90 Glass, William
91 Glass, Mary Pontus (born 1612; married 1644 and 1657) (see De la Noye)

92 Hopkins, Stephen (1585–1644)
93 Hopkins, Catherine Wheldon (married 1639)
94 Hopkins, Damaris (1617–1669; married 1646)
95 Hopkins, Giles (1607–1690)
96 Howland, John (1592–1672)
97 Howland, Elizabeth Tilley (1606–1687; married 1624)
98 Hatherley, Timothy (died 1666)
99 Hatherley, Alice Collard (died 1642)
100 Hatherley, Lydia Tilden (married 1642)
101 Hatherley, Nathaniel
102 Heard, William
103 Hilton, William
104 Hilton, Mary (born 1600)
105 Hilton, William the younger (born 1618)
106 Hilton, Mary the younger (born 1620)
107 Hicks, Robert
108 Hicks, Margaret
109 Hicks, John (born 1605)
110 Hicks, Sarah (born 1607)
111 Hicks, Samuel (1615–1675)
112 Hicks, Phoebe (born 1610; married 1635)
113 Holman, Edward

114 Jenney, John (1594–1644)
115 Jenney, Sarah Carey (married 1614; died 1655)

116   Kempton, Menassah (1600–1663)
117   Kempton, Juliana Carpenter Morton (1584–1665; married 1627)

118   Little, Thomas
119   Little, Anne Warren (born 1612)
120   Long, Robert

121   More, Jasper (1614–1656)
122   Masterson, Richard (1590–1633)
123   Masterson, Mary Goodall (1600–1650)
124   Masterson, Nathaniel (1620–1665)
125   Maverick, Moses
126   Maverick, Remember Allerton (1614–1655; married 1633)
127   Mitchell, Experience (1609–1689)
128   Morton, George (1585–1624)
129   Morton, Thomas the younger
130   Morton, Nathaniel (1616–1685)
131   Morton, John (1616–1673)
132   Morton, Sarah (1618–1694)
133   Morton, Ephraim (1623–1693; born on voyage)

134   Oldham, John (died 1636)

135   Palmer, William (1570–1637)
136   Palmer, Frances
137   Parks, Richard
         Parks, Sarah Collier Brewster (married 1634 and 1652)
138   Partridge, George
139   Partridge, Tryphosa Tracy (born 1600; married 1638)
140   Pratt, Joshua
141   Pratt, Mary Priest
142   Pratt, Phineas (1593–1680)
143   Prence, Thomas

144   Prence, Patience Brewster (1600–1634)
145   Prence, Mary Collier (1614–1662; married 1636)

146   Ratcliffe, Robert
147   Rickard, Giles
148   Rickard, Hannah Pontus Churchill (1614–1690; married 1669)
149   Robinson, Isaac (1610–1704; arrived 1632, son of John)
150   Robinson, Margaret Hanford (married 1636, niece of Hatherley)
151   Rogers, Joseph (1608–1678)
152   Rogers, Hannah (married 1644)

153   Sampson, Henry (1614–1684)
154   Sampson, Ann Plummer (married 1636)
155   Sowle, George (1599–1680)
156   Sowle, Mary Becket (1605–1677)
157   Standish, Miles (1584–1656)
158   Standish, Barbara (died 1650)
159   Snow, Anthony
160   Snow, Abigail Warren (born 1618; married 1639)
161   Snow, Nicholas (1605–1677)
162   Snow, Constanta Hopkins (1605–1677)
163   Southworth, Constant (1615–1679)
164   Southworth, Elizabeth Collier (born 1616; married 1637)
165   Southworth, Thomas (1616–1669)
166   Southworth, Elizabeth Reyner (married 1637)
167   Sprague, Francis (1600–1676)
168   Sprague, Anne (1602–1660)
169   Sprague, Mercy (born 1621)

170   Tracy, Stephen
171   Tracy, Anne Palmer
172   Tracy, Rebecca
173   Thomas, William (1573–1651)

174   Thomas, Nathaniel (born 1608)

175   Warren, Richard (1580–1628)
176   Warren, Elizabeth (1583–1673)
177   White, Peregrine (1620–1703)
178   Winslow, Edward (1595–1655)
179   Winslow, Susanna Fuller (1594–1680)
180   Winslow, Kenelm (1599–1672)
181   Winslow, Ellen Newton Adams (married 1634)
182   Winslow, John
183   Winslow, Mary Chilton (1605–1679)
184   Waller, Ralph
185   Waller, Joyce
186   Willet, Thomas (1610–1674)
187   Willet, Mary Browne (1616–1670; married 1636)
188   Wright, William (born 1588)
189   Wright, Priscilla Carpenter

Afterword

Nothing in this book has been invented. All incidents, opinions, comments, conditions of weather, and states of mind, public or private, given here have documentary support.

Having said that, it must be admitted that many details are missing in the foregoing account. Research that can call upon the aid of newspapers and letters, films and broadcast programs, is a very different matter from that which depends upon fragmentary documents riddled with maddening gaps, their authors having been so little concerned with posterity's interest in their everyday doings that they did not even bother to name the ship in which they crossed the Atlantic. It proves impossible to track down the precise name and age of every passenger.

It is therefore of the utmost importance to resist the strong temptation to make assumptions, to write in what is known as the "he must have" style. If a fact is unknown I have said so.

None the less, it has been a rewarding piece of work. The founding of America in both of its great stages, 1607–1630 and 1776, undoubtedly ranks among the noblest of human aspirations. That it has often fallen short of the original ideal is human too. No backsliding can detract for long from the immense and splendid concept of both groups of those forefathers who "brought forth upon this continent a new nation, conceived in liberty, and dedicated to the proposition that all men are created equal." It is sometimes a little difficult to remember this when the United States shows its less attractive face to the world, but the great design is there for all that, a glimpse of what America can do when she really sets her mind to it.

The dates mentioned throughout this book are old style, ten

days behind what they would be now. But it seemed preferable, as well as fitting, to go by the Pilgrims' own datelines. I have not attempted to change their seventeenth-century pounds into twentieth-century pounds or dollars: after three centuries this seems unrealistic.

The title of Part IV suggested itself to me because the *Alumni Gazette* of the College of William and Mary in Virginia, which uses colonial-style terminology whenever it can, so entitles its news of former students, among whom I have the honor to belong.

It is a matter of the deepest regret to me that, in the dedication of this book, it is only to the memory of Bryen Gentry that I can offer my thanks.

It might at first sight appear strange that I have selected the *Queen Mary* for purposes of comparison with the *Mayflower,* since the *Mary* is no longer sailing and might be thought obsolete. But she is, to me at any rate, *the* transatlantic liner, as much a legend in her way as the *Mayflower* is in hers, and to place the 81,000 tons of the *Mary* against the 180 of the *Mayflower* proved irresistible.

There have been many moments of interest during the writing that had nothing to do with the subject. One of these was early on, when I came upon the name of the Indian chief Massasoit. At once I remembered that it was at the Massasoit Hotel that Lilly Page ate so many waffles, watched in admiring astonishment by Katy and Clover Carr, on their way to Hillsover School. I had first met the name at the age of ten, and thought it sounded French. At any rate it was exotic; and when I first saw waffles on an English menu, I ordered them instantly on Lilly's recommendation (though not by tinkling a fork against a glass). I record here with pleasure that neither in waffles nor in Chief Massasoit have I been disappointed.

It is tempting in a book like this to draw conclusions, important to resist doing so. Yet perhaps I may be forgiven for touching on two points that I hope have stood out clearly in the preceding pages. The *Mayflower* company, small as it was, certainly started something; and, in the matter of founding fathers, a nation could do a lot worse.

London, 1973–1974   Kate Caffrey

Acknowledgments and Sources

My greatest debt in writing this book has been to William Bradford (1589–1657), governor of the Plymouth Colony, whose journal, published under the title *Of Plymouth Plantation,* proved *the* source book. Hardly less is my indebtedness to Admiral Professor Samuel Eliot Morison, who in 1952 superbly edited the journal, producing the incomparable volume that reveals Bradford's work as a great classic by any standard.

Much invaluable information came from the writings of Edward Winslow (1595–1655), upon whose accounts, principally in *Mourt's Relation,* I have also drawn heavily.

To the following people I am particularly grateful. To the late Nicholas Tomalin, Esq., whose provision of a specimen bibliography saved me endless time and worry. To D. G. Williams, Esq., librarian of my local public library, whose interest supplied me with many books. To the Staff of the British Museum Reading Room, and to Dr. F. Taylor and his assistants at the Rylands Library in Manchester, for making books and documents available to me. To Dr. Stephen Doree and Dr. Michael Martin, of the Department of History at Trent Park College of Education, for information, advice, and kindly interest on many occasions. To Robert Druce, Esq., for enabling me to visit Leyden. To all those people in Plymouth, Devon, Dartmouth, and other places I visited who answered questions so courteously. To my publishers, both British and American, and especially to Esther Whitby for all her encouragement and assistance; and to my agents, Elaine Greene and Ilsa Yardley, for making the whole thing possible.

Apart from two or three brief and irresistible examples, I have used modern spelling throughout for quotations. As all the quotations used are from seventeenth- and eighteenth-century sources, I have simply to acknowledge my debt to the works listed below, in alphabetical order of authors.

SEVENTEENTH-CENTURY WORKS

Bradford, William: *Of Plymouth Plantation.*
Hakluyt, Richard: *Discourse of Western Planting.*
Morton, Nathaniel: *New Englands Memoriall.*
Mourt, G.: *A Relation or Journal of the Beginnings and Proceedings of the English Plantation settled at Plymouth, New England.*
Purchas, Samuel: *Purchas His Pilgrims.*
Smith, Captain John: *A General History of Virginia, New-England and the Summer Isles.*
Winslow, Edward: *Good News from New England.*

OTHER WORKS

Addison, A. C.: *The Romantic Story of the Mayflower Pilgrims and Its Place in the Life of Today* (Boston, 1911).
Ames, Azel: *The Mayflower and Her Log* (New York, 1901).
Anderson, R. C.: "A Mayflower Model," *Mariners' Mirror* (1926).
———: "Have the *Mayflower*'s Masts Been Found?" *ibid.* (1933).
Archer, G. L.: *Mayflower Heroes* (New York, 1935).
Bartlett, W. H.: *Pilgrim Fathers, Founders of New England* (London, 1864).
Boorstin, Daniel: *The Americans: The Colonial Experience* (London, 1958).
Brown, J.: *Pilgrim Fathers of New England and Their Puritan Successors* (London, 1895).
Burgess, Walter: *John Robinson, Pastor of the Pilgrim Fathers* (New York, 1920).
Carpenter, E. J.: *The Mayflower Pilgrims* (London, 1918).
Cawley, R. R.: *The Voyagers and Elizabethan Drama* (Boston, 1938).

Charlton, Warwick: *The Voyage of Mayflower II* (London, 1957).

Dillon, Francis: *A Place for Habitation: The Pilgrim Fathers and Their Quest* (London, 1973).

Gardiner, Samuel Rawson: *The First Two Stewarts and the Puritan Revolution, 1603–1660* (London, 1899).

Garrett, E. H.: *The Pilgrim Shore* (Boston, 1900).

Gill, Crispin: *Mayflower Remembered* (Newton Abbot, 1970).

Goetzmann, W. H., ed.: *The Colonial Horizon: America in the Sixteenth and Seventeenth Centuries, Interpretive Arts and Documentary Sources* (Reading, Mass., 1969).

Harris, J. Rendel: *The Finding of the Mayflower* (Manchester, 1920).

————. *The Last of the Mayflower* (Manchester, 1920).

Hills, L. C.: *History and Genealogy of the Mayflower Planters and First Comers to Ye Olde Colonie* (Washington, D.C., 1936).

Jones, Howard Mumford: *O Strange New World* (London, 1965).

Langdon-Davis, John, ed.: *Mayflower and the Pilgrim Fathers* (Jackdaw series; London, 1964).

Marsden, R. G.: "The Mayflower," *English Historical Review* (London, 1904).

Morison, Samuel Eliot: *The European Discovery of America, volume I, The Northern Waters* (Oxford, 1971).

————: *Colonial New England* (Oxford, 1956).

Notestein, Wallace: *The English People on the Eve of Colonisation, 1603–1630* (London, 1954).

Parry, J. H.: *The Age of Reconnaissance* (New York, 1963).

Quinn, D. B.: *Raleigh and the British Empire* (London, 1947).

Rowse, A. L.: *The Elizabethans and America* (London, 1959).

————: *The Expansion of Elizabethan England* (London, 1955).

Simpson, Alan: *Puritanism in Old and New England* (Chicago, 1956).

Smith, H. J.: *The Master of the Mayflower* (New York, 1936).

Starkey, Marion L.: *Land Where Our Fathers Died: The Settling of the Eastern Shores, 1607–1735* (London, 1961).

Vaughan, Alden T., ed.: *The Puritan Tradition in America,
              1620–1730* (San Francisco, 1972).

Villiers, Alan: *Give Me a Ship to Sail* (London, 1958).

——: *The Western Ocean* (London, 1957).

Willison, George F.: *Saints and Strangers* (London, 1946).

Wright, Louis B.: *America of the Pilgrim Fathers: Colonial Civilisation
              of North America* (London, 1949).

——: *Atlantic Frontier, Colonial Civilisation of North America*
              (New York, 1959).

——: *Everyday Life in Colonial America* (London, 1965).

——, and Fowler, Elaine W.: *English Colonisation of North Ameri-
              ca: Documents of Modern History* (London, 1968).

ALSO

Dana, Richard Henry: *Two Years Before the Mast.*

Kipling, Rudyard: *Captains Courageous.*

Longfellow, Henry Wadsworth: *The Building of the Ship.*

——: *The Courtship of Miles Standish.*

Trevor-Roper, E. R.: *The European Witch-Craze of the Sixteenth
              and Seventeenth Centuries* (London, 1969).

Index